OTHER BOOKS BY JAY NEUGEBOREN

IMAGINING
ROBERT

Jay Neugeboren

IMAGINING

ROBERT

My Brother, Madness, and Survival · A Memoir

Rutgers University Press
New Brunswick, New Jersey

First published in hardcover in 1997 by William Morrow and Company, Inc.

First published in paperback in 1998 by Owl Books

Reprinted in paperback in 2003 by Rutgers University Press,
New Brunswick, New Jersey

Library of Congress Cataloging-in-Publication Data

Neugeboren, Jay.
Imagining Robert : my brother, madness, and survival : a memoir / Jay Neugeboren.
p.   cm.
Originally published: New York : William Morrow, 1997.
ISBN 0-8135-3296-5 (pbk. : alk. paper)
1. Neugeboren, Robert—Mental health.   2. Neugeboren, Jay.   3. Mentally ill—
United States—Biography.   4. Mentally ill—Institutional care—United States.
5. Mentally ill—United States—Family relationships.   I. Title.
RC464.N48 N48 2003
616.89'0092—dc21
[B]2002036746

British Cataloging-in-Publication information is available from the British Library.

Manufactured in the United States of America

For my friends
Robert Goldstein and Richard Parks

List of Illustrations

Acknowledgments

Portions of this book have appeared, in different form, in *The American Scholar, Tikkun, Moment, Congregation* (ed. David Rosenberg), *Expect a Miracle* (ed. Dan Wakefield), and *Psychiatric Rehabilitation Journal*.

IMAGINING
ROBERT

I

AT 3:00 A.M., on a cool summer night—a few hours after my youngest son has graduated from high school—I find myself cruising the deserted streets of Northampton, Massachusetts, searching for the fifty-year-old man who is my brother. I have considered calling the police, but I know that if a policeman actually finds my brother and approaches him, Robert might, as in the past, panic and become violent.

My brother Robert has spent most of his life, since the age of nineteen, in mental hospitals and psychiatric wards in and around New York City. The list is long: Hillside, Creedmoor, Elmhurst, Gracie Square, Bellevue, Kings County, Rikers Island, Mid-Hudson Psychiatric Center, South Beach Psychiatric Center, and others.

Until the time of his first breakdown in 1962, Robert had been a delightful, popular, and gifted boy and young man— talented at dancing, acting, and singing, invariably winning the lead in school and camp plays and skits. He'd had a love and talent for many things, including tennis, writing, art (painting, drawing), and chess. (He was in a chess club with Bobby Fischer at Erasmus Hall High School in Brooklyn, but Fischer refused to play with him; " 'With you, Neugeboren, I don't play,' he always said to me," Robert says. Why not? "Because," Robert says, smiling, "I played crazy.") He was a good if erratic student in high school, won a New York State Regents Scholarship to college, and successfully completed his freshman year at the City College of New York.

He was, in short, a bright and idiosyncratic young man with a sense of life and humor all his own, a person who showed no signs, until his first breakdown (except for those that, look- ing back, any of us might find in ourselves), that such a break- down was at all likely, much less inevitable.

Robert's diagnosis has changed frequently in the past thirty years, depending largely upon which drugs have been successful in keeping him calm, stable, and/or compliant. He was schizo- phrenic when enormous doses of Thorazine and Stelazine calmed him; he was manic-depressive (bipolar) when lithium worked; he was manic-depressive-with-psychotic-symptoms, or hypomanic, when Tegretol or Depakote (anticonvulsants), or some new antipsychotic or antidepressant—Trilafon, Adapin, Mellaril, Haldol, Klonopin, risperidone—showed promise of making him cooperative; and he was schizophrenic (again) when various doctors promised cures through insulin-coma therapy or megadose-vitamin therapy or Marxist therapy or gas therapy. At the same time, often in an attempt to minimize side effects, other drugs were poured into him: Artane, Bena- dryl, Cogentin, Kemadrin, Symmetrel, Prolixin, Pamelor, Na- vane . . .

During these years, Robert also participated in a long menu of psychotherapies: group therapy, family therapy, multifamily group therapy, Gestalt therapy, psychoanalytically oriented psychotherapy, goal-oriented therapy, art therapy, behavioral therapy, vocational rehabilitation therapy, milieu therapy, et al. Most often, though—the more chronic his condition, the truer this became—he was treated solely with drugs, and received no therapy at all.

It is as if, I often think, the very history of the ways in which our century has dealt with those it calls mentally ill has, for more than thirty years now, been passing through my brother's mind and body.

Robert and I talk with each other almost every day, and see each other often, sometimes in New York and sometimes in Massachusetts, and though our visits are not without their difficulties (why should we be different from other brothers?), visits in my home, with my children, have invariably been without incident.

I've never seen Uncle Robert this way, each of my three children said to me in the hours before and after my son Eli's graduation. Is he going to be all right? Can I help? And then: And what about you, Pop—are *you* going to be all right?

Robert spent the day and evening of Eli's graduation in and out of the house, withdrawing hundreds of dollars, ten dollars at a time, from automated teller machines; buying secondhand clothes at local thrift shops; leaving trails of clothing, coins, cigarette butts, small paper bags, and crumpled snot-filled tissues in virtually all the rooms of my (eleven-room) house; going from room to room and turning lights on and off; showing me pieces of paper upon which he had written indecipherable messages while demanding that I understand what they meant; and, whenever my children and their friends arrived home, hurrying from sight and hiding.

Eli returned home from his all-night (supervised) graduation party at the local county fairgrounds at about 6:00 A.M., and Robert, whom I had not seen since we had left for Eli's graduation ceremonies at about 6:00 P.M. the night before, arrived not long after that, and ordered me to put him on a bus for

New York immediately. He looked ghastly (he had—inexpertly—given himself a haircut, and had shaved off his mustache), and seemed totally disoriented: his hands and arms were flapping uncontrollably, his body was hunched over, his eyeglasses were covered with a milk-white sticky substance ("Scum!" he declared, when I asked), his movements were jagged, and he kept turning on me, ordering me around, screaming things that made no obvious sense.

Whether I did or did not reply, he became more and more enraged, telling me again and again that I wasn't *listening* to him, that I never listened to him, and that if I didn't do what he said he didn't know *what* he might do. "I want *letters!*" he kept shouting. "I want *letters!*"

At the bus stop he scurried around wildly, virtually on all fours, picking up cigarette butts and searching for money. He wore a wide-brimmed straw hat, a tuxedo vest over a T-shirt, tight white extra-short pants, bright knee-high red socks. He went to each of a half-dozen sidewalk newspaper kiosks and began putting quarters in them, taking out papers, and either stacking them on top of the kiosk or putting them in a mailbox. He went back and forth to a pay phone, dialing for information about people on Staten Island and yelling at the operator; he walked across the street to a parking lot and shouted questions at me; he wept and he screamed, and I found myself hoping that the bus would come on time (or ahead of time), that he would be allowed to board it, and that he would somehow get back to his halfway house (located on the grounds of South Beach Psychiatric Center) safely.

I had been in situations like this with Robert before—dozens of times through the past four decades—and though, as I said to my children, seeing Robert like this was not new for me, each time it happened it did still take me by surprise, and each time it happened, it seemed unutterably sad and heartbreaking.

How could it be that somebody who was so warm and loving, so charming, happy, and seemingly normal one moment—

one day, one hour—could become so angry, wild, and lost moments later? And how could it be that each time it happened—no matter the years gone by—it felt as if it were happening for the first time?

Though, with the years, I've learned to cope with these situations—to be able to help me *and* Robert get through—and though, with the years, Robert has actually reversed the path his life had been on (despite dreadful prognostications, he had come, in the eight or nine years preceding Eli's graduation, to be able to spend more time out of hospitals than in them, and had made more of a life for himself than most people had dreamed possible), I still found myself going through litanies of familiar questions and doubts: Should I call the local police and have them take him to a hospital and deal with getting him back to New York City? Should I ask Robert where he was all night, and if he had been drinking and/or doing drugs, and if he thought he could get back to the city by himself? Should I leave my children and try to drive Robert the two hundred miles back to Staten Island? Should I call the hospital on Staten Island? Should I call some local psychiatrists and social workers I knew? Should I stay with Robert, or leave him alone? And how should I respond to his outbursts of anger, his bizarre behavior, his accusations, his questions, his tears?

What could I do, I wondered, now as ever, that might ease his pain and confusion—that might minimize damage? If he was in free fall, as it were, was there anything I could do to help buffer the fall, so that, instead of plummeting downward ten stories before he crashed, he could bounce down gently after, say, only falling a few steps? Should I say anything at all, and was there a right thing or wrong thing to say, and was there anyone I could call upon who could help get us through, or was it better to say nothing and to just leave him be?

How much of what was going on with Robert was frightening my children, or taking away from *their* celebration and reunion, and was it best to shield them from the worst of Robert's troubles, or to inform them in fuller detail of what was happening, and of my own fears, and intentions? In a situation like this, despite the many times I'd been here before, what I felt most of all was an overwhelming sadness and help-lessness. Who knew if there was anything at all that might ease things, or make them less awful? Who knew, really, *what* to do?

What I did, finally—what I found myself doing—was what I've been doing more and more through the years: simply trust-ing my instincts, and Robert's. I found myself acting on my belief that, despite all, Robert still knew himself—even at a time like this—better than anyone else did, and that if he was determined to get back to Staten Island by himself, he would.

Robert had stayed away from my children most of the time during his three days with us, and—his innate kindness, as ever, at work—had kept both his anger and his confusion hid-den, for the most part, when in their presence. Still, each of my children noticed what a hard time he was having, and each came to me and offered sympathy, and help.

When, while changing from cap and gown into casual clothes, for his graduation party, Eli asked if he could do any-thing to help, and I told him the best thing he could do was to go off and enjoy the party, that Robert was my responsibility and not his, Eli had replied, "But he's mine too, Pop."

I smiled. "Maybe," I said. "But today is your day. This one's on me, okay?"

My sense of the fear and humiliation (along with the logisti-cal problems) that would result from having local agencies deal with getting Robert from Massachusetts to New York, or my trying to deal with him in a locked car for four or five hours (a week before his first breakdown in 1962, he had, while we were going seventy miles an hour on a highway, opened the car door, stuck a leg out, and threatened to jump), reinforced my instincts—to believe that the best immediate solution was the simplest one: to let Robert get back to his home by himself, and as quickly as he could.

So I did what I usually do when things get bad for Robert. I tried, gently and firmly, to be as patient and direct with him as I could (telling him, for example, that I would call ahead to his halfway house to let them know he was on his way; asking him, again, if he did, in fact, want me to drive him back to Staten Island), and, when he came near to me—and when he walked off and seemed especially lost—I put my arms around him, and told him I loved him, and talked with him about whatever came to mind—his meals (I'd packed him a lunch), the bus, the trip back, the weather.

While people waiting for the bus stared, or tried not to stare, or moved away, Robert stayed close to me and seemed to be listening: I was glad he'd been able to visit, I said, and I wished he wasn't having such a hard time again, and we'd talk on the phone that evening after he was back at his halfway house, and I was very glad he'd been able to be here for Eli's graduation and had seen Miriam and Aaron, and we would see one another again soon.

Robert navigated the eight-hour trip home—bus, subway, ferry, and bus—successfully. We spoke that night—he cried a lot, complained about the hospital and the medications, and then he was off on flights of words that, because I knew the reference points (events and people from our childhood, jokes we loved, experiences we'd been through together), seemed more poignant than strange. "I didn't embarrass you, did I?" he asked at one point. "I didn't embarrass the children, I hope. . . ."

The following morning, for the first time in a year, and for at least the fiftieth time in his life, he was hospitalized. When I called the doctor in charge of Robert's ward and he asked what I thought had precipitated Robert's break, I said that there were some immediate causes that seemed obvious, but that the real precipitant, it seemed to me, was simply the fact of Robert's life—of the last thirty-one years of his life. If you'd been where Robert had been, and suffered all the drugs, abuse, incompetence, and pain he'd suffered, the wonder, it seemed to me, wasn't why he'd broken again, but why he hadn't, like so many others he'd known, died or killed himself or deteriorated completely.

But after I said this, I did name some of the things that had been going on in Robert's life that might have precipitated this break. There was the graduation itself, and being with family (but Robert had been in this situation dozens of times before and had had no difficulties). There were his desires and fantasies about living in my home with me in Massachusetts, now intensified because Eli would be going off to college and I would soon be living alone (but I'd been the single full-time parent of my three children for nearly a decade, and though Robert often asked about moving in with me, I'd never encouraged him, and he himself had begun saying he didn't think it was a good idea). There was the fact that, a few weeks before, Robert's best friend had been moved out of the home in which he and Robert had lived together for two years and into which Robert had been hoping to return (so where would he live now?). There was the fact that he had been out of the hospital for eleven months, and the better he became—the more alert, the more himself—the less the make-work activities of the hospital's day center interested him, and the more bored he became. There were all the feelings (of failure, envy, love, resentment) aroused by being with me and my children—seeing Eli graduate (and at the age Robert was when he had his first breakdown), and seeing us move ahead with our lives while his life seemed, still, to be going nowhere.

Though I could, as ever, talk about what I thought had caused Robert's condition, long-term and short-term, the more important question, it seemed to me (or was I thinking this way in order to give myself heart, in order to find *something* good in a situation that was godawful?), wasn't what had caused this breakdown, or any of the others, but what, given his life, had enabled him to survive, and to do more than survive—to retain his generosity, his warmth, his intelligence, his pride, humor, and his sense of self. This, it seemed to me, was, as ever, the true miracle and mystery.

I had, not long before, asked Robert the same questions the doctor asked me. Did he ever have any sense of what made him go off the way he did sometimes—of what the difference was, of what made things change for him, or in him? He had been silent for a long time, and then had said, "No answer."

These were, I said at once, afraid my questions might have hurt him, questions *nobody* seemed to know the answers to.

"So why should I know?" Robert said then. "Am I different from anybody else?"

The doctor at South Beach Hospital concluded that Robert's breakdown had been precipitated by alcohol and substance abuse. Robert had admitted that on the way up to visit me he had had a few beers and had inhaled amyl nitrite. The amyl nitrite ("poppers") was "part of the gay lifestyle," the doctor said, and was taken by homosexuals to increase sexual pleasure. The alcohol and substance abuse, he concluded, had clearly "destabilized" and "unhinged" the parts of Robert's brain that his medications—lithium and Depakote—had stabilized. The problem, therefore, was "noncompliance."

I had heard this from doctors before, and I responded with an obvious, if rhetorical question: Okay, but what was it that had caused the noncompliance? If mental illness was as debilitating and awful a condition as it seemed to be (as surely it had been for Robert), and if the medications alleviated that condition, why would anyone ever stop taking the medications, or do anything to interfere with their beneficial effects?

As my father had once put it, to a doctor who refused to continue treating Robert because Robert had stopped taking his pills, "So where, Doctor, is the pill to make him want to take the pills?"

•   •   •

When I visited Robert after his breakdown—on a locked unit at South Beach Psychiatric Center (a New York State facility where he has been hospitalized, on and off, for the past twenty years, and which is located on Staten Island, a half-mile or so from Staten Island Hospital), he was, as before, on isolation: living, day after day, twenty-four hours a day, in a bare room in which there was nothing but a sheetless bed and an empty dresser. This was called, by the staff psychologist, Henry Grossman, "reduced stimulation."

When I had, previously, questioned, as gently as I could, whether being on isolation, and on heavy doses of Thorazine (the medication Robert hated above all others), and not being permitted to make or receive calls, or to have visitors, might not feel to Robert like punishment instead of therapy, Henry Grossman had replied that this might temporarily be the case. "But our experience," he said, "is that in retrospect patients come to appreciate the reduction of stimulation—the limits and boundaries that have been set for them."

He had also assured me that Robert was not just locked away in a room—that every hour on the half hour, for five minutes, Robert was taken to the bathroom and for a walk down the hallway. When I asked if Robert had had or would be receiving any therapy—if he was talking with anybody in any regular way about what he was going through—Henry's reply was abrupt: "Robert cannot tolerate therapy."

This seemed to me an absurd statement—*Robert* couldn't tolerate therapy? You mean *you* can't tolerate trying to work with him, I wanted to scream. Why are you a therapist if you don't want to work with patients, to listen to them? And when will Robert be able to "tolerate" therapy—when he's *well*?

But it was the same old story, and I was in the same old quandary: if I complained too much, or confronted Robert's health care workers with their inadequacies, or sent off the long letters I often composed in my head (to *The New York Times,* to hospital and state officials, to doctors, etc.), I feared they would only take out their resentments of me upon Robert—that they would (as had happened before) simply talk with me less, care for Robert less, and/or ship him off to a ward where he would receive even less attention (and more drugs) than he was now receiving.

Robert had been here, in this ward and ones like it, and in worse places, before. (One time at Mid-Hudson, a forensic facility, when they had him in a straitjacket for a long period of time, I remembered him telling me, he asked for a smoke, so he could let the ashes fall on the jacket and set himself on fire. He succeeded. After the aides got him out of the straitjacket, one of them took him to the basement, where he beat him up and warned him never to do what he had done again.)

Now, on a warm summer day in July of 1993, because of my visit, Robert has been granted courtyard privileges, and we sit at a picnic table by ourselves. He opens the bag of food I've brought him for lunch, but his hands are shaking so badly that when he tries to eat an egg salad sandwich, the egg salad sprays everywhere. He is frustrated, apologetic, embarrassed. I talk with him easily, we joke back and forth, and after a short while I scoop up pieces of egg, tomato, lettuce, and bread, he takes his false teeth out, and I feed him with my fingers, placing the food directly into his mouth.

When he cannot tolerate his tremblings any longer, he walks away. He calls to me, and I go and sit next to him on a different bench, and we talk about the ward, and the doctors, and my trip down, about Eli's graduation, and the floods in the Midwest, and our cousins. We have more than three dozen first cousins (both our parents came from large, extended families), and I fill Robert in on who is where and doing what—our cousins, and the children of our cousins, and the children of our cousins' children—and which relatives I've seen or heard from. Suddenly Robert turns, leans down, and, with great gentleness, kisses the back of my hand several times, after which he begins weeping.

"Oh, Jay, Jay," he cries softly. "They're barbarians here. Barbarians, barbarians! Pavlovians . . ."

He presses his mouth to the back of my hand, and I take him to me, hold him close. A few minutes later, we walk around the courtyard, and then he tells me that he likes to walk back and forth, in a diagonal, between two trees—they are about ten yards apart—and count the number of times he can do this. So we walk back and forth together, and I sing to him, and then he joins in—putting his arm around my waist, leaning on my shoulder—and we go back and forth again and again, loudly singing old camp songs, in English and Hebrew, that we remember from our childhood.

He eats some more, and then we walk again, side by side, our hands clasped behind us, mimicking two diplomats, trading stories and news. He clutches his dentures in one hand, a piece of bread locked in their bite, and when he puts the top bridge back in his mouth, I say something about his being on uppers.

He starts giggling, inserts the lower bridge.

"And now you're on lowers," I say, and add that I don't understand why, since he's on uppers and lowers, which probably balance each other, the hospital has to give him any other medications.

"It's how they make their profit," he says.

When I call Robert from Massachusetts after our visit, he is flying—repeating everything he says twice, rambling on about people living and dead as if they were there with him on the ward, thanking me for visiting him and for the things I brought him, giving me lists of all the foods he has eaten and all the things he wants me to send him, mixing these lists with references to scenes in movies and to scenes from our childhood, talking about Adlai Stevenson and Bill Clinton (who is, he says, his son) and how the whole country is in a very big depression—and every few seconds he tells me that he has to hang up, he has to hang up (though he never does). And then, when he finally takes a breath, and I tell him I love him, his voice suddenly drops and slows down, and he talks to me in a way that is totally natural.

"Oh, Jay," he says, "don't you see? There's nothing better in my life than what's happening! You don't know. You don't know, Jay. You don't *want* to know . . ." He weeps freely, keeps talking. "This life of working here and there in hospitals, or as a volunteer, and being here now, and doing nothing— isn't there ever going to be anything *better* for me? Please get me out of here, Jay. Please, please . . ."

When, later in our conversation, I tell him that I called him the day before but nobody could find him, he asks me what I called him, and when I say, "I called you my brother," he laughs, says, "That's an old one, Jay. That's an old one— but listen, I'm going to switch the phone to my good ear, all right?"

"There," he says, a few seconds later. "Now can you hear me better?"

Moved as I am by Robert's situation and his life—and his plea for a life different from the one he has—I find, after our visit and our talk, that I am feeling relieved, and, even, mildly exhilarated. (I am also feeling exasperated, yet again, with the treatment, and lack of treatment, he receives from the staff; when I talk with his new prescribing psychiatrist, his fourth since his hospitalization, I discover, for example, that this man—"So why are you calling me?" are his first words to me after I identify myself as Robert's brother—has been prescribing and changing Robert's medications for a full week without having spoken with or examined Robert. When I complain about this to a part-time staff psychiatrist who has previously treated Robert, she is appalled, though not surprised.)

But I am feeling better about Robert and his situation because the truth (I shrug when I realize this, as if to say to myself: What can I do? That's the way it is) is that when Robert and I are together, whether in my home or on his ward, whether on the West Side of Manhattan (where we lived next door to each other in the mid-sixties, during his first year out of Creedmoor), or in Atlantic City (where, six weeks before Eli's graduation, Robert and I went together for two days, at his request, to celebrate his fiftieth birthday), we're happy. Not always, and not without a pervasive sense of loss and sadness, but happy to be with each other, no matter the context, because it seems good, simply, in an often frightening and miserable life, to be *known*—and to be able to be near the person who knows you and is known by you.

During the weeks that follow Robert's hospitalization, we talk regularly, and I visit him and send notes and a few small gifts, and whenever we talk, Robert asks about each of my children— his niece and two nephews—and though our talks sometimes last for less than a minute, and though sometimes he is angry (at doctors, at me—at life!) and sometimes sad, and sometimes high—and though sometimes I am nearly swept away by grief, from my sense of all that *he* senses his life has become and has not become, I find, strangely enough, real pleasure—as ever— in these talks and in our time spent together.

This happens not only because I know Robert's patterns, if patterns they are, fairly well, and know that once his sense of humor returns (and once he begins talking with me in direct ways about his feelings and needs), his recovery will follow— that he will be back before long, for better or worse, in the "real" world most of us live in—but simply because, for better or worse, our lives, in a crucial time for each of us, have once again been joined.

In a few months, I think to myself, I'll drive my youngest son, Eli, out to start his freshman year in college, and then I'll return home and, for the first time in more than two dozen years, I will be alone. And I realize, to my surprise, that this prospect, if intermittently, has been depressing me. I have become so habituated to having my children with me all these years—so used to the simple sharing of the infinite complexities of any hour or day of family life—that when friends ask what I expect I might do after Eli is gone, I find myself going blank. (The habit of parenting, and of parenting alone, is a habit I love, in part, I later think, because it allows me to believe, even in the most difficult times, what I sometimes fear is not so: that I am, in fact, *useful* to others, and that, because of this, my life matters.)

I've seen my three children through these years, and though I did so without a partner and they did so without a mother (she left them and moved away, definitively, in 1986), and though the four of us have had our hard times (drug problems, suicide attempts, depression), we've all gotten through some-how. My daughter, just graduated from Scripps College, in California, has begun work in Washington, D.C., as adminis-trative assistant to the director of Habitat for Humanity Inter-national; my son Aaron is driving across the country with a friend, to Albuquerque, New Mexico, to begin his second year of college; and Eli is about to begin his first year at Ohio University's School of Fine Arts.

In a few months, as in the past, I assume, Robert will get out of his ward and return to his halfway house, and if things go well there, he will move from the halfway house into a supervised apartment, and we'll go to Atlantic City together again, and, my on-site parental responsibilities now diminished, Robert and I will see each other more frequently. We'll talk and laugh and trade jokes, argue and complain and become irritable with each other, reminisce and make plans and go on trips—and he'll gradually tell me, without my asking (as he has already begun to do), about what he did and where he went on the night of Eli's graduation, and that too will become part of the history we share.

And the more I know about him, and the more time we spend together, the more I'll wonder, as ever, about how he came to be who he is and to have had the life he's had. What continues to surprise, though—but why?—is that the more I know Robert and know about him, the more I'll continue to want to know, and that this will only, as ever, increase for me, not the sadness of his life, but its wonder.

Several weeks after Eli's graduation, while Robert is still on isolation at South Beach, I come across a full-page advertisement in *The New York Times* sponsored by NARSAD (the National Alliance for Research on Schizophrenia and Depression), an organization founded by the four most prominent mental health groups in the United States (the National Alliance for the Mentally Ill, the Schizophrenia Foundation, the National Depressive and Manic-Depressive Association, and the National Mental Health Association), that talks about "the many urgent scientific projects that are paving the way for better treatments and the cure we all hope for."

Suddenly, all the years of Robert's life—the breakdowns, the treatments, the horrors, the frustrations and failures and hopes abandoned; images, memories, nightmares—seem to take up residence within my mind. *The* cure? I want to scream. *The* cure?

"New hope of a breakthrough cure is on the horizon," the ad proclaims, "as we start to identify the genetic markers that cause depression."

The ad sets forth the current and conventional wisdom about mental illness and (especially) depression: its symptoms, the suffering it brings, the numbers of people afflicted ("In any six-month period, 9.4 million Americans will suffer from depression . . ."). What the ad says echoes what I've read in most literature put out by mental health professionals, organizations, and agencies: that mental illness is a "biochemical illness" and a "no-fault biologically based brain disease." (Thus, for example, the former director of the National Institute of Mental Health is quoted in the organization's newsletter, the *NAMI Advocate,* as having presented research at the 1993 NAMI convention which "establishes—irrefutably and unequivocally and forever—that mental disorders are brain diseases." And the president of NARSAD begins a November 1994 letter with the following: "I am thilled to report progress in the search for which you and I pray—the search for the magic bullet for schizophrenia, depression and other severe neurobiological disorders.")

Surely, thinking of mental illness in this way—believing

that biology causes it (in the same way it causes cancer, diabetes, or heart disease, illnesses to which it is frequently compared), and that nobody's to blame ("Remember this is a biochemical illness," the National Depressive and Manic-Depressive Association states in each of its publications. "It isn't yours, or anyone else's fault")—does enormous good: it reduces anxiety, stigma, and guilt; it inspires hope; it allows for increased coverage under (some) insurance plans; it provides (through organizations such as NAMI) forums and practical assistance for families; it enables useful legislation and research, and so on.

What it does *not* do, however, is to deal directly with the major fact of mental illness for those who suffer its larger devastations: its generally long-term chronic character and how this is experienced, as on Eli's graduation night, by the mentally ill and those who care for them—for those who must cope, over the course of a lifetime, with a condition which invariably, by its insidious, unpredictable nature and course, tears families apart, and for which condition, most of the time, there are no solutions, long- *or* short-term.

Robert and I have been hearing talk about "breakthrough cures" for more than thirty years now. First it was electroshock, and then it was psychoanalytically oriented psychotherapy, and then it was insulin-coma therapy, and then it was family therapy, and then it was the new range of antipsychotic drugs, and then it was megadose-vitamin therapy, and then it was lithium therapy, and then it was anticonvulsant therapy and then it was clozapine and risperidone. . .

And for more than thirty years any questions (or reservations, or complaints) I've had about these forms of treatment have been met, by and large, with the following response from Robert's doctors: We know more than you do about Robert's condition, and what we are doing for him is the only thing that can be done, and if you don't encourage Robert to obey our rules, you will be doing him harm.

Thirty years ago, my mother (a registered nurse), in *her* helplessness, was crying out, again and again—after virtually every hospital visit (and there were often five or six visits a week), "Some day they'll discover it was all chemical—you'll see! Some day they'll discover it was all chemical. . . ."

But eight years after Robert's first breakdown, when she was sixty-two years old, she left Robert in New York and moved to Florida. "I've done all I can do," she said. "Let the state take over. You be in charge from now on, Jay—I just can't handle it anymore. Nobody knows. Nobody can know what it's like to have a mentally ill child. Nobody! It's worse than death. . . ."

What upsets me in the *New York Times* ad—what upsets me whenever I hear language about breakthrough cures and genetic markers and brain disease and new miracle drugs ("the magic bullet!")—is not the possibility that Robert's condition is chemical (which it surely is, in part), but the belief so many have in its corollary: that if the condition is chemical, it can be corrected with chemicals. How easy it would be for everybody if there were chemical causes and chemical cures! How free of responsibility we might all be then. . . .

But even if we find cause and cure, what then do we do with the life lived, and the history—and fear, and shame, and doubt, and despair, and sheer misery—that has accompanied that life? If behavior and feelings can change the chemistry and patterns of the brain (the principle of neural plasticity— e.g., the feelings and physiological changes in athletes, musicians, stockbrokers, writers, artists, and others when in intensely productive periods), just as chemicals can change behavior and feelings, how can we know which is cause, and which effect?

The instant I see the words about breakthrough cures, and read about how NARSAD has provided financial support to 315 doctors and scientists in seventy-eight leading universities, medical schools, and research institutions, what I also see, but more vividly, is my brother, in a room by himself, lying on a bare mattress, hour after hour and day after day, doped up, groggy, and trembling from medications, fear, and loneliness.

In a realm where the relation of mind to body remains so complex and mysterious—where, still, we know so little (the evidence concerning organic brain substrate for gender differences, for example, is far more convincing than the evidence of an organic basis for schizophrenia, yet most of us take it for granted that male and female brains are more similar than different, and that what differences exist are largely socioculturally determined)—why, again, such a fierce belief in an *exclusively* neurobiological view of mental illness, and why so much time and money spent in the search for chemical and organic causes and cures, while back on the ward patients languish and die for the simple lack of human attention to their ordinary, daily needs?

(In what editorial writers, politicians, and mental health advocates praise as "landmark legislation," and an economic "boon" for the mentally ill, New York State, early in 1994, passed laws intended to reassign, over a five-year period, an estimated $210 million—savings from the closing of mental hospitals and the discharge of patients—to community mental health services. When I read about how dozens of mental health organizations worked to bring the bill to reality, and of how thrilled they, along with the governor and other politicians, are with the results, I note that this sum, which *may* someday be expended for the benefit of tens of thousands of mental patients over a period of five years, will come to less than what a single drug company spends, on average—$231 million—to bring a single new drug to market.)

For even if we do one day separate out the gene or the neuron that proves to be the cause of what we decide is this or that species of mental illness, what, then, will we do about the life that has come before and will continue after the moment of diagnosis and medication, and of how the fact of having this condition has affected an individual's history?

Hope and research are fine, and genuine gains have been

made. Hundreds of thousands of human beings, plagued by various forms of madness—mania, depression, hallucinations—have, thanks to medications and psychotherapy, been able to lead productive and ordinary (and sometimes extraordinary) lives in the world outside mental hospitals. But hundreds of thousands of other human beings, like Robert, despite all forms of treatment and medication, continue to lead grim lives of madness, misery, and despair.

Medication and research are fine, I think, but meanwhile, back on Robert's ward, he has to sneak out of his room to telephone me, and his doctors rarely call me to inform or confer, and the only link to the outside world for thirty or so acutely psychotic patients is a single pay phone. Meanwhile, back on the ward, Robert has been forgotten and abandoned by virtually everyone who knew him (despite all the friends and relatives we have living in the New York City area, Robert has, in the last two decades, received fewer than a half-dozen notes or calls from them). Meanwhile, back on the ward, important messages don't get through (thus, when Robert, for the first time in his life, threatened suicide, and I informed one of the nurses, and I called back a few days later to speak with Robert's doctor, I discovered the doctor had never been informed of Robert's threat). Meanwhile, back on the ward, when Robert breaks a tooth, it takes more than three months for him to get his dentures back, during which time he must eat with his gums. Meanwhile, back on the ward, the major activities are TV and card games, the staff is outnumbered and overworked, the refrigerator is padlocked, and the only time patients can get snacks is when an aide unlocks it twice a day at "refrigerator time."

As it was, for the most part, thirty years ago, I think, so it is now: the little that passes for therapy is simply reward and punishment done up, if at all, in the guise of crude behavior modification programs (smoking "privileges," courtyard "privileges," grounds "privileges," phone "privileges") whose aim is not enhancement, but containment and neutralization. As ever,

custodial needs—getting meals and pills out on time, minimizing disruption and noise—take precedence over human needs.
In the world Robert lives in too often, ordinary habits and
idiosyncrasies (sloppiness about clothing, loud talking, hostility
toward roommates) become psychological deficits for which one
receives demerits, and worse. In the world Robert has been
living in for too many years, model patients seem not very
different from model prisoners.

At least, I say to Robert during one conversation, they don't
use straitjackets anymore, and when I say this, we both laugh,
and talk about the time he asked a friend visiting him at
Creedmoor if she could take his dirty clothes home for him
and get them washed. The friend took Robert's laundry bag
to a Chinese laundry and started removing the clothes, only to
find that mixed in with the dirty socks and underwear was
Robert's straitjacket.

"In the old days it was straitjackets and wet sheets and
electricity," Robert says, "and now, I guess, it's isolation and
injections."

A few weeks before Eli's graduation, I had asked Robert why
he thought it was that he had survived when so many others
he knew, from Creedmoor and Mid-Hudson and South Beach
and Hillside, never got out, or killed themselves, or deteriorated to the point of no return.

"First of all," he joked, "I realized that God is black and
that she loves me."

But really, I persisted: had it ever occurred to him to wonder
why, despite all he had been through and all the drugs and
therapies that had been poured into him, he had not gone
under—why he was able, more than three decades after his first
breakdown (when he tried to kill our father; when he hallucinated extravagantly; when he believed he was being taken, by
ambulance, to my funeral; when he tried to chew his tongue
out of his mouth; when he was straitjacketed and shot up with
large doses of Thorazine; when he had catatonic seizures), to

make a life for himself that was so much better than often, during these decades, seemed likely?

"Well, I had wonderful parents!" he exclaimed. He laughed, then was silent for a while. When he spoke again, his voice was warm, thoughtful. "I just wanted to survive and persist," he said. "That's all. And—I don't know—but it's like Faulkner said in the speech he made, for the Nobel, remember?—I wanted to *endure* somehow. I never really wanted to stay on the wards, but I'd get there and then the minute they locked the door on me, I would think, 'Oh my God—I've got to get out of here!' But then I'd throw fits and stuff.

"And also," he added, smiling, "because my brother didn't want to keep visiting me in hospitals."

2

IN THE WEEKS and months following Robert's breakdown, I speak several times with Dr. Kaluri, a young Indian psychiatrist who fills in part-time for Robert's regular (and regularly changing) prescribing psychiatrists. She is the only staff member who returns my calls regularly, and she tells me that, as in previous years, Robert is recovering quickly, and will soon be ready to leave the locked ward for a Beacon of Hope halfway house.

Beacon of Hope, a charity run by the Catholic Archdiocese of New York, has two halfway houses on the South Beach grounds and also sponsors other supervised residences and independent living units around the city. During the previous decade, Robert has been a resident both in its halfway houses and, for nearly two and a half years—his best and happiest times in more than twenty years—in one of its supervised homes on Staten Island, in which home he and two roommates lived by themselves (a social worker visited several times a week), taking care of all their own basic needs: cooking, cleaning, shoveling the walk, etc.

I tell Dr. Kaluri what Robert has been repeating to me: that he is very scared he has tardive dyskinesia, a condition caused by antipsychotic medications that results in constant and increasing tremors, not only of the hands and arms, but of the eyes, legs, feet, and head. Dr. Kaluri is aware of Robert's fears (tardive dyskinesia is usually irreversible), and concerned about his tremblings. After so many years and so many medications, she says, he has almost no reactions to dosages, and so it is hard to know what will and won't work, and what the side effects will or won't be. She intends to discontinue lithium and Haldol, and then to reintroduce them, in small doses, a bit at a time, after which, she believes, if the tremors subside, Robert will be ready for discharge.

"Psychologically," she says, "Robert is quite sound." I tell her I appreciate her concern, and her attempts to get the side effects of the medications under control. But what I wonder about is the following: While you are working to regulate the chemicals that pass in and out of him, who is dealing with his *human* concerns—day after day, alone in a locked ward and, often, on seclusion in a bare room—who talks with him or listens to him concerning his ordinary (and extraordinary) fears, his anxieties, his despair? Is *anyone* talking with him in any regular way about *anything*?

Not really, she says. She herself tries to find time to spend with him each day; sad to say, however, she has only ten minutes per patient. She also agrees that when Robert begins to regain his sense of humor (and self), as he has been doing, he becomes bored and irritated with the ward's activities, and with the kinds of low-level jobs the various social workers steer him toward. Robert is, she says, "much too bright to be happy with working as a part-time volunteer in a hospital gift shop." Robert is, she believes, capable, still, of making a good life for himself away from the wards and halfway houses of South Beach, and she hopes to see this happen.

South Beach Psychiatric Center is one of a small number of hospitals built in the late sixties by New York State when it thought it would be emptying its large mental hospitals and building a series of smaller hospitals that would look not like hospitals (or prisons), but like college campuses, and that would be located not out of sight, but within residential communities. It was "considered the jewel of New York's state mental hospitals," *The New York Times* reported in 1980, in a series of articles exposing the deteriorating conditions there.

When I visit Robert at the end of August, and walk from the bus stop to his ward, I am struck once again by how pleasant the hospital grounds are: small two- and three-story modern buildings set apart by well landscaped lawns. Robert's ward itself is clean and spacious, with many healthy-looking houseplants set in front of large windows, which windows let in bright light and provide a view, beyond abandoned, overgrown fields, of the Verrazano Bridge. The ward's bulletin boards are covered with colorfully lettered announcements, schedules, and charts (including one that lists the purposes, effects, and possible side effects of psychiatric medications), and the constant mix of sounds—TV, stereos, the chattering of residents—makes the lounge area seem very much like a college dormitory . . . except that the ward is locked by a thick and windowless metal door, that it has a medical station at its center, and that most of the people living in it look ghastly.

The patients sit around zombielike, for the most part, or pace back and forth, or sleep across lounge chairs. After Robert and I embrace, patients begin approaching and shying away, pestering him for food and soda. One man, grotesquely thin, stands immobile next to a wall, hugging himself tightly. Another man sits in a chair nearby, raking furiously at his hair, while next to him an elderly woman keeps weeping and wailing, her mouth wide open, yet without any sound emerging, and I am struck, on this visit, more by the sickly, drugged pallor of the residents—their half-closed eyes, their jaundiced, splotched skin, their stringy hair—than by their behavior.

Robert's tremors have diminished, but, since there has been no movement at all toward getting him out of Baltic and into Beacon, my concerns for his life have increased. (A year and a half before, when he was ready to leave this ward for a halfway house, the staff had "lost track" of things, Henry said, and so the halfway house had given away Robert's place. Forced to remain on Baltic's locked ward when he was well, Robert had become hostile and agitated, had broken down again, had been heavily medicated, and had wound up spending an additional five months there.)

Before my visit this time, I have called ahead and pushed for an appointment for the two of us with Robert's primary therapist, Henry Grossman. I've also asked about talking with Robert's social worker ("*I'm* Robert's social worker," Henry informs me). A few minutes after I arrive, the three of us meet in Henry's office (windowless, with two desks and barely enough room for the three of us to sit), and Henry opens the discussion with a question. "How," he asks Robert, "do you feel about your brother not letting you live with him?"

I am taken aback not only by the question, but by Henry's abrupt manner. I say nothing, though. If I challenge things Henry says in front of Robert, I'm worried this might frighten or upset Robert even more; and what is Robert to do—with Henry, with his feelings, with his life on the ward—after I'm gone, and Henry remains in charge? Robert, however, merely shrugs, looks away, and says that he's lived in New York City his whole life, and what would he do in Northampton anyway? He does, however, repeat that he wants to get out of Baltic, and that he wants to get off all the medications. "They zonk me out so I can't think straight about anything, or do *anything*!" he says. "It's as if my whole head's in a straitjacket. . . ."

Henry asks Robert what he thinks his options are after discharge, and Robert rambles a bit about where he would like to live—he talks about Section 8 housing (where the city provides rent subsidies), and living in an apartment on his own, or with his former housemate and best friend in a Beacon apartment—and Henry interrupts and tells Robert that "there is *only* one option" for him: the Beacon halfway house located on the South Beach grounds.

Robert looks at the floor and says nothing. I reach across, put my hand on his. I have the urge to ask Henry if he really thinks his harsh manner and seeming lack of kindness (for Henry does, I know, want to help Robert get out of Baltic; he does, he often says, really *like* Robert) can possibly be helpful to Robert. We're all silent for a few seconds, and then Robert raises his eyes, and speaks in a strong, clear voice.

"I am fifty years old," he declares, "and I have none of my own teeth, and I am not a member of the Communist Party, and I like girls *and* boys, and I am an American . . ." He pauses, then continues in a voice that trembles with indignation and passion: ". . . *and I don't have any rights!*"

When Henry asks more questions and, to Robert's replies, keeps pointing out the ways in which Robert contradicts himself, Robert sighs and shakes his head. "I am tired of answering questions," he says. "I have been answering questions for over thirty years. Why is everyone so *concerned* about me?"

We talk about other things, including our childhood home, and I am astonished to discover that Henry, who has been Robert's therapist for extended periods of time during three hospitalizations that span a half-dozen years, does not seem to know the basic facts of our family history ("So what did your mother do?" he asks at one point), or of Robert's childhood, or of his early hospitalizations: that our mother was a nurse who supported our family financially, often working night shifts and double shifts; that our father failed in business after business; that our parents fought bitterly and daily, using Robert and me as confidants in their battles; that our mother *and* father, by turns, regularly threw violent tantrums; that Robert was enormously gifted, when a child and young man, as a dancer, actor, and writer; that Robert has endured insulin-shock therapy, gas therapy, megadose-vitamin therapy . . .

Several years before, when Henry was a graduate student working at South Beach, he had taken a special interest in Robert and had told me he thought it a shame Robert was not receiving any kind of psychotherapy. I had, at the time, offered to pay for individual and/or private sessions, but Henry was never able to arrange for them. Now, Robert says that he very much wants to be in therapy again, that he wants to be able to talk with *somebody* once or twice a week—but Henry tells Robert what he has previously told me: "There is no way to do it through the present mental health system."

Henry asks Robert if he thinks I am "exploiting" him (I have, with Robert's approval and collaboration, begun work on this book). He asks Robert what kind of relationship he'd like to have with me, and—without either Robert or me mentioning phone calls—if Robert would like me to telephone him "less often." When Robert talks about all the memories he carries around, and the feeling he often has that he is forever living in the past, Henry says, "Then you feel you have no present or future?"

Henry also turns to me, frequently, and talks about Robert in the third person, as if he were not there. I am appalled, and I do what I can to ease the pressure of what seems, at times, a cross-examination, and to tell Robert what I believe: that he does have a future, though it may not always be a happy one, or the one he once dreamed of having. I talk about things he and I do share: the memories we have of experiences we've been through together, the plans we have to do things together in the future, and the warmth and affection (and, sometimes, hostility) we've had toward each other. To Henry's questions about how close Robert wants to be with me, I say something about feeling as if Robert and I live our lives on separate roads, but that sometimes I cross over and walk with Robert on his road for a while, and that sometimes he does the same and walks with me on my road, and that sometimes, for varying periods of time, our roads join and we walk along together.

Given all you've been through, I say to Robert, how could you *not* be afraid of the future?

Robert nods vigorously.

"Then you feel you never fulfilled your potential—is that it?" Henry asks.

Robert says he is angry with me for not letting him telephone our mother, and I explain, again, that our mother has been losing her memory and does not always know who I am— I have already made one emergency trip to visit her in Florida, and may soon have to return, to see about a nursing home.

During my last visit, she had proudly pointed to a shelf of my books. "My son wrote all these books," she said, then looked right at me, smiled brightly. "Have you ever met him?" she asked. When I told her that *I* was her son Jay Neugeboren, she laughed like a child, clapped her hands. "Of course!" she exclaimed. And then: "But it really is terrible, the way I forget things—it's a terrible mental handicap." When I mentioned my children—her grandchildren—she went around her apartment, showing me their pictures (though she did not know their names, or who was who). And when I mentioned Robert, she beamed. "Oh, Robert!" she exclaimed. "He's doing wonderfully, you know. He's somewhere in the South, and he has a very big job. Very big. He's very important—he has lots of people working for him and under him. He's *very* successful and happy, my Robert." After the third or fourth time she said this, it occurred to me that "the South" might be a reference to "South Beach," and I told her that Robert was living in the *North,* but at *South* Beach Psychiatric Center, on Staten Island. Was he married? she wanted to know. Did he have children? When I answered her questions, and added that Robert was doing well, as he was at the time, she asked if I ever saw him. I told her I saw him frequently, and that we talked with each other almost every day.

At this news, her memory seemed to return fully, and her eyes filled with tears. "Oh, Jay," she said. "I worried about him so—you don't know. You don't know." She stood, put out her arms, to embrace me. "You don't know how happy it makes me to know this." While she wept, I held her close. "He had his problems, and it was awful—so awful—but now that I know you and he are in touch, I feel better."

Now, in Henry's office, I tell Robert what I've told him before: that he's certainly free to call our mother whenever he wants, but since she probably will not know who he is, this might prove upsetting for him. (In the dozen or so years that preceded our mother's loss of memory, she had only telephoned Robert once, and had, during these years, made only one brief visit to him—for an hour, in 1981. In a letter I received from her a few years back, she had added a note along the letter's edge: "P.S. Please give my love to your brother.")

Our talk with Henry lasts for nearly an hour. It is only the second time in six years we have had a talk with him (our first talk lasted twenty minutes), and this is also, I realize, the longest session we have ever had with *any* therapist at South Beach (where no staff member, to my knowledge, during the previous twenty years, has asked for or taken a family history), and though I am amazed—and pleased—at Robert's ability to sit through the session—at his tolerance for such a wide-ranging discussion—I am also concerned that talking feelingly about so many matters from his past might stir up emotions he will have difficulty handling, especially after I head back for Northampton.

A week or two after our visit, then, when I return from taking Eli out to Ohio, I call Henry and ask if he's been able to have any follow-up talks with Robert since our session, and he says he has not, and that he will not. "Robert has such complicated and ambivalent feelings toward you and the family that it's hard to know what to make of them," Henry says. "And his mental state is so unstable that I'm not sure he knows what he really means." But Henry is glad we met and talked—perhaps we can do it again the next time I visit, he suggests—and it is good, he adds, to have some reference points now about the family, so he can understand Robert a bit better.

By early October, Robert has, either through Baltic's inefficiency or Beacon's inflexibility, lost his place at Beacon's halfway house (again), and his tremors have returned, as has his hostility. When we talk on the phone, he often yells at me or hangs up abruptly if he doesn't receive the answer he wants, or if I haven't done exactly what he's told me to do. He has now been on a locked ward for over four months, and when he gets into a fight there, he is put on higher doses of Thorazine, and, again, on isolation.

In the meantime, I am exploring other possibilities for Robert, both in New York City and in Massachusetts. I talk often with Milton Klein, a psychologist and lifelong friend who has known Robert since he was born (Milton lived in our four-family building on Martense Street in Brooklyn all through the years of our growing up), and has visited with Robert, several times recently, in his office. Milton declares that it is the hospital that is making Robert crazy ("We're not born crazy," Milton says. "People make us crazy"), that he himself will be Robert's therapist (if Robert agrees), and that the first order of business is to get Robert off the medications that are poisoning him. (Milton refers me, as he has before, to Peter Breggin's *Toxic Psychiatry*.) As before, I agree with Milton in principle—the hospital and drugs don't seem to be doing Robert much good—but what do we put in their place? Robert has done well on medications, and has broken when he has stopped taking them. How, simply, remove them from his mind and body without disastrous and unpredictable results? If and when Robert leaves the hospital, what will he do with himself, say, from nine to five, Monday to Friday? What will he do, and where will he go, and who will talk with him and care for him, if, as is probable, hard times return? And what medical doctor can Robert see for follow-up with regard to medications, blood tests, and the rest?

I ask Milton if he can locate a knowledgeable social worker for me in New York City, someone I can sit down with and to whom I can explain Robert's situation and history, so that when Robert is ready for discharge this time, we can know what options, if any (outside of South Beach's system), in terms of jobs, housing, follow-up, medications, and therapy, might be available. Milton says he will take care of it.

I have no illusions that we are, in any definitive way, going to make Robert *better,* I say, but I do believe Robert can have a better *life* than the one that has been his in recent years.

I talk with people in Massachusetts about halfway houses and programs in my area (none seem viable, either psychologically or financially), and I talk with Dr. Kaluri occasionally, even when she is no longer assigned to Robert. I point out that Robert has now been on a locked ward for nearly half a year, has had dozens of changes in medications, has experienced awful side effects (tremors, incontinence, dizziness, constipation, diarrhea, insomnia), and is becoming increasingly frightened, angry, and impatient. If he has to wait indefinitely to get out, he'll surely break again, I say. What, if anything, can be done?

Dr. Kaluri has no answers, but tells me, in confidence, that, despite its high cost, she is thinking of recommending clozapine. She also says that the staff know Robert well, are tolerant of his behavior and sensitive to his needs. Despite the trouble Robert often causes—how difficult he can be when he begins screaming, spitting, and striking out—the staff *like* Robert, she says. She does agree, though, that some kind of talk therapy is essential, and suggests I call Baltic's "Team Leader" (the ward's administrator), Nick Farini.

I do, and he repeats what Henry says: that therapy is not an option, but that the staff interact well with Robert, and *like* him. (Robert is, to be sure, enormously likable; given the treatment he often receives, though, it occurs to me to wonder what happens to patients whom the staff does *not* like.) I offer to help in any way I can, ask that I be kept informed, and tell Nick that nobody ever calls to let me know about major changes in Robert's situation. He promises to stay in touch.

He does not. In the meantime, Robert, on new medications (Klonopin and Ativan), and with yet another new prescribing psychiatrist, is put on seclusion more frequently and, groggy from the medications, spends most days alone in his room, sleeping.

"So I hear you've been talking to everybody and getting them to do things for me," he says, when I call one night in early November. We talk about ordinary things—his meals, my children, Chanukah, his finances, the flu that's going around. Everybody's sick these days, I say. "Especially here!" he exclaims, then laughs. When I say that I don't think he's sick, he replies, "But I am! I am—want me to prove it?" He tells me that Henry keeps giving and taking away privileges, and that every time he tries to talk with Henry, Henry is in his office, eating, and that Henry always tells him to go away. Robert thanks me for calling, and for the money I sent him for Chanukah. "I wish I could respond," Robert says, "but money doesn't mean anything to you"—he pauses—"and it means *everything* to me!"

Toward the end of November, Robert does begin to recover, is given passes to leave the ward (we spend a day together, outside the hospital, the weekend before Thanksgiving), and he is, once again, put on a waiting list for a bed at Beacon.

Though he can now roam around the city by himself during the day, he returns at night to a locked ward, and in our visits and talks I begin to fear the recurrence of an old fact of his life: that his periods of medical and psychological stability offer fleeting opportunities that need to be seized and acted upon, or else, inevitably, he becomes restless, bored, frustrated, nervous, angry, violent, manic. . . .

In the meantime, seven weeks after Eli leaves home, he telephones, sounding frightened and disoriented. "I did it again," he says. We talk for a while, and the next day I fly out to Ohio and spend a week with him while he comes down from a bad LSD trip, one in which he has had strong suicidal impulses. He is, by turns, confused, lost, hostile, and—the good news—determined to deal with long-standing drug habits, some of which he has kept hidden not only from me, but from the therapist he was seeing during his last two years of high school. (Gifted as Eli has been at many things—art, music, sports, science—he has also been gifted, sometimes to a fault, at knowing how to please others; unlike his brother, Aaron, who tests me constantly and ingeniously, Eli has worked hard most of his life—often, as now, by concealment—at figuring out how *not* to get me upset or angry.) Eli is very affectionate and witty, very happy I am there with him (when he is not surly), very open with me about things he's done and has kept secret, and very, very scared by what he has been through.

He blinks often, and keeps shaking his head, as if by doing so he will be able to jiggle things back into place. After we check him out medically (he may, the doctor says, have recurring "flashes" for a year or so), and after he has set himself up for psychotherapy at the student counseling center (we go to a session together), and after we have, at his initiative, met with the dean (Eli is on probation), and when he seems on his way to recovery, I decide to return home.

Shortly before I leave, he turns to me and, swallowing hard, asks if I know what his greatest fear has been during the past few weeks. I shake my head sideways.

"That you would have to take care of me for the rest of my life the way you've been taking care of Uncle Robert," he says.

A few days after my return from Ohio, my son Aaron telephones from New Mexico and tells me he has good news. "At least I think it's good news," he adds. He says he wants to transfer to the University of Massachusetts, where I teach. I note that he has previously talked about transferring to UMass at some point, and he says, "No—not at some point. For the spring semester—in January." He asks if I can help him with his application, and with logistics. I groan inwardly—I have had seven weeks alone and, to my surprise (and relief), have found that I enjoy living alone (though I *have* had seven weeks, I tell myself at once, and not many single parents get even seven weeks). What about dormitory applications and deposits, I ask. *"Dormitories?"* Aaron replies. "Why would I want to live in a *dormitory?"*

We also talk about Eli, and what he's been through (Aaron has his own more overt history of drug problems and academic difficulties), and I ask if he's ever been worried or frightened that he might be like his Uncle Robert in some ways.

"Are you *kidding?"* he replies. "Of course I have. Lots and lots of times." He laughs. *"I* know I'm insane. I've just been working hard to keep other people from finding out."

We talk some more—now and later on—and I think of how, even when Aaron was first born, I was aware of fearing for him the way he now tells me he has been fearing for himself. Like Robert, Aaron was the second child born; like Robert, he was, at birth, underweight and golden-haired; like Robert, he was, in his early years, less physically resilient than his older sibling. And later on, when, like Robert, he developed somewhat strange sleeping and eating patterns, various addictions, phobias, and eccentricities, and when, like Robert, his performance in high school became erratic and his mood swings severe, I would sometimes find myself slipping: when I called him to come down to supper, or talked about him to friends, or became impatient or angry with him, I would hear myself calling him Robert instead of Aaron.

When, during our conversation now, I say something to him about respecting his privacy (I've asked if he's aware that he has what might be called an addictive personality, and he laughs and says of course he's aware—*"Might* be?" he responds), he replies, as he has before, with an easy, "But what do you mean? You're my *father*! You can always ask me anything. I'll never lie to you, Pop."

Three weeks after I return from Athens, Eli comes home for intersession. Five weeks later, on January 1, the day before Eli heads west for the start of his second semester, Aaron arrives home to stay, and during these weeks—between Thanksgiving and the New Year—Robert's release to Beacon delayed again and again, the inevitable occurs: Robert deteriorates steadily, rapidly.

He spends his time outside the hospital buying lottery tickets, opening and closing bank accounts, finding and cashing in empty soda cans, visiting the two or three friends he has. He goes to a day center on South Beach's grounds most days, as the hospital requires, but this only increases his restlessness and—especially—his anger.

When I ask him what it is about the place that makes him so angry, he replies quickly: "I'm angry because I'm being treated like a second-class citizen—like a subpatient—and always told to wait. I'm treated like a sub*moron*! Like the most important thing in the world is their lunch hours! And the people there, the other patients, I don't mean to condescend, but their mentality is so *low*. I mean, they're nice and all that, but there's nothing to do there all day but wait until I can get out. They keep telling me I'm raising my voice, and I am. *I am!* But the schedule's for idiots—Monday it's 'Gym and Leisure' and 'Weekend Review,' and Tuesday it's a movie that's so godawful I wouldn't even watch it if it was on TV, and there's something called 'Vocational Planning,' which is really just group therapy, and I'm not in group therapy. I mean, I'm not good at it: I tend to dominate or to do nothing. I've never received any help from group therapy, in all the years I've been sick. . . ."

When I ask if he's talking with the young man assigned to him at the day center as therapist, he laughs, and tells me that this person, who has only a bachelor's degree (without a major in psychology), is grossly overweight, smokes all the time, asks stupid questions, and is very, very dumb.

"He *means* well," Robert says, using an expression our father used to use for relatives none of us could stand, "and I'll show up for my appointments, I guess, but when he asked about doing therapy with me, what I told him was that I thought neither of us was qualified."

Robert becomes increasingly bored, combative, and confrontational, loses his "privileges," is put back on isolation, has his medications (along with his psychiatrist) changed (again), and the dosages increased.

At the same time, I am receiving calls from Florida, telling me that my mother has become a danger to herself and others: that when she wakes in the middle of the night, she runs from her apartment, battling anybody who tries to restrain her, and goes out onto roadways and highways, trying to stop cars. (I recall, when I was a boy, being asked to walk her father—my grandfather—to the bus stop, so he could return to his old age home in Manhattan; when we got to the bus stop, however, he would push me away, walk into the middle of the street, and begin rapping on car windows, asking people if they were going to Manhattan. When he found somebody who said yes, he would open the car door and get in.)

And so I find myself spending a large part of each day on the phone to nursing homes and home nursing agencies, social workers and lawyers, to get round-the-clock care for my mother until I can get a nursing home placement for her. I speak frequently with her friend Marty Kaplan (a man her age, eighty-two, who has been her companion for ten years, but whom she refuses to marry or live with), and he sometimes telephones me late at night or before dawn to tell me, in detail, about his bleeding (from cancer) and his bowel movements, and to warn me that if I don't come right down—the next day!—and take care of things, he will call the state welfare board and have them come and cart my mother off.

I locate several nursing homes for my mother (this proves a

lot easier once the homes find out—and the information is always solicited early in our conversations—that my mother has the wherewithal to pay on a private basis, and is not a Medicaid case), fill out applications, get the necessary documents in order, and my mother, too, like Robert, is put on waiting lists.

Though I continue to call Robert nearly every day (and to visit him every four or five weeks), I find that I'm often tired from the calls—weary, exhausted—even before I make them, and I also find, especially when Robert takes off on lengthy, nonstop accounts of his daily life (how much he received for the soda cans he collected; how much he won and lost on lottery tickets; how many showers he's taken, how many times he has or has not masturbated), that I have taken to holding the telephone receiver away from my ear, or setting it down on a table, or making up reasons for getting off the phone before he finishes his monologues. ("But listen, *Jay!*" he immediately says each time. "Jay . . . ? *Jay—?!*") Sometimes, however, I simply say that I love him and that I'll call him again soon, and—before he has time to reply—I hang up. My patience, too, I realize, like Robert's, is rapidly, steadily disappearing.

Nor does Aaron's return home give me the ease I long for. During his first few weeks home, he reverts to his old habits— never saying hello or good-bye, never cooperating on basics of living together, and resisting my every request (e.g., to turn down his stereo, to wash some of the pots after dinner). He spends most of his time in the darkness of the TV room, and if I even attempt to talk with him, or to get him to talk with me, he begins cursing angrily—calling me a shithead, a fucking this or that—and, after walking out on me, slamming doors loudly (ways of acting that, he claims, he learned from me).

When I am able to get his attention, and to tell him that I don't think his living at home again is going to work—that if we are living in the same household, we need to have a minimum of cooperation, civility, and communication—that I am not an innkeeper—he walks away, saying that he knew this would happen, he knew I would kick him out of the house. "I'm not kicking you out," I say. "But you're twenty-one, and if living here makes both of us miserable . . ."

A few minutes after this, though, he knocks on my door, comes in, tells me that when he was in New Mexico, his friends thought he was nuts to want to return home and live with his father.

"But I thought it would be a *good* idea," he says, his voice quivering with emotion, and, something I have rarely seen, his eyes brimming with tears. "I mean, I don't expect us to be pals or anything, like I would be with roommates in a dorm, but I honestly thought it would be good for the two of us to live together, just you and me, and to get to know one another . . . and to—well—to just be together here for a while. . . ."

At these words, I open my arms for him—"I love you, Aaron," I say—take him to my chest, kiss him; he hugs me hard, kisses my cheek, and I say that I think it's just fine that he has come home.

When, on December 29, 1993, nearly eight months after Eli's graduation, I telephone Robert's new psychiatrist, Dr. Aldrich, a doctor who has known Robert for many years and is filling in until a new full-time psychiatrist is assigned, the doctor agrees with me that Robert is sound psychologically, and that it's a shame to keep him on a locked ward. He, too, is surprised to learn that Robert and I talk with each other most days. (Do these doctors *ever* talk with Robert, I wonder, or look at his chart, or review his history? One of his previous psychiatrists, announcing to me that he was going to try "a brand-new drug" on Robert—Depakote, an anticonvulsant—is surprised to learn from me that Robert had, in fact, been taking Depakote, and for more than a year, immediately before his present hospitalization.)

When I ask Dr. Aldrich how long it might be before Robert can leave the ward, he says this isn't his department. I say that I know Robert is fifth on the waiting list for Beacon's halfway house, and I wonder if there's anything that can be done to move him up on the list. The problem, the doctor says, is that there simply aren't enough facilities. I ask if there is anything I can do to help. "Talk to the governor," he replies, and he hangs up.

I sit at my desk, staring at the phone. *Talk to the governor?* I'm appalled, enraged, stupefied. And I am also tired. I'm tired from my talks with Robert, and I'm tired of having hospital personnel ignore me and/or treat me this way, and I'm tired of raising three children by myself, and I'm tired of dealing with my mother's situation and Marty's tantrums, and I'm tired of struggling to make ends meet financially. And I'm also tired, as with Robert and his doctors (and with Aaron, at times), of holding back—of not saying what I feel and think when, as now, I'm feeling especially furious, beleaguered, depleted, and helpless.

You bastards, I keep thinking. Oh, you fucking bastards! There was a window of hope there, when Robert was lucid, happy, and full of energy, and Robert pressed you to do something, and I kept asking you to do something, and you did nothing, gave him nothing really—just the same old stuff: drugs and passes and a locked ward. Out of sight and out of mind. Out of mind *so* out of sight. Goddamn your eyes, all of you . . . just goddamn your eyes. . . .

And afterward, when my rage and frustration subside, I find sadness rising up, especially during and after conversations in which Robert's sweetness, in the midst of crisis (and tantrums), shines through—when he asks me to please call often and tells me how much our talks mean to him; when he asks me about Aaron, Miriam, and Eli ("I don't know Aaron the way I know Eli. I want to know him. Do you think he can visit me here? Would that be a good idea, or would it upset him?"), and talks at length about how he wants to help put my children through college; when he suddenly weeps about our mother ("I'm never going to see her again, am I? That scares me, Jay— that I'll never see her again!"); when he jokes about having his privileges taken away ("It's like a Jewish concentration camp here, Jay, except I'm keeping kosher"), or teases me, without trying to hide his hostility (to my usual statement at the close of our phone conversations—"I love you, Robert"—he now takes to replying, "I wish the feeling were mutual. You love me and I don't love you. See? Life is *not* fair, Jay . . .").

My talk with Dr. Aldrich, then, throws me into a state in which my inability to get anyone to help me to help Robert (Milton, despite his promises, never locates a social worker for me), along with my inability, often, to see how I am going to provide for my children (I experience some major rejections in my literary life, for books I've been working on for a half-dozen years), begin to feed upon each other. And our talk has also, I realize, stirred up feelings of helplessness and sorrow which I recognize as being very much like those I felt more than thirty years ago, when Robert first broke down.

I find myself, again, recalling my visits to Robert during his first hospitalization, in February 1962, two months before his nineteenth birthday, and I find myself seeing Robert again as, in midsentence, he would sometimes freeze into catatonic positions—arms and legs bent at acute angles, mouth wide open, eyes closed tight, as if, I thought then, he resembled, in bone structure, a deadly and beautiful prehistoric bird. I would stand by while aides lifted him and carried him off—he was so rigid, it seemed as if he had been starched and folded—and tied him into a straitjacket, or strapped him down to a bed.

Before and after visits—he was on a locked ward at Elmhurst Hospital, in Queens—I used to imagine that Robert was a small, starving bird, his mouth eternally open, waiting for his mother to return to the nest and give him food, but that, instead, a large funnel had been inserted into his mouth, and an endless river of pills was being poured into him.

I recall looking into his mouth—at raw, grotesquely swollen flesh—on the day after he tried to chew his tongue away, and I recall wishing more than anything in life that I could trade places with him—that he could be out and I could be in—

that I could do something—*anything*—to bring him back, to help him become the brother I had known only a few days before.

I recall, too, being scared that his fate would soon be mine. I recall, during drives to and from his ward, wondering if my writing was itself a more insane enterprise than anything Robert had ever done—wondering if my intense desire to make sense of life through words and stories, along with the actual madness and violence I sometime conjured up *in* my stories, and the endless river of rejections these stories brought back to me, was not itself the clearest sign of my innate perversity, my lethal self-absorption. I recall imagining that my mind was a house in which my feelings, memories, and thoughts, caged until now in separate rooms, were going to blast forth, knocking down walls and doors, shattering windows, rushing around murderously, exploding into flames, and destroying everything I had ever been, known, or felt.

In January 1994, as in February 1962, I find myself feeling not only that I can't do anything to keep my brother from deteriorating, but that all my efforts to help may be useless, and worse than useless. I find myself wondering again—as I did, sometimes suicidally, thirty-two years ago—whether my own seeming survival has been bought at the expense of my brother's life. ("This is my love child," our mother would always say about Robert, while lavishing affection and kisses on him. "That one," she would say, pointing to me. "That one's a cold fish. That one's selfish and mean. All he ever thinks about is himself. Who could ever love *that* one? Mark my words—that one's a killer.")

I know that my feelings and fears, now as then, are irrational, but this doesn't stop them from being mine, and from possessing a bewildering and terrifying power. And so, in the hours and days following my talk with Dr. Aldrich, I find myself once again fearing that I may, in my own way, be as mad and lost as Robert.

Dr. Aldrich's words—*Talk to the governor?!*—stay with me, insinuating themselves into my waking hours, my sleepless hours, my conversations with friends, my conversations with myself. I wonder too: Am I mad to walk around, as I often do—at home, in my office, in the street—talking aloud to myself? Am I mad to have spent tens of thousands of hours living the lives of people who have never existed—the imaginary characters in my novels, scripts, and stories?

And the ongoing drought in my literary life intensifies my sense that, no matter what I try to do—for myself, or for those I love—I am going to be rejected. Though since when, I quickly ask myself, have I been a stranger to rejection? Before I published my first story, I had acquired, by count, 576 rejections; before I sold my first novel, at the age of twenty-eight, I had written eight unpublished books and had received more than 2,000 rejections. For most of my adult life, the fact of rejection has been a constant that has, if anything, usually served to inspire me. I've rarely *taken* rejections of my work personally, though I have, to be sure, often *felt* them personally. . . .

But then, after a few days in which the doctor's words continue to repeat themselves inside my head, I find myself smiling. *Talk to the governor?* You bet I will! After a few days, I find that my fear and fatigue, along with my feelings of humiliation, shame, and failure (for not being the writer, father, and brother I keep imagining I *should* be), give way to rage, and that the rage transforms itself into the sweetest, most inspiring of muses—that I can, that is, make use of the rage within me to fuel my imagination, my will, and my prose.

So I do exactly what Dr. Aldrich has told me to do: I talk to the governor. I put aside the manuscript of this book (along with the manuscript of a new novel) and spend several days working to produce a letter, and to keeping the letter to a single page.

Dear Governor Cuomo:

A week ago, when I asked my brother Robert's psychiatrist at South Beach Psychiatric Center, on Staten Island, if there were anything I might do to help get my brother out of the locked ward he has been on for more than six months (since for several months now there has been no medical or psychological reason for him to be on such a ward), the psychiatrist said, "Talk to the governor," and hung up on me.

So I am, by this letter, talking to you. My brother Robert, who has spent much of the past thirty-two years as a patient in New York State hospitals—but who has, in recent years, been spending increasing time out of hospitals, and functioning well while out—had a breakdown this past June, and was put on the Baltic Unit at South Beach. For several months now, according to all reports, and by my own observations (we talk nearly every day and see one another frequently; I have been his caretaker for the past two decades), he has been doing well. He is coherent, animated, funny, warm, and very eager to get off this locked ward—a ward where his activities are gravely restricted: he cannot even have toiletries (since other patients might drink them); visitors to the ward are turned away; passes to get off the ward are given and taken away depending upon his levels of "irritability" (but who wouldn't be "irritable" if locked up with 30 psychotics 24 hours a day?); snacks are kept in a padlocked refrigerator which is opened twice a day at "refrigerator time"; phone messages are not given to him; he can keep no personal possessions; etc.

Three months ago his previous psychiatrist stated that Robert was psychologically sound, and that the only reason he needed to stay on the Baltic Unit was so that some troublesome side effects of medications (severe trembling) could be brought under control. That happened a while ago, yet the staff at Baltic says there is no alternative but to continue to keep Robert locked up until a bed becomes available at Beacon of Hope House (a private halfway/recovery house, on the South Beach grounds), and they seem, during the past few months, to have failed fully in being able to reserve and/or secure a place for him at Beacon, while offering no alternatives. So Robert languishes on a locked ward, and he continues, needlessly, to cost the New York State taxpayers considerable sums of money because, in truth, the staff has messed up in handling his case and transfer.

I realize how busy you are, but here is a very fragile and very human life—my brother's life—that is dying a bit, day by day, because of bureaucratic ineptitude. I love Robert very much, and want to do anything I can to help, and since his doctor told me there are no alternatives but for him to stay locked up indefinitely and/or for me to "talk to the Governor," perhaps, I hope, the second of these alternatives can provide a way out of the darkness and frustration to which he has been condemned.

I mail the letter, and find that the very act of writing it, shaping it, and sending it—of believing, again, that I am not yet totally powerless to help Robert—restores me. When I talk with Robert in the weeks that follow (and when I write, and when I deal with my children), I am more patient, less tired— more accepting of those situations (with hospital, with children, with the literary world) about which I may not be able to do much—and, at the same same time, more determined than ever to continue trying.

3

ON A WEDNESDAY AFTERNOON in late January, a few minutes before I begin teaching (and three weeks after I have sent off the letter to Governor Cuomo), I check my answering machine at home and find a message on it from Nick Farini, Baltic's Team Leader, saying he wants to talk with me about Robert. Worried that Robert's situation has become grave (this is the first time a staff member from Robert's ward has *ever* telephoned me without my having telephoned first), I return Nick's call, and it turns out (but why am I surprised?) that he wants to talk with me not about Robert, but about my letter to Governor Cuomo, a copy of which he has received from Albany. I tell him I'm about to teach, and we set up a time for us to talk the next day.

By the time I get home that night, Robert has called (collect) three times, and when I return his call, he sounds dreadful—he weeps and he screams, he babbles in Hebrew (calling me by my Hebrew names, identifying himself by his Hebrew names), and he tells me he's been *very* upset because Nick Farini came onto the ward from his office, and that *Nick* was very upset. "He told me he wants to talk to you about a letter you sent to the governor," Robert says. "Did you really write to the governor about me?"

I tell Robert that yes, I did write a letter to the governor, in the hopes of persuading someone in his office to help speed up Robert's discharge. "Good, Jay. Good," Robert says. "Thank you. Thank you." We talk for a while (I keep picturing Nick— an overweight, heavy-smoking, nervous man—rushing onto the ward to give Robert the news about my letter to the governor, and I shake my head. Is the man mad? Is there a chemical, I wonder, that can cause or cure chronic bad *judgment*?), and after I get off the phone, I check my journal entries: the last time I spoke with Nick, when he promised to keep me informed regularly, was four months ago.

The next morning, I telephone Nick, and he immediately tells me that he is *very* disturbed that I wrote to the governor— my letter has upset him greatly, and has been the cause of a thorough reevaluation and "rejustification" of all of Baltic's practices; he adds that he simply cannot believe *anybody* at Baltic would ever say what I claim someone said. Can he ask who it was? I tell him it was Dr. Aldrich, and Nick says he is "shocked." In truth, he now allows, he would not have been surprised if I had told him it was one or two other doctors, but Dr. Aldrich is "the nicest guy in the world," a devoted "patient advocate" who "really likes Robert." Dr. Aldrich is an "ideal" to everyone here at South Beach, Nick says, the kind of guy who "can't walk down the street without trying to help somebody."

Nick keeps me on the phone for an hour or so, going

through my letter sentence by sentence. The letter is "very unfair," he says, although, he admits, "nothing in it is not true." But there are, he claims "always two sides to every story" (e.g., the refrigerator is padlocked because otherwise patients would steal one another's food; the staff like Robert so much that instead of throwing out some of his possessions they are using part of a staff closet for storing them). Nick claims that he did, in fact, do everything possible to get Robert into Beacon, but that Beacon was "inflexible" and "inconsiderate."

I tell him I wish I'd known he had worked so hard to get Robert placed there. But Robert is still on the waiting list, and my only concern remains his well-being. If Beacon is closed to him indefinitely, what, if any, are our other options? Nick says that other city and state halfway houses Robert is eligible for are, in a word, "terrible." Because Beacon's halfway house is on the South Beach grounds, and because Robert is familiar with it, they feel it is the only option, and the *best* option. It provides structure, familiarity, and convenience, and therefore the staff kept hoping they could get Robert a placement there.

But if you can't, I ask, what do we do?

Nick says they will keep trying to get Robert into Beacon, and he assures me the staff at Baltic *like* Robert, and adds: "I think our team has done a terrific job with Robert."

The next day, Dr. Aldrich telephones me, and he is livid. He tells me he has seen my letter, that I took his remark out of context, that I slandered him—that I made him seem like a schoolteacher accused of abusing children—that he now has to go through an "inquisition" at the hospital, and that his "entire professional life is being called into question." He calls me a liar, demands a retraction, and wants to know why I didn't call him back if I was so upset, and why I didn't call Beacon, where the real problem is.

I listen patiently, and somewhat wearily—I am tired of these conversations and confrontations (whether real or imagined), and tired of expending energy that, in the end, as now, seems to make so little difference for *Robert*—and when Dr. Aldrich finally stops spewing forth his fury, I say, "But you said it. You told me to talk to the governor, and then hung up."

When he screams, again, about how I took his remark out of context and didn't write about all the other things he said, I say that my letter was only one page long. Perhaps, I suggest, he was simply the wrong man saying the wrong thing to me at the wrong time, and I ask him to consider the context in which I *received* his remark: that I have been trying, unsuccessfully, to get people at the hospital to talk with me; that Robert keeps being wait-listed indefinitely and I know that if he doesn't get into a halfway house soon he'll have another breakdown; that my calls are never returned; that when I asked about holding on to Robert's bed at Beacon, I was told "there was no problem" and if there was, that "Henry could handle it"; and that though I can hear how upset Dr. Aldrich is about my letter—surely I am aware his work is often thankless, grueling, and has *its* frustrations—what I care about most of all is my brother, and when I asked what I could do for Robert, and he told me to talk to the governor, the limits of *my* frustration gave way.

But Dr. Aldrich is so enraged that he hears little of what I say, and, in truth, he does seem to me to be a decent man, doing the best he can in a difficult situation, so that by the end of our talk—he *demands* several times that I write a letter to the director of the hospital, and to Albany—I say that nothing in our conversation (the first I have ever had with him, though he has been assigned as Robert's doctor, intermittently, for at least a decade) indicates he is a man who would make the kind of thoughtless and gratuitous remark he did in fact make.

Several minutes after my talk with Dr. Aldrich, Nick Farini telephones. "Are you all right?" he asks. Dr. Aldrich was so furious, Nick says, that he is calling just to make sure I'm okay. I tell him I'm fine, and he says something about not everyone at Baltic having people to care and fight for them the way he and Henry have fought for Robert. (Henry is on vacation; when he returns, he calls to tell me how upset he is that I didn't call *him* before writing to the governor; he too promises, again, to keep me informed regularly.)

I get off the phone, and I think: It's like asking a monotone to be an opera singer. I have been dealing with people like Nick and Henry and Dr. Aldrich for over thirty years. The sad truth is that gifted therapists do not often work for the state, and if and when they do, they soon wear down. How not? They work with meager and ever-changing budgets, without adequate professional and technical resources, with restrictive bureaucratic rules, and with patients whom others—families *and* institutions—have often given up on.

The people who have worked with Robert are sometimes caring and sometimes competent, but they have rarely provided him with what he needs most of all in this world: constancy and continuity. In a life filled with so much *in*constancy, one of the great needs in Robert's life has been for some professional or professionals who knew him and his history, who would stick by him, and to whom he could turn, in good times and bad, no matter where he was.

Though I can appreciate the difficulties and constraints under which the staff at South Beach work (e.g., their need to control the ward and protect its residents), what I wonder about most of all is the simple and sheer paucity of imagination that now, as thirty years before, winds up instituting, for complex and troubled adults, a reward-and-punishment system that is as ineffective as it is crude. Isn't it, at the least, foolish, for example, to keep *demanding* delayed gratification from those who are where they are precisely because, genetically or otherwise, they *cannot* delay gratification?

And Robert is, to be sure, a lot more experienced at being a mental patient than people like Henry and Nick are at helping mental patients; Robert is clearly—no asset—a lot brighter and more imaginative, despite all, than most of those who have, for thirty-two years, been paid to care for him, and a lot more adept, alas, at manipulating others (to his own destruction) than others are at working to help him learn to care for himself. (What do people like Henry and Nick think they are proving when they describe, at length, how *bad* Robert has been, and how uncooperative, resistant, and disruptive he is? Since Robert is where he is precisely because he is unable to care for himself, or to have much insight into why he feels and acts the way he does, why continue to fault him, and to punish him for lacking insight into his condition, and for not taking responsibility for it?)

I spend the next few days drafting a letter to the director of South Beach, in which letter—two pages long this time—I spell out my concerns, my frustrations with the staff, the context of Dr. Aldrich's remarks, and my hopes for the future ("the better informed I am, on a regular basis, the more helpful I can be to my brother").

Though the staff at Baltic are, for a while, a bit more solicitous (Henry calls two or three times, to report on Robert's condition), Robert's deterioration continues. He becomes increasingly agitated, hostile, and disoriented, loses all his privileges again, and is placed, yet again, on isolation ("reduced stimulation"). When I am able to get through to him, he talks endlessly about money, and screams at me for virtually anything and everything I say.

One evening, though, when he is calmer (he has been whimpering and pleading: "Please get me out of here, Jay. Please . . . Please . . ."), he suddenly starts yelling at somebody else, shouting that he *received* the call from me—that he didn't *make* the call. A moment later, an aide takes the phone away from him and demands to know who I am and if Robert telephoned me.

When I say that I am Robert's brother and that I telephoned him, the aide gives the phone back to Robert.

In mid-February, a few weeks after my talks with Nick and Dr. Aldrich, a bed becomes available for my mother in a nursing home in West Palm Beach, and I fly down to Florida. My mother *looks* wonderful—she is eighty-two years old, yet appears to be a strikingly athletic, energetic, happy, silver-haired woman in her early sixties. Her blue eyes are more radiant than ever, and though she does not seem to know who I am at first, once she learns that I am her son, she is overjoyed, and constantly hugs and kisses me. "I just want to touch you," she keeps saying. "I love you so much, so much."

Physically, she remains in excellent shape: her blood pressure is 120/70, her pulse 72, and full sets of lab tests (required for her admission to the nursing home) reveal no evidence of either previous heart attacks or brain hemorrhages (both of which, for many years, she claimed to have suffered). She paces from room to room most of the day, picking up lint from the carpeting, reaching down and, without bending her knees, staying bent over for minutes at a time as she moves along at her self-appointed task.

Her short-term memory is all but nonexistent (if she turns away, and then turns back, she will ask me who I am, when I arrived, and why I am there), but her long-term memory remains fairly intact. She remembers her mother and father clearly, and when I ask about them, she talks easily.

"My mother hated me—oh did she hate me!" she says. " 'I hate you,' she used to say to me. I was her fourth daughter, you see, and she would say to me, in Yiddish, 'I needed you like a hole in the head.' And she hit me and smacked me around a lot, and then two years after I came into the world my brother was born—that was Izzie—and I wasn't even allowed to *touch* him, he was such a prince. But she hated me. She beat me up a lot."

And her father?

"Oh no—he was a sweetheart. He worked hard—twelve hours a night in the bakery, and he came home tired. I worked twelve hours too, you know—oh how I worked. Double shifts and split shifts, and you couldn't just keep working, so I had to come home from the hospital, and then go back as if it was another day, with four hours in between, and then work another four. I worked very hard. But she hated me. Oh, did she hate me."

She has no understanding of where she lives, or what day it is, or why I am there. "I never hurt anybody," she tells me, over and over again, "and I never wanted to be hurt. If people wanted to fight, I walked away. And I never took from anybody either. How I put it together—our home—I don't know. People thought I was rich, but they didn't know what I did—how I connived. And nobody has to know—here too, when I go outside and people ask me how things are, I tell them they're fine, that everything is fine. Nobody has to know my business."

She asks several times if I am married and if I have children, and I keep repeating that I am divorced and have three children—her grandchildren. She is surprised by this news and when I say I am raising my children and putting them through college by myself, she keeps asking about their mother, and if I visit the children when they are with their mother.

So I tell her, again—this on the morning I am getting her ready for her move to the nursing home; the last morning in which she will ever live outside an institution—that my children live with me full-time.

"What happened to their mother?" she asks.

She left them, I say.

When I say this, my mother gasps and clutches at her blouse, above her heart, and begins weeping freely. "Oh my God!" she cries out. "Oh my *God*! How could she? How could any mother do such a thing? How could she? How could she . . . ?"

When we arrive at the nursing home, which is small and pleasant—with colorful posters on the walls, lovely gardens, a small, well-kept library and crafts room, a staff that seems bright and attentive—and show my mother to her room, and when I set up some photos on her night table, and put a few familiar objects around (a Chagall print, one of my novels), her confusion suddenly vanishes.

"This is *not* my home!" she cries. "What are you doing to

me? I am *not* going to stay here. Don't you put my things in that closet. You can't make me stay here. What are you *doing* to me? This is *not* my home!"

I talk with her gently—tell her that since her friend Marty is ill, and I have to go back home to my job and to my children, nobody can be with her at night, so we wanted her to be in a place where she would be well taken care of—but she keeps insisting that this is not her home, and then she starts to run down the corridor. "I'm getting out of here!" she cries. Some of the staff members see what is happening, and they distract her, get her talking about herself (I hear her saying that oh yes, she was a nurse too, once upon a time, and worked very, *very* hard), and they tell me to leave—that they will take over.

But less than an hour later the head nurse calls, complaining about how difficult my mother is, saying they can't handle her—that my mother keeps trying to get out, that she won't take her Haldol (prescribed by somebody who has not yet met her)—and that she is responsible for twenty-nine other patients. Can "the girl" who was with me (Maria Gomez, a certified nurse's assistant who has been taking care of my mother during the day) come and stay with her? The head nurse has dealt with Alzheimer's patients before, she says, but never with a woman this active and this resistant.

This active and this resistant. I smile. That's my mother! Has anybody *ever* been able to tell her what to do, or to get her to do something she didn't want to do? But I stop smiling when I recall, instantly, the sessions we would have in her Queens apartment after visits to Robert, sessions in which my mother would, literally, be banging her head against walls and tearing out her hair—wailing, screaming, weeping about what the world was doing to her and to Robert! When I would try to console her—to tell her how I sympathized with her for what she was going through—she would turn on me. "*Nobody* knows what I'm going through. Nobody!" she would declare. "Don't you *dare* tell me you know what I'm going through." When I would suggest that perhaps it would help if she saw a therapist—if we all did—she would turn on me. "*Me* see a therapist? Never! I'm not the crazy one," she would snarl. "You think anybody is ever going to get *me* to change? Not on your life, mister." And when I said I wasn't accusing her of anything, that I just wanted to help ease things for her, she would come close and wag a finger in my face. "I'm not the one who has to change," she would say then. "I'll *never* change, do you hear me? The whole world can go and change before I'll change. I'll *never* change. Never, never, *never* . . ."

An hour after I have put my mother in the nursing home, I return, with Maria, and I try to calm my mother down, to reason with her and reassure her—I will come back in the morning, she will not have to stay here forever, Marty will visit her as soon as he is well—but no matter what I say, she keeps repeating that this is not her home. After a while, however, she begins to tire, and to let Maria and me help get her ready for bed. She touches my hand very gently and, tears running down her cheeks, she whispers, "I just want to die. I want to die. . . ." She takes her medicine and gets into bed, Maria at her side, holding her hand.

I make my way out of the nursing home slowly, looking around at the other residents—in their hospital beds, or lined up, in their wheelchairs, in the corridors—and trying to understand how it can be that all of these people, like my mother, had full lives once upon a time—families, jobs, histories, hobbies, struggles. Few of the residents seem alert—those who are not lying in bed sit passively in wheelchairs, their eyes glazed by drugs, or by age, or by who knows what. Some of them tremble and shake, some stare at TV sets, others cry out as if in the midst of nightmares, repeating phrases over and over again. It occurs to me that the residents, most of them Jewish, look very much like people in photographs of concentration camp survivors: pale, thin, maimed, misshapen (many residents lack legs, arms, fingers, noses), and oh so weary of this world.

Leaving the nursing home, and driving to my mother's

empty apartment in Century Village, the senior citizen enclave (a walled-in community of about fifteen thousand residents) in which she has lived for more than twenty years, I wonder how it can be that such a full, difficult, and complicated life can end in such a small space. I think of Robert, a thousand miles away, and imagine him asleep on his ward. Sometimes—especially at South Beach—when I look at him, or hold him, I wonder, too, how it can be that so much history, pain, and memory can be contained in such a small body, and that this person I am looking at or holding is the same person I once held, in my bed and in my arms, fifty years ago.

Back then, after I thought our parents were asleep, I would often get out of my bed, lower the side of Robert's crib, lift him out and take him into my bed with me, so we could play and snuggle, so I could tell him stories and touch his skin, skin whose soft silkiness never ceased to amaze me. If our mother found us out, as she often did, she would put Robert back in his crib and yell at me—accusing me of not loving my brother, of having woken him up and taken him into my bed because I wanted to hurt him and be mean to him.

Aaron, who drove me to the airport, is waiting for me when I return from Florida. On our drive home, he asks about his grandmother, and I tell him about my time with her. "I'd like to go to Florida with you the next time you visit her," he says. He tells me that Robert sounds pretty good—that he has been calling frequently. I talk about how, years ago, most people never thought Robert would have even the semblance of the life he now has—that he would be forever shut away on some back ward.

"Well, maybe," Aaron says, "that didn't happen because of some person I know who's been doing things for him all these years."

A week after I return to Northampton, I receive a call from Doris Kelly, director of social services at the nursing home, who tells me she has had to have my mother transferred to the psychiatric ward of Bethesda Memorial Hospital, about a half hour away, in Boynton Beach. Doris tells me my mother was out of control, manic, and delusional—that she kept trying to run away, kept banging on windows, kept fighting with nurses.

So I am on the phone most of the next few days, finding out about her medications, talking with her psychiatrist, talking with the staff at Bethesda Hospital, talking with lawyers, financial consultants, and health insurance companies, faxing consent forms and authorizations (before leaving Florida the week before, I went to court and received emergency guardianship powers). The hospital and nursing home keep me closely informed—call me, in fact, each time they give my mother a new medicine (she is taken off Haldol and, irony of ironies, put on Klonopin—the same *new* medication Robert is on), or each time she falls down, or, sometimes, just to report on how she is doing.

A social worker from Jewish Family Services, Art Strauss, visits my mother frequently and reports to me regularly. He is doing what he can to get my mother moved up on the waiting list at the Morse Geriatric Center—a much larger home, with more facilities and staff, more wherewithal to care for a woman in my mother's condition. Art has, in fact, been a godsend during the past half year—not only checking out nursing homes, home nursing services, lawyers, and Realtors (we need to sell my mother's apartment in order to fund her upkeep in the nursing homes), but often anticipating needs and situations (e.g., as now, challenging what seems to be excessive sedation of my mother), and making sensible suggestions about how to handle matters. And he has also called often, as he does late on the night I first put my mother in the home, and a day or two after I return to Northampton—simply to find out how *I* am doing.

When I visit Robert a few weeks after my return from Florida, he is shaking terribly again, and is very upset about our mother. He is angry at me for bringing him all the wrong things (and then grateful to me for bringing him all the right things), and keeps talking about all our old friends and relatives who are now living with him in his hospital (and pointing them out to me); at one point, while we are alone in the courtyard, and just after several dozen patients have filed back into the ward following their hourly five-minute "smoking time" (the patients enter the yard in single file, an aide standing at the door, lighting a cigarette for each patient as the patient passes by), and after I have tried to ease Robert out of his gloom with a joke, he turns to me and—the first time he has done this since we were boys—he slaps me.

I am more surprised than hurt (though I *am* hurt, and say so), and Robert is, afterward, almost inconsolable. "I just have all this *rage* in me sometimes," he says, "and I don't know what to do with it." I put my arm around his shoulder, and he cries, though while he does I notice that he has his fists clenched tight, and that he keeps opening and closing them.

"I like to bite people when I fight," he tells me. "Did you know that? And I get envious of you, Jay, and of the life I don't have." He pauses. "What I think," he says then, "is that you matured, and I never did."

That week I also receive a call from my mother's sister Evelyn, who lives in Florida, an hour's drive from West Palm Beach. Evelyn, ten years younger than my mother, and also a registered nurse, tells me she visited my mother, who is back at the nursing home after a ten-day stay in the psychiatric ward—and that she found my mother all by herself at the end of a corridor, strapped into a wheelchair, sitting in her own piss and shit. I telephone the nursing home, my Florida lawyer, Art Strauss. . . .

A few days after this, when I call Robert, I am told that he is not allowed to receive any calls, and that he has been "four-pointed." When, nearly a week later, Henry returns my calls, and I tell him I've been unable to speak with Robert for six days, he says that Robert has lost his phone privileges because he "abuses the phone" and was out of control.

"Are you surprised?" he asks.

Henry then tells me (again) about how impossible Robert

is—how he curses loudly, screams at telephone operators, keeps demanding refunds from the phone company, dials 911 and tells the police or fire department there is an emergency on the ward (and to come get him out!), spits at aides, scratches them, strikes other patients. This is why Robert was considered dangerous, and not allowed out of his room. I tell Henry that I know how difficult Robert can be, but why, I ask, wasn't he allowed to talk with me once a day on the staff phone, as Henry and I had arranged? What possible *medical* reason can there be, especially when Robert is doing poorly, for depriving him of any contact with the world beyond the ward—of the right to receive even a single phone call?

Henry says he won't dispute the fact that there was some miscommunication—that he *had* given Robert permission to talk with me once a day—but, he adds, "between us," that the "caliber of help" on night shifts is not especially good: the people are not well educated, and often don't look in the "special privileges book." Henry also asks if I understand what being four-pointed means. I say that I assume it refers to a series of demerits—four points and you lose your privileges.

No, Henry says, it means that Robert was physically restrained on a mattress, with his arms and legs tied down at four points—at the wrists and ankles. As a general rule, Henry explains, no patient is allowed to be four-pointed for more than two straight hours, and while being four-pointed the patient is checked every fifteen minutes.

Two days after my talk with Henry, I fly to Florida again— to appear in court for a guardianship hearing, and to pack up and close my mother's apartment (which has been sold). I spend four days there, cleaning out the literally tens of thousands of packets of ketchup, mustard, maple syrup, salt, sugar, pepper, and salad dressing my mother has taken from restaurants and squirreled away in drawers and closets, along with hundreds of used yogurt cups, and thousands of paper napkins—each one unfolded and rolled into a tube—all items neatly arranged and stacked, row after row, layer upon layer. I go through closets

and dressers, through books, photo albums, and papers, deci
ing which items to save (I send most of the usable furnitι
to Miriam, for her apartment in Washington, D.C.), and wh
to give to charity.

Alone in my mother's apartment, surrounded by the remaining artifacts of her life—by objects I've known since I was
a child, items that have traveled from Brooklyn to Queens to
Florida—cookie tins, silverware, and cutting boards; ashtrays,
lamps, and linens; books, newspaper clippings, decks of cards,
stationery supplies, sewing supplies, letters and post cards
going back forty and fifty years (and some items—a wooden
spoon; several prayer books; family photos—that made the journey from Poland—Galicia—to America before my mother was
born), I find myself lost in time and in memories. I find locks
of my brother's hair, and of mine, from our first haircuts; I
find a chair from the 1939 World's Fair (I recall going there,
and being carried around on my father's shoulders); I find letters my mother wrote and never sent ("For my Grandchildren—I hardly know you, but I remember how much you love
me, and how you looked when I first saw you—and how happy
I was . . .").

I go through box after box of buttons, photos, letters, documents (tax records, birth certificates, a copy of a handwritten
page from the "Thirteenth Census of the United States: 1910
Population" that lists the names, birthplaces, and occupations
of my father's family—his parents, his eight brothers and sisters), I wonder about all those parts of my parents' lives I will
never know anything about—about all the stories that have
gone and will go to the grave with them—and I become lost
not only in imagining what these stories might be—who were
these people, and what were their lives like, day by day?—but
in discoveries: I am surprised, for example, to find that though
my mother has had no contact with Robert for many years,
she has, in Florida, been an active member of the National
Alliance for the Mentally Ill.

I find myself remembering, as if it happened the week before, a summer evening in 1946, when I was eight years old and Robert was three. My mother and her four sisters have taken me and Robert and our cousins to Kenoza Lake, a farming community a few hours north of New York City, for the summer. Each family rents separate rooms in small cottages (there is a communal kitchen), and our fathers arrive for weekends, or for a week or two of vacation.

I see myself, in bathing suit and striped polo shirt, sitting on the grass beside a wooden dock and watching my mother and Evelyn swimming far out in the middle of a lake. I watch them make their way silently through the water, in a straight line, one behind the other. My mother is doing the backstroke, and I watch her arms move gracefully through the air and back into water, again and again. The sun is about to disappear behind low hills—its slanting rays make the lake's surface appear calm, hard, black—and, watching my mother and Evelyn slice clean, quiet lines in the surface of the lake, I cannot believe how beautiful, happy, and peaceful they seem.

They were young women then, my mother and her sister—they were young nurses, wives, and mothers, with young children (one of Evelyn's four children would, years later, at the age of nineteen—the age Robert was when he first broke down—jump from a building in Queens and kill himself). That women who worked so hard—that women who, at home or away from home, never ceased moving and doing, could seem, at the end of this summer day, so at ease with themselves and the world, and could let me be with them while this was so—this seemed amazing to me, as magical as it was improbable. And on that evening nearly fifty years ago, my mother was, I now realize, twenty years younger than I am on the evening I sit in her empty apartment, remembering her.

I talk with my children by phone each night—Aaron at home in Massachusetts, Miriam in D.C., Eli in Ohio—and I tell them about items I find, about things I'm saving for them, or shipping to them, or want to show them someday—things I remember from my childhood that will be gifts to them from their grandmother—and I find myself feeling a tenderness toward my mother I have not known for years.

When I visit my mother at the nursing home, though, I am stunned—she seems to have aged twenty years in a single month: her color is awful (jaundiced, pale), her eyes are lackluster and half closed, her speech slurred. Her equilibrium has been so unbalanced by medications that she cannot stand by herself. The staff try to get her to stay in a wheelchair, yet she is, even in her drug-induced stupor, determined to remain independent. (After this visit, with help from Doris Kelly and Art Strauss, I am able to get my mother's medications reduced. After this visit, too, when I go through hundreds of pages of Medicare and insurance papers, and discover that the home's consulting psychiatrist has already been paid for more than a dozen forty-five-to-fifty-minute "psychotherapy sessions" at $180 a session—these in addition to thousands of dollars paid to him for "medication management," "nursing facility care," and "subsequent hospital care"—I call him and inquire; he claims the hours listed as forty-five-to-fifty-minute psychotherapy sessions were used to evaluate my mother, and to instruct the staff on how to deal with her.)

On our first afternoon together, while I am walking with my mother along a corridor, she suddenly grabs at a door, and when I try to help, she pushes me away. But the door, painted red, is a locked supply closet. A minute later my mother mumbles something and looks down, and I realize she thought the closet was a bathroom, and that she has just soiled herself. She breaks away from me, finds an abandoned wheelchair, sits down in it, and begins, furiously, tearing off her slacks and her underpants. Two nurses try to stop her. They tell her that they will take her to her room and change her, but she fights them off.

A third nurse arrives, and the three nurses take my mother away. I follow them and enter my mother's room, but the nurses ask me to please leave while they change my mother's diaper and get her dressed. Now and afterward, I talk with staff members—they are exceptionally patient, concerned about all the "wandering" my mother does; they try hard to involve her in activities, and their dedication to their work, and to the individuality of each resident, is touching. Still, it is clearly easier in this home, with its limited facilities and staff, to control the ward and its patients, and to get the meals and pills out on schedule, if the patients are sedated and in wheelchairs. As it is on Robert's ward, I think, so it is here: if you are active or manic or demanding or resistant, you are given more drugs, made more helpless and dependent. Passive, depressed, and compliant patients rarely lose privileges, or suffer the wrath and abuse of those paid to care for them.

Once, while I sit quietly beside my mother in her room—she has been calm and sleepy for a while, and her chin is at her chest—she reaches over, caresses my hand warmly. "I love you, Jay," she says, but without lifting her head or looking at me.

When, during our walks together, I ask questions—Do you remember Kenoza Lake? do you remember Martense Street?—she sometimes nods yes and sometimes shakes her head sideways. On several occasions, when I mention the names of people—her husband, David; her sister, Evelyn; her best friend, Mary—she nods, bites her lip, squeezes my hand, and cries.

In the shuffling way my mother drags her feet while we walk along the home's hallways, and in her stooped posture, and in the pastiness of her skin, and in the way her eyes stay half closed, in the way spittle runs from her nose and mouth, and in the very feel of her hand when she clutches at me or pushes me away . . . in the streams of seemingly unconnected words she speaks, in the quality of her voice, and in the particular way she whimpers and heaves when she cries, she is so like my brother—her son—and so unlike the woman I left here a month before, so unlike the woman I have known my whole life long.

Without much memory of her past, she seems, too, free of the bitterness, grudges, resentments, and anger she has carried with her most of her life. In any one hour I receive more affection from her than I have received during the previous fifty-five years of my life.

On my last night in Florida, driving from the nursing home to her apartment, I find myself wondering, too: Do I somehow love being responsible *for* her more than I love or ever loved *her*? Am I now, in caring for her—as for Robert and for my children—merely trying to prove (to her? to myself? to the universe?) yet again that I am not the mean and selfish boy she always told me I was? Do I care for others, still, in the hopes that if I do a good enough job, somebody will, still, come along and care for me in the way *I've* longed to be cared for my whole life long?

After the movers have come and gone—on my last night in the apartment—I telephone Robert. I tell him about the guardianship hearing (the court has, by law, been obligated to send him a notice, which notice has upset him greatly): the social worker, lawyer, and doctor who visited our mother all agreed her loss of memory is so severe that she can no longer live by herself. I tell him I have moved her to a nursing home. He asks me questions about the home, and I tell him she has a private room, and that the people who work in the home seem very caring, and have lots of activities planned for the residents (bingo, a newspaper, outings).

"Remember what I once wrote?" he asks, and then recites a line he has frequently recited for me through the years: " 'Home is there which now is here.' "

I tell him I'll be flying home back the next day and intend to visit him the following weekend, and he begins telling me the kinds of sandwich, soda, and cigarettes I should bring, and a list of other things he needs: sunglasses, a pocket watch, new underwear, socks . . .

I also tell him that I have had a call from a man who works for the New York City office of the state Department of Mental Health. The man's name is Dan Farrell, and when I come down to New York City next week I am going to meet with him. I tell Robert what Dan has told me: that when Robert is ready for discharge, Beacon will *not* be the only good alternative for him—that when Robert is ready for discharge, some kind of regular therapy definitely *will* become a possibility.

Dan has also told me that until Robert stabilizes again—while he remains in Baltic, that is, and until he can pass the screenings required for admission to a halfway house or some other program—there is little we can do. He agrees about "windows of opportunity"—when anyone has had the history Robert's had, he says, the duration of these periods is usually brief, and if you don't seize them, the patients usually decline again. "But let's meet and strategize," he says. In the meantime, he adds, if I have any concerns, I am to call him—and I should feel free to let the people at South Beach know that, in his words, "the state has taken a special interest in Robert."

Robert tells me again that he is sorry he hit me, and sorry he criticized me for putting Mother in a nursing home. "You did the right thing, Jay. You did the right thing. A home is best, a home is best," he says. Then he starts crying again and talking through his tears: "A home is best—yes, yes—but listen, Jay, I would love to see Mother one more time before she dies. Can we, Jay? *Can* we? Do you think maybe, when I get out of here, that we could take a train ride together to Florida, Jay—do you think we could do that?"

He says he can't wait to see me—"Hurry, Jay. Hurry!"—and that he already knows where he would like to live when he leaves Baltic.

"Where?" I ask.

"In the nursing home with Mother," he says.

"Oh, Robert . . ." I say. We talk some more, and I repress the urge to make a joke—to talk about getting him and Mother some kind of a two-for-one deal—and while we talk, and afterward, I think of my mother and my brother, on their separate wards (and on the same drugs), one in New York and one in Florida, and I let my mind float free and wander—so many memories, I think: so many years, so many losses, so many feelings, so many words, so much sadness and disappointment. . . . Still, my minutes and hours alone in the near-empty apartment—like the chance to take care of my mother when she hardly knows I am doing so, like the hours spent with her these past three days (which hours, I suspect, are the last I will ever spend with her)—seem a gift: they allow me to remember, to reflect, and to grieve for all that was, and was not, and may never be. They allow me to wonder again how lives that were full of so much hope once upon a time— so much energy, so many dreams, so much desire—could have come to so little.

4

DURING THE WEEK in which Robert was born, I stayed with the family of one of my father's three older sisters—with my Aunt Esther; her husband, Sol; and their four children— and what I remember most about that week is pieces of paper: those upon which I drew pictures—World War II warplanes mainly, B-24 bombers, Flying Fortresses, Flying Tigers, Messerschmitts, fighter planes like the Corsair, with wings that folded up—and those upon which my mother wrote to tell me I now had a brother whose name was Robert Gary, and who, for the rest of my life, was going to be my "best friend."

She wrote the letter from Bushwick Hospital, on April 18, 1943, the day after Robert was born, and I remember looking at the names Robert and Gary again and again, and being thrilled because these were the same names as those of two of my best friends on Martense Street—Robert Schneider and Gary Brody—friends who lived in the two large four-story apartment houses that lay between our small four-family house and the near end of our street.

I was almost five years old, and as happy during that week, my last as an only child, as I can ever remember being. I loved the adventure of being in my Aunt Esther's home (and away from my own home), I loved being doted on by my older cousins, I loved seeing my father each evening when he arrived for supper, after work, and after he had visited my mother and brother in the hospital, and I loved conjuring up in my mind the physical presence of the golden-haired infant my mother described for me—a brother who looked like me, she said—a brother I could help take care of, a brother who would somehow be *mine* for the rest of my days.

(Before Robert was born, I had an imaginary friend I often played with, and so intense was my relationship with this friend—so real his imagined presence—that once, while my father's three sisters were visiting—my mother was serving them coffee and cake in the living room—I burst into tears and carried on inconsolably until, pointing at my Aunt Molly, who was sitting on our couch, I cried out that she was sitting right on top of my friend.)

At first I believed Robert had been named *for* my two friends, but my father told me he was named for his mother, a grandmother I had never seen. Her name was Bela Gittel, and she had died before my father met my mother (my parents were married when he was thirty-two and she was twenty-five). My father had registered for Brooklyn Law School the week before his mother's death (he never attended college; in those days one could go straight to law school from high school), but after his mother died, and after the week of mourning, he canceled his registration, got a job, and never returned to school.

I didn't understand. Why was my brother being named for a dead woman? My father explained that it was a Jewish tradition to name newborn children after loved ones who had passed away—that this was our way of keeping these people alive in our memories, and in our lives. Just as I had been named for his father, Yakov Mordechai, so Robert was being named for his mother. Since she was a woman, however, my parents used the initials of the name only—a common practice at that time among American Jews—and then selected equivalent masculine Hebrew names. Thus, Bela Gittel became Boruch Gershon (Robert's Hebrew name), and Boruch Gershon became Bobby (Robert) Gary.

(For the first three days of my life, my American name had been Jacob Mordecai. But my parents fought over this name— my [nonreligious] mother wanting me to have a Jewish name, my [religious] father wanting me to have an American name. Three days after I was born, the name Jacob Mordecai was crossed out on my birth certificate and the name Jay Michael written in above it.)

In name and spirit, then, Robert and I began our lives married to each other, as it were, he with the gender-modified name of our grandmother, I with the Americanized name of our grandfather.

My father was next-to-the-youngest of nine children, and my mother was third-from-the-youngest of eight children (two older brothers died as infants in Poland). My parents' brothers and sisters were all married (before and after his mother's death, several of my father's older siblings lived, with their spouses and children—and with their brothers and sisters—in his parents' home), and they all, with one exception, a family with an only child, had at least two children—so that I grew up with thirteen sets of aunts and uncles, and more than three dozen first cousins, almost all of whom, along with dozens of my parents' aunts, uncles and cousins, lived within walking distance of our home in Brooklyn, and *all* of whom I saw regularly.

(Now, one generation later, in what seems a curious new diaspora, I have cousins living in Israel, Brooklyn, and the Canadian Rockies; in New York City, upstate New York, and on Long Island; in Pennsylvania, California, New Jersey, New Hampshire, Wisconsin, Florida, Maryland, Ohio, Texas, Nevada, and—since I have, through the years, lost touch with virtually all first cousins on my father's side of the family— who knows where else. But, like my children, who have no first cousins, no aunts, and only one uncle [Robert] and one grandparent [my mother], and like virtually all my friends, I have no relatives living anywhere near me. Now, most of the time, it seems, social services have come to perform functions that family, synagogue, and neighborhood once performed, and they seem to perform them—as with my mother and brother, on their wards—in settings far from anything resembling home.)

The attitudes and beliefs that marked family life for me and Robert in the years during and immediately following World War II—the near-worship of education and hard work, along with the supreme value put upon loyalty to family and to the Jewish community—also marked our communal life. About our lives as first- or second-generation Jewish-Americans Robert and I were taught to believe two things simultaneously: that the freedoms we enjoyed could enable us to prosper in ways rarely known by Jews in any time or place ("I *love* America!" my father would cry out when he could not abide our criticisms of our government's policies. "Do you think you would be free to criticize the government this way in Russia?"); and that these freedoms were, as ever, conditional—that anything we achieved or possessed (actual or emotional) could at any moment be taken from us (though our father sang praises to freedom of speech, he also warned us frequently, especially during the McCarthy era, "never, *never* to sign petitions").

Our family lived in the same apartment, at 221 Martense Street, from 1940, when I was two years old, until 1959, when I graduated from college and Robert was in his third year of high school. Our own block and neighborhood, in a lower-middle-class area of the Flatbush section of Brooklyn, were not, as it happens, mostly Jewish. About a third of my classmates throughout elementary school were black, and a majority of the families who lived on our block were Catholic (Irish, German, Italian). No matter our origins, though, what seemed true for me and Robert seemed true for our friends, Jewish and non-Jewish, white and black: those beliefs and attitudes given to us at home, and in our extended families, were echoed in the world beyond our family—not only in our churches, synagogues, and schools, but in the schoolyards, alleyways, museums, libraries, movie houses, candy stores and on the stoops, apartment-house roofs, and ballfields where we spent our free time.

Thus, the world into which Robert was born on April 17, 1943, now seems, at least in memory, whole to me, largely because what was in place—whether family or friends, luncheonettes or commandments—for the most part stayed in place, day after day and year after year, and because the people with whom we interacted, at home and on the street, were not strangers.

My parents' friends were the parents of my friends, and the brothers and sisters of my friends were Robert's friends; the owner of the fruit-and-vegetable store around the corner was the father of my friend Steve, who lived next door to me, and with whom I hung out with after school, and whose sister Gloria was Robert's classmate; our butcher, Mr. Klein (Milton's father), who lived in the apartment above us in our four-family building, brought our meat orders to us evenings when he came home from work, and Milton gave me weekly guitar lessons when I was ten years old at a dollar a lesson; my father brought home our eggs—three dozen at a time, wrapped in newspaper (a dozen or more of them double-yolkers set aside for me)—from his older brothers, Harry and Manny, who had a butter-and-egg business on the Lower East Side; my Hebrew School teacher, Mrs. Berg, lived two houses down from me, and I played football and stickball with her son, and wondered about her daughter, who seemed different—slow-witted, awkward—and who often disappeared, without explanation, for months at a time; our mailman, Ralph, spent most mornings in the kitchen of the elderly bachelor brothers, Leo and Phil Rubensohn, who lived in the apartment next to ours, so that a steady stream of neighbors would come knocking at the Rubensohns' door to get their mail; our landlord, Mr. Schoenemann, a German Catholic housepainter, lived in the four-family building connected to our building (with his brother, he painted our apartment every three years), and his wife worked at a bakery a block away where I sometimes bought our bread; Mrs. Demetri, my favorite elementary school teacher, lived around the corner from me, and I took oil painting lessons from her at night in her living room; Jimmy, the delivery boy for our grocery store (which was next to the butcher shop, which was next to the fruit-and-vegetable store, which was next to the candy-store-and-bookie-parlor), molested me and my friends sexually, on separate occasions (as we later learned), in the lobby of my best friend Gary's apartment house (Mrs. Berg's building), two houses down from mine; Gary's younger brother Burton, Robert's age, was Robert's best friend throughout elementary school, and would, during the early years of Robert's hospitalizations, visit him regularly. . . .

The world into which Robert and I were born, then, and in which we grew up together, did not contain any more mystery, conflict, joy, or unhappiness than, say, the place in which I live now (the Amherst-Northampton area—a rural New England region that is home to five colleges; The University of Massachusetts, Mount Holyoke, Smith, Amherst, and Hampshire), and in which I have lived, taught, written, and raised my children for the past quarter century, but its elements do seem, at least in memory, to have been connected to one another in an ongoing, natural, and daily way, and to have remained so throughout the course of my growing up, so that, just as I came to know and be known by my aunts, uncles, cousins, friends, and neighbors in the ordinary course of the ordinary round of life (births, illnesses, deaths, holidays, graduations, weddings, feuds), and through an extended period of time, so too did I come to know and to be known by others in the community in which I lived.

I have been living in the Amherst-Northampton area and teaching at the University of Massachusetts for twenty-four years, and I have been living in my present home for ten years. My home sits on a quiet, tree-lined street of handsome (mostly Victorian) private homes, one block from the Smith College campus, in a city and region that is culturally rich and physically beautiful. I have been living in this area longer, in fact— *astonishing* fact—than I lived in Brooklyn, yet I share little with anyone on my street or in my neighborhood other than an occasional hello. What, then, I've often wondered (this was especially so in the weeks and months following Eli's graduation and Robert's breakdown), am I doing here—a Jew from Brooklyn, one generation removed from the Old Country— living in the land of Emily Dickinson and Jonathan Edwards?

My synagogue is a five-minute walk away, and all through my children's growing up our family went there each Sabbath. I had been active in the synagogue—had led the youth group, chaired the education committee, served as president for two years, and been on the board of directors for a decade. And yet, after my children's mother and I divorced, and I became a full-time single parent, for nearly a half-dozen years—shortly after my term as president, and during the time of my children's Bat and Bar Mitzvahs—no member of a synagogue of some two hundred families ever invited me and my children for a Sabbath or a holiday meal.

How could this be, I sometimes wondered, and was the problem mine in some way? Did the lack of connectedness I felt to the world beyond my home come from whatever it was in me that had struggled, and thrived, in the tens of thousands of hours of solitude that came with my life as a writer, or from my somewhat anomalous family situation? Was the port from which I set out and which I was headed toward still the essential isolation of my life, no matter my seeming efforts through the years at joining with others for communal enterprises, whether in family life, or in writers' groups, or on athletic teams, or in the synagogue, or at the university, or in political and social action?

Did what seemed a lack of neighborliness and community in my life derive merely from the accident of those who happened to be my neighbors, or from the nature of academic life, or from something in the New England character—from its extreme regard for privacy, its reticence, its love of good fences? Whatever the origins and reasons for my feelings and speculations, what seems clear is that the place in which I have come to live is vastly different from the place in which Robert and I grew up largely because the family (nuclear *and* extended), as we knew it when we were boys, has ceased to be an active presence in our lives.

Back then, for better or worse, husbands and wives stayed married to one another for life; senile parents lived with their children, or with their brothers and sisters, until they died; and troubled, eccentric, or retarded family members (though often mocked and miserable) frequently grew up and grew old with their families, and within the neighborhood communities into which they had been born.

Thirty-two years ago, when Robert was first hospitalized in New York City, a steady stream of aunts, uncles, cousins, and friends visited him and wrote to him. Now, entire years go by, one following the other, in which he receives not a single letter, note, call, or visit from any of his former friends, or from any of our dozens of relatives.

Though I am, on occasion, as capable as anyone of singing hymns to the Brooklyn of our childhood—to that world usually associated with the Brooklyn Dodgers, Coney Island, bagels, egg creams, and the rest; to a world in which illness and eccentricity were not automatically banished from daily life—I also know what I did not sense back then: that such exercises

in nostalgia can sometimes be veils for rage and resentment—
for suppressing and repressing the actual unhappiness and cru-
elty that often lay at the heart of our growing up. (For every
afflicted family member who lived at home, there were also
daughters, sons, brothers, and sisters who lived on the back
wards of state mental hospitals, and whose presence there—
stigma, guilt, and shame at least as powerful then as now—
was never talked about.)

Still, whatever misery and tragedy lay in wait for us, or
existed, overt or hidden, in the world around us, near or far
(the Warsaw Ghetto uprising by Jews against the Nazis began
on April 19, 1943, two days after Robert was born), few intimations of such unhappiness seemed present during the week
of Robert's birth.

When my father brought me home to our apartment, the
door to my bedroom was closed, and he urged me to open it.
I did, and there, on a chair in the middle of my room, bright
sunlight pouring down upon them, were my mother and
brother, my mother cradling Robert in her arms while he
sucked at her breast.

My mother had never seemed so relaxed to me, and my
father had never seemed so animated. I was surprised. Throughout most of my childhood, and especially at home, my mother
was forever frenetic—forever *doing,* rarely able to sit still for
more than a few minutes—while my father was an angry and
withdrawn man whose major purpose in life, most days, seemed
to be to get me to be good to my mother—to obey her wishes,
and to anticipate her desires: to be quiet when she slept, considerate and adoring when she was awake. But on this day, like
a child set loose in a toy store, he was moving here and there
in what seemed a frenzy of delight. My mother laughed at his
antics (he bent over, I recall, and kissed her on the mouth,
then kissed Robert on the forehead), and asked me if I wanted
to hold my brother.

I said yes, and I sat down on my bed. My mother lifted
Robert from her breast, placed him in my arms. I touched his

face, and when I did I could not believe how smooth and soft, like warm satin, his skin felt. I recall too—especially—the motes of dust that slanted down from two rear windows into my bedroom, and how the light filled the room and flickered among the frail wisps of Robert's hair.

My mother seemed to me then what she rarely seemed before or after: a truly happy and satisfied woman, and my father seemed transformed too—boyish, surely, but proud and confident in a most uncharacteristic way: as father, husband, and man. Do I idealize? Perhaps. But in my memory it is as if there was a happiness in that room as tangible and weightless as the motes of dust that floated lazily in the air and drifted down upon my hands and upon my brother's hair and skin. It is as if Robert and I were in that moment like those golden, airy motes—as if we could, as in the dream of my namesake, ascend and descend upon them forever.

For an extended moment in time, the four of us were a *happy family*—the happy, united family my mother and father had always dreamed we would be. (Years later, during Robert's first long-term hospitalization, my father would write, in a single-sentence postscript to one of my mother's lengthy letters, "As for your Dad, I am well, and as long as my family is ONE I am happy.")

My mother allowed me to carry Robert across the room, and set him down in his crib. I remember smoothing the blanket over him, drawing its satin edge to his chin. A short while later I ran out into the street, to find my friends so I could bring them home with me and show them my new brother.

My mother's mother, the eldest of eight children, had escaped from Russia to eastern Poland during a pogrom. My mother's father, one of seventeen children, from the village of Burshtyn, in the Carpathian Mountains, had been taken in by her mother's family, in Tarnopol, while doing his military service there in the Austro-Hungarian army (or, depending upon which relatives one listened to, while fleeing *from* his military service).

Her mother's family, in the dairy business, sold milk to the soldiers.

My mother's father fell in love with a young daughter in this family, but in a replay of the story of Jacob, Leah, and Rachel, he was, he maintained, tricked into marrying the eldest daughter—my grandmother. To the grave, he spoke bitterly of the dowry he was promised more than a half century before, for marrying my grandmother, and had never received.

My mother did not speak with her own mother for the last eight years of her mother's life; because my grandfather attended my Bar Mitzvah, my grandmother, my Uncle Izzie (my mother's only brother), and my Aunt Ethel (her eldest sister) did not come. My mother's greatest fear, as a girl growing up in the Williamsburg section of Brooklyn, was that the police would be in her apartment when she came home from school, as they often were, to break up the battles between her parents. Several times she described watching in awe while her mother lifted her father bodily and threw him down the staircase. She claimed to have lived her entire life horrified by any kind of violence, and to have hated religion of any kind because all religion ever did, as far as she could tell, was to make people go to war against one another.

Her parents' major occupation, as far as Robert and I could tell (we rarely saw our grandmother, and our grandfather never knew us well enough to get our names straight), seemed to lie in the intrigues they wrought by dangling minuscule legacies, to be dispensed after their deaths, in front of their children. They had no inhibitions about choosing favorite children (Izzie belonged to the mother; Esther, a few years older than my mother, to the father), and about making the children choose sides in their ongoing war.

Unlike the grandparents of our friends—of *everyone* we knew back then, Jew and gentile, white and black—our grandparents did not live together. Our grandmother lived in a narrow storefront building she owned and took care of: fixing the furnace, repairing the roof, cementing the sidewalk in front of the house. Our grandfather, a baker, lived on the Lower East Side, in a large, dormitory-style room at the Bialystok Home for the Aged, in which room he had nothing of his own but an iron bed and a narrow metal locker. When I visited him I was surprised to discover how much he was admired by the other men, for his storytelling and for his learning.

He would, I was told, sometimes sit in Prospect Park and gather people around him so he could, in Yiddish, entertain them with extravagant tales and extemporaneous poetry. When Izzie, his only son, died at the age of thirty-eight, he gave the eulogy in rhymed Yiddish.

At intervals, he would visit our grandmother and, for the right to sleep with her overnight, pay her fifty cents. At intervals, too, my mother, her sisters, and Izzie would try to get their parents back together. I recall, in particular, the year we were all invited to attend a family Seder at Izzie's house. For weeks before the Seder, like a child telling me about a party she'd been invited to, my mother kept clapping her hands and jumping up and down and repeating: *Momma and Poppa will be together again. . . . Momma and Poppa will be together again. . . .*

But the Seder was cut short by a major family battle— screaming and shouting about who had done what to whom, and why, and when—and all the way home, I recall (after Robert had vomited in the backseat), our father chided our mother, who kept sobbing and chewing on her knuckles, about how silly she was to have hoped for what would never be. When, he kept asking, would she ever learn?

Before Robert was born, my father was doing fairly well in what was known as the "installment business." Partners with his brother-in-law Hymie (Molly's husband), my father had clients he referred to fur, clothing, and linen stores on the Lower East Side that were not open to the general public. He paid the stores for the purchases, then collected the charges (in installments, with interest) from his clients.

Not long after Robert was born, however, my mother went back to work, and my father started various stationery and printing businesses. I remember him proudly showing me, on a new set of business cards, the name he had created for his company, which name combined his and my mother's names: *DavAnn Stationery and Printing Company.* He also bragged often about having voted for Roosevelt (who was like a god to him, as to most Jews of his generation), even though he knew that voting for Roosevelt meant voting for legislation that would bring an end to his career as an installment dealer.

If, before Robert was born, my mother had worked occasionally in order to supplement my father's income, she quickly came—within the first year of Robert's life—to *have* to work full-time. Our father never earned a living from his businesses, and was forever borrowing money from friends and relatives simply to keep from going bankrupt, or—more often—to keep our mother from discovering just how poorly he was doing. He could never earn or borrow enough, however, to fool her, or to pay our bills. Without her income, that year as in the years to come, we would have been unable to pay our rent, or to buy food—a situation that, through all the years of our growing up, made him ashamed, and her resentful.

On weekends, when she returned from her shifts at the hospital, she would lay into him with tirades that became as familiar as they were venomous: Why did he just sit there in his chair like a lump? Why didn't he go out and get another job— she didn't care what it was or how little it paid: an usher in a movie theater, a janitor, a door-to-door salesman—why didn't he do *something* instead of nothing, so that she could stop working, so that she could get out of the tiny, stinking apartment we lived in, so that she would know that he *really* loved her?

On Saturday mornings, my father, Robert, and I went to synagogue together, after which he would spend the rest of the weekend sleeping on the living-room couch, or sitting in an armchair, hour after hour, like a dead man.

I recall standing over him one time while he snored away (I was in college then, commuting two hours a day by subway to Columbia), trembling with a rage I felt was going to blow my head open—feeling so consumed with hatred, I wanted to smash him to pulp, to throw him through windows, to kill. Instead I went into my bedroom, and wrote out the words— three pages of penciled scrawl—that were marching through my head. ("To come home and see him sitting entombed in that chair, his arms folded across his chest & his feet crossed. Hours & hours he sits there doing nothing. Nothing nothing nothing while all of life passes him by. . . . I hate him. I hate him. He has no right to sit there year after year & kill us all. . . .")

I wrote that he was a lump, a failure, and a coward, that he was not a man and didn't know how to be one, that his "sickness" was the cause of my mother's suffering, that he was killing her, and—the part I felt I was carving into the paper as if with the blade of a linoleum knife—that I would *never never never* grow up to be a nothing like him.

"Do you know how come I know I'm the smartest man in the world?" he would often ask me and Robert, and, in our mother's presence, he would grin, and answer his own question: "Because I married your mother—that's how come!" Then he would get us to join with him in frenzies of adoration—to tell her she was the most wonderful woman who ever lived, more beautiful than the most beautiful movie star.

With her dark curls, full mouth, high Russian cheekbones, and gorgeous deep-set blue eyes, I did not have to lie, for I believed she *was* incredibly beautiful, and while Robert and I would join in flattering her, our father would try to get her to let him kiss her.

Most times she would turn away, or, were he able to trap her lips with his, she would set her mouth rigidly shut, keep her eyes wide open, and stare past him. When he let her go, she would open her arms and Robert would race into them and spread kisses all over her neck and face. "This is my love-child," she would cry. "This one is the light of my life! This one understands me. . . ."

At other times, our father could make us giggle by pleading with our mother to stop fondling her bare breasts while we ate, or to stop walking around the apartment naked—to stop parading in front of open windows, to stop giving the men in the backyard, there washing their cars, "free looks." I recall, too, how embarrassed I always felt when I went shopping with her, or for walks, for during these excursions she would start conversations with anyone and everyone—friends, acquaintances, strangers we met on the street, or at bus stops, or in the park, or in stores—and would be personal with them (touching them, hugging them, telling them about my achievements, her troubles) in ways that made me want to disappear.

For the first five years of my life—until Robert was born—my mother told me at least once a day that I should have been a girl. She would touch my face and hair, remark on the smallness of my nose and ears, my blond curls, and then shake her head from side to side. "What a waste!" she would cry out. "What a waste! You should have been a girl!" And she would say the same thing to neighbors or to strangers we met on the street, trying to get them to agree with her that I should have been born a girl.

I found nothing strange in her repeated cries; if I imagined anything back then, it was that *all* mothers who had sons with small features and blond curls wished they had given birth to daughters, that they all said so on a daily basis, and that they all regarded boys like me as being, somehow, mistakes.

From the moment Robert was born, he became, in my mother's words, her "love-child"—her "sunshine," the "light of her life." Robert was sensitive, creative, considerate, loving, lovable, warm. I was a "cold fish." She would caress him while sneering at me: "That one—" she would say, "—who could ever love *that* one?" While I watched my mother paint Robert's nails with polish, put lipstick on his mouth, and dress him up in little girl's dresses, I seethed with envy and rage.

I became famous in the family for the speed with which I wiped away kisses I received from my mother and my aunts. I had a ferocious temper, and before I was a year old, to resist doing things my mother wanted me to do I would lie on the ground and hold my breath until I nearly passed out. Several times, storming out of the house, I slammed doors so hard that the plate glass in them shattered. "Someday," my mother constantly warned me, "mark my words, but someday you're going to *kill* someone with that temper of yours!"

I was furious with my mother for mocking me and favoring Robert; I was furious with Robert for accepting her caresses and affection; I was furious with my father for doing nothing to stop what was going on; and, above all, though I hardly knew it then, I was furious with myself not only for showing forth my anger, my desires, and my jealousy—for behaving in those ways that made her scorn me more and cut me off even further from the love I craved (if she didn't love me, did I *exist?* And what did I have to do—what parts of my true self did I have to express or repress—to gain her love?)—but for the part of me that wanted and did not want to be like her. I was, that is, quite literally sick with rage—and I was frightened too, without quite understanding why, because in part of me I feared that I was, by my willfulness if by nothing else, more like her than I cared to know, and because in part of me, too, I wanted, quite simply, to be loving, sensitive, tender, and womanly, but was scared to death of acknowledging the existence of these feelings, much less expressing them.

Through the years people have often asked me why I think it is that I somehow survived and my brother did not. How could it happen that two sons, born five years apart from the same parents, and raised in the same household—two sons with so many similar characteristics (we were both bright, both talented as athletes, actors, musicians, artists, and writers, both about the same height and weight, etc.)—could have wound up having such different lives? And through the years, though I have never wanted to answer the question (how different are we, really, I've often responded—and how different, in the years to come, might we yet be?), and have never been able to come up with anything resembling a sufficient answer, for others *or* for myself, I do sense that though I may have often resisted my mother's attempts to get me to be somebody I did not want to be (somebody, that is, who would, as I perceived things, submit to her will), and rejected her attentions and affection as intensely—and, at times, as venomously—as I felt she had rejected me, still—in all kinds of ways, and especially by my very opposition to her—my own willfulness, anger, resistance, and independence (like her, I too loved having things *my* way; like her, I too was driven, and in ways I barely understood, by my fear of being forever unloved)—I was putting on those very characteristics that had enabled her to survive, and that could, I must have sensed, do the same for me.

During the first year of Robert's hospitalization, I recall telling a therapist during a family therapy session, when he asked why I thought I had not broken down and Robert had, that the answer seemed clear to me—Robert had identified with and internalized our parents' weaknesses and I had internalized their strengths. I said that I had often, while growing up, acted on my belief that the world was divided into the strong and the weak, and that in such a world the strong survived and prevailed, while the weak succumbed and perished (small wonder that my favorite novel, when I was a freshman in high school, was Ayn Rand's *The Fountainhead*).

I said that whereas Robert had identified with our father's failures, shame, and servile mentality, I had identified with his stronger qualities (his intelligence—for we all agreed he was *smarter* than our mother; his ability to concentrate—for he would arrive home from work some evenings with two or more novels from a book rental library, and have them all read by the

morning; his knowledge and judgment in worldly matters—fo
he had an amazingly retentive memory when it came to history
politics, sports, and Judaism). While Robert had identified
with our mother's suffering, complaining, and sickness (he
migraines, her crying fits, her insatiable needs for attention and
love), I had identified with her work habits, her persistenc
(she *never* stopped doing things, and never gave up once sh
set her mind to achieving something), her rage (against ou
father, the world, and anyone who stood in her way, or let he
down), and her worldly successes.

For whatever else our mother was, she was surely a capabl
woman who (like her own mother, who was doted on by neigh
borhood friends) had enormous reserves of energy, stamina
charm, and determination: not only did she support our famil
financially by often working double and triple shifts at hospi
tals, but, while doing this, she was also a full-time mother and
housekeeper, and a full-time caretaker and counselor to dozen
of friends and relatives who came to her for consolation and
advice. She cooked and cleaned, helped us with our homework
and tended to us when we were sick; she took us to museums
zoos, and concerts (she was a "private duty" nurse all through
our growing up in order to pick and choose her cases so she
could be at home for us during school and summer vacations)
she encouraged us to take music lessons and art lessons and to
read (when I was seven years old, I recall her handing me a
thick book—a real *novel* just like the ones she and my fathe
read—*The Voyages of Dr. Dolittle,* by Hugh Lofting—and saying
"I think you're ready for this now"); she dressed us, mended
our clothes, knitted our mittens, scarves, and sweaters, and
took us shopping with her; she drove our car, took care of it
maintenance, and made all household repairs (e.g., stripping
repairing, and painting furniture; I never saw a paintbrush
screwdriver, or hammer in our father's hands); she made u
birthday parties, prepared a beautiful table for us each Friday
night for the Sabbath, and for all holiday meals (Passover, Rosh

Hashanah, Thanksgiving), and took us to sleepaway summer camps (where she worked in exchange for our tuitions, while also receiving twenty-five-dollar commissions for each camper who went there because of her recommendation).

Though she obsessed so about the smallness of our apartment that several times a week I would come home to find she had, yet again, rearranged all the furniture and rugs (moving the heavy furniture herself), the apartment itself was always clean, and handsomely furnished and decorated; on weekends and holidays its rooms were full of our aunts and uncles, our cousins, and our parents' friends—with their laughing, their talking, their arguing.

Though my mother could go on lengthy tirades against our father, or against me, or against the world ("Why is everyone against me?" she would wail. "Why does everyone turn against me when all I want to do is to love them?")—and though she would, daily and bitterly, complain about our lack of money, and how difficult it was to make ends meet (she would let us know, in lavish detail, about all the conniving she did, with hand-me-down clothing, used furniture, food bargains, household repairs, deals she'd struck with merchants and others— an Emerson radio and fifty dollars, in 1943, for a 1931 DeSoto—buying only things that were on sale, etc., in order to "stretch" our money so nobody would *ever* look down on us), when others came to our home, I was constantly amazed not only at how gorgeous our kitchen and living rooms looked, how elegant and ample the cakes, cookies, Jell-O molds, and platters of food, but, most of all, at how happy our mother seemed—how gorgeous and well-dressed she always was, and how much, quite simply, she loved having a good time: laughing, telling jokes, playing games (mah-jongg, canasta, Scrabble), arguing politics, and talking about me and Robert, and of how proud she was of us, and of the great hopes she had for our futures.

And when our apartment was filled with my parents' friends

and relatives (this seemed most magical and mysterious of all), I could never understand how it was that these grown-ups, who saw one another several times a week, and spoke to one another more often than that (my mother was on the phone at least three or four times a day to her sister Esther, who lived a few blocks away), were forever talkative and animated (the women especially), and how they seemed never to run out of things to say to one another, and of stories to tell to one another.

My mother also took time off from nursing, many years, to run campaigns for charitable organizations (local fund-raising drives that involved luncheons, raffles, dances, auctions, rummage shops, door-to-door solicitations, and so on)—campaigns in which she was in charge of hundreds of workers and volunteers. Whenever I stopped by her office, or met the people who worked for her, they would tell me what an extraordinary woman she was, how proud she was of me, and how lucky I was to have a mother like her.

The same thing would happen whenever I met the patients, families, nurses, and doctors my mother worked with at hospitals. They praised my mother in language not so different from the language my father used: there was nobody quite like her—she was the most wonderful nurse in the world, the most caring and loving person they had ever encountered.

The bedroom Robert and I shared from the time he was born until I left home sixteen years later was so small that when Robert outgrew his crib and our mother bought us a high-riser, and when we opened it at night, to sleep, the twin beds filled all remaining space in the room, so that to get from one end of the room to the other we had to walk across the beds.

On Saturday and Sunday mornings, Robert would put on shows in bed—dancing and singing, doing pratfalls and somersaults, prancing around with cane and top hat, doing imitations of movie stars. He called these performances (for reasons neither of us can recall) the Robert Shalita Shows. And while he would be singing and dancing and making me laugh, our parents would usually be screaming at one another on the other side of our bedroom wall—fighting about the two things they always fought about: money (and the lack of it), and the inconsiderate way my father treated my mother.

Our parents fought and made up, and fought again, and they drew Robert and me into their battles, even as my mother's parents had drawn their children into their battles. When I was eight or nine, my father began asking me, in confidence—and with the hope, I realize now, that I might actually provide him with a usable answer—how he could make my mother happy.

"You're a bright boy, Jay. You're smart—so maybe you can tell me what I can do to make Momma happy. Please tell me what to do. Just tell me. . . ."

While I was rushing home from school to get the mail first, so I could remove letters from my father's creditors and pass them to him secretly, my mother was telling me the ways in which my father maltreated her ("I don't care if he never earns a living, but if he *really* loved me—it's all I ask—he'd learn how to talk to me in the right way. When he criticizes me— when I feel criticized, I don't know why, but something inside me just breaks"), and she was confiding in me the ways in which she was, with friends, and in secret bank accounts, hiding from him the extra money she was earning.

Such games, along with constant threats of divorce, along with our father's periodical leave-takings in the morning with a small suitcase, and his staying away from home overnight (usually with one of his sisters), along with our mother's retreats to "milk farms," to rest from her labors and prevent the "nervous breakdowns" she kept threatening to have—were the easy ones for Robert and me to deal with. They smacked of intrigue and absurdity (what in the world could Jewish women from Brooklyn be doing at places called "milk farms"?), and they were, at least, overt.

Behind the closed doors of our bedroom, or taking walks

together in the neighborhood, Robert and I could laugh about our parents, could mock them and imitate them, could complain about them and argue about them without suffering, from each other, what we feared from them: rejection and the withdrawal of love. We would frequently compare our relationship—how little we fought physically, how much we had in common and did together, how close and affectionate we were—with the relationships of our friends, and we would take great pride in concluding that of all the sets of brothers and sisters we knew, we got along best.

The things that were more difficult came to us in grotesque disguises—presented to us in the name of love, though we sensed they had little to do with love. But how make sense of what made no sense? And how confront or argue or disagree with one's parent, when the price of disagreement was the withdrawal of love and affection—or an avalanche of anger and words that left one feeling wiped out?

We were witness, daily, to scenes that now seem extraordinarily and excruciatingly mad—more mad because at the time they seemed so ordinary, even normal (didn't mothers and fathers in *all* families act this way?), and because they occurred, in one guise or another, or so it seems in memory, virtually every moment of every hour of every day of our childhood.

I recall being awakened one night by noise, getting out of bed, walking through the living room to the foyer, standing there, and watching my father pull dishes from the kitchen cabinet and smash them, one after the other, into the sink, while he blubbered and pleaded—"What do you want of me, Annie? Tell me! What is it you *want* of me?" And I recall Robert standing next to me, slipping his hand into mine.

Another night, after supper, Robert and I were summoned to the living room by our father, who declared that he was going to prove, once and for all, how much he loved our mother. "I love her so much I not only worship the ground she walks on, but I'd lick her feet, that's how much I love her."

While our mother laughed—her blue eyes aglow with a happiness little else seemed to provide—my father got down on his hands and knees, crawled across the living-room rug and, to prove to us that he was a man of his word—"Robert! Jay! Watch this now!"—he began licking my mother's shoes and kissing her feet.

"What I think," Robert says (we are sitting on my porch on a summer afternoon, a year or so before Eli's graduation), "is that Mother had Dad in a straitjacket. She was a simple woman, but she had common sense. Only she had no sense of direction. Remember how when she was driving and came to a one-way street, she would always say, 'The street is going one way against me'?

"One time she was taking me to the Bronx Zoo and she made a wrong turn somewhere and I kept asking if she knew how to go, and we kept driving and driving and about an hour later, I said, 'Isn't that our house over there?'

"And I remember one time I heard Dad screaming and I went into the bedroom and he was standing in the corner—he was fast asleep—and he kept screaming and screaming, and mother was all done up in white cotton, and had a night hat on like the pilgrims wore, and she had a pot of boiling water in her hands and I was scared she was going to throw it at him. When he didn't stop screaming, I went up to him and slapped him in the face and he asked me to get him a drink, whiskey or bourbon, and I did. 'Thanks for the drink,' he said, 'but you didn't have to slap me.'"

Robert leans toward me, a hand cupped to the side of his mouth, and he whispers: "I used to come home from school and see her sitting in a car with a young doctor."

What did he think they were doing in the car?

"What do you *think* they were doing?" Robert says, then shrugs. "But they were on *our* street, and in a car. But I found Dad jerking off when I came home one time, and—listen, Jay, listen—worst of all was coming home and finding a scum bag floating around in the toilet.

"And yes, yes, I remember how she paraded around the house naked all the time, but who was really running the home?" he asks. "That's what I never understood. What was Dad's role? There was no money, there was no *money,* Jay! That was very confusing to me. And when they were going to get divorced—when they talked about it and Mother said she'd had enough, and I believed them—I heard them one night making arrangements, and this is what Mother said: 'You take Jay and I'll take Robert.' That's what she said.

"And do you remember when Dad used to throw furniture around? And he spit on me too—did I ever tell you that? All the news that's fit to spit—that was him. He had some temper, our father! Sometimes he would hit me—lightly, lightly—and when I asked why, he'd say, 'That was for nothing—so can you imagine what you'll get from me if you do something?'

"And I remember visiting Grandpa with her, and how his place—the Bialystok Home—was like a nightmare movie. It reminded me of Creedmoor. It was the scariest place I ever visited. And Izzie and Grandma died a month apart, you know, but what I remember is that before she died, she spoke. 'He pushed me,' she said—but nobody knew who 'he' was."

We reminisce some more, talk about how I liked to boss him around, and slap him across the face when he didn't do what I wanted, and how he would tease me and taunt me (mocking me for being his know-it-all *big* brother), spit at me, and steal money from me ("You *knew* I stole from you? That's terrible. And all the time I thought I was fooling you")—and when Robert tells me he always thought I was the favorite son, I laugh and tell him I always thought *he* was the favorite son.

Robert says he thought I was the favorite because I was always such a success at things, and I say I always thought that though I was loved for what I could *do,* he was always loved for who he *was.*

"That's very funny, you know," Robert says.

I laugh, after which we're silent for a few seconds.

"Oh, Robert," I say then, "how did we ever live together in that one small room for all those years?"

"Maybe," Robert answers, "we were the same person."

IMAGINING

ROBERT

5

A MONTH OR SO before Robert's fourth birthday, on what I recall as a cold late-winter evening in 1947, my father announced that after supper we would all go around the corner to the Granada Theater to see a movie about the greatest entertainer in the history of show business, a man my father had seen perform when he himself was a young man.

Going to a movie was always a treat (because we observed the Sabbath, Robert and I could rarely go to the Saturday-afternoon matinees most of our friends went to—matinees that, in addition to two feature films, would have cartoons, an installment of an ongoing serial, a short subject, coming attractions, and door prizes), and for the four of us to go together, as a family, and on a weekday night, made it an extraordinary occasion.

The movie was *The Jolson Story,* and during the movie our father kept whispering to us about all the songs he remembered, and how the actor who portrayed Jolson—Larry Parks—looked, acted, and danced exactly the way Jolson had. On our way back home, my father and mother actually held hands, and, walking behind them, Robert and I giggled and did the same.

After we were in our apartment, and while our father continued to go on and on about when and where he had seen Jolson, Robert suddenly got down on one knee, threw out his hands, and began imitating Jolson's version of "My Mammy."

He danced around the living room, clapping his hands in front of him patty-cake-style, mimicking Jolson's raspy voice and minstrel gestures, singing bits of other songs—"California, Here I Come" and "Toot, Toot, Tootsie!" and "April Showers."

A day or two later my father arrived home from work with a gift-wrapped package: a 78-rpm album of records from *The Jolson Story.* Robert played the records over and over again, memorized the songs, invented routines to go along with them—imitating Larry Parks imitating Al Jolson (who, himself a Jew, had been imitating other white men, in blackface, imitating black men)—and belted out the tunes.

In the months that followed, Robert became famous in our neighborhood, performing his songs and dances on street corners and in schoolyards, in local candy stores and luncheonettes, and being rewarded not only with applause and praise, but with money and candy that people threw at his feet.

That spring, my mother decided to give him tap-dancing lessons at the Robert Stone Dance Studio. The studio, at the corner of Church and Nostrand avenues (a hundred yards or so from the Granada Theater), was a large, bare second-floor room that contained a few mirrors, a small phonograph, and some wooden folding chairs. Stone, a former vaudevillian, would take children singly or in groups, show them some steps, then send them to an empty part of the room to practice while he taught whoever was next. There were no set times for lessons—you came when you could, danced and practiced for a while, paid a dollar or two. Robert took a lesson once a week, picked up steps quickly, improvised on them, and soon became the boy wonder of the local dance world.

Once a year, Stone rented out a theater and put on a full-length show in which his students participated. He and his teenage son carried most of the show with vaudeville-style routines, but it was Robert who stole the show: as dancer, singer, comedian. His timing was exquisite, his dancing extraordinary, and when he went to the front of the stage in blackface and white gloves, got down on one knee, and crooned "My Mammy," he brought the house down.

Encouraged by our parents, Robert performed everywhere: at family gatherings, school, summer camp, the houses of friends. In later years, billing ourselves as the Brothers Neugeboren, Robert and I performed as a duo—me playing guitar, and sometimes singing, and Robert dancing. While I dutifully played notes and chords as written (I had little gift for improvisation), Robert would perform a traditional soft-shoe routine. Less than halfway through any performance, however, he would break out with flamboyantly athletic flourishes and Chaplin-like turns that were as delightful as they were surprising: he might suddenly rise on his toes in graceful and comic imitation of a ballet dancer—or come flying across the stage, arms and legs fully extended, and then, while in midflight, reach down to his crotch with one hand and scratch his balls.

"I never practiced, you know," Robert says. "It was just something I did. I never had good tap shoes either—just taps the shoemaker put on my regular shoes."

We reminisce about our shoemaker, Mr. Fiala, whose store was on Rogers Avenue, a few doors away from our meat, grocery, and vegetable stores, and about how, without giving out receipts, Mr. Fiala could remember where everyone's shoes were, and the days on which he'd promised to have them ready. We talk about seeing Mr. Fiala walking to and from work each day dressed in suit and tie, and how he could fit people for shoes and boots he would actually make himself. Robert is surprised that I remember Mr. Fiala's name.

"And I could never get the street names straight, either," Robert says, of the two streets Rogers and Nostrand avenues— that bordered Martense Street. "I could never remember which was which, but I remember that I had a key to our mailbox, and after you were gone—oh were you gone, Jay: you were far gone!—I would get the mail and bring it to Dad at work— his bonds and insurance papers and the people he owed money to—and he would take me up on the balcony of his building and give me a pep talk about what I should do with my life. He could give some pep talks, our father."

Robert says that the annual Robert Stone shows were held, not as I remember them, in a narrow, run-down theater that had no center aisle, but at the large and elegant Brooklyn Academy of Music.

"I remember that I kept saying, 'Can I do it now—can I do it now?'" he says. "And finally I did it, but I don't remember what it was I did, except that everybody laughed."

While Robert was becoming our neighborhood's Al Jolson, I was losing myself in sports, magic, and books. I was usually one of the two or three best athletes in my class, and I loved spending whatever free time I had in local schoolyards, streets, and backyards, playing stickball, punchball, handball, basketball, or football with my friends. On afternoons when I was not playing ball, I would be at the library: I would usually bring home four books—the limit—and, usually, too, have them all read within a day or two. I remember being lost in the stories—all sense of time and self dissolved—and wondering how it could be that a single human being could imagine, know, feel, and describe—and make me feel—what all these different people, in so many different times and places, could feel, think, and do. I remember, too, weeping (secretly) while I read novels, and wondering how anybody was ever going to discover that I was the kind of person who could, living within the lives of others, feel what I felt.

A few months after we saw *The Jolson Story,* I decided to become a writer like the writers I had been reading (Howard Garis, John R. Tunis, Hugh Lofting, Charles Dickens, Mark Twain), and I wrote a seventy- to eighty-page novel, which our mother typed out for me (the typewriter ribbon, I recall, printed my words so that the top halves of the letters were black and the bottom halves red), and which I read once a week—a new chapter each Monday morning—to my fourth-grade class. (I recall, too, the unease I felt, while everybody was praising me, because I was frightened somebody would discover I had borrowed the plot of my first chapter from one of my comic books.)

I also became a magician. I read through all the magic books in our local library, constructed my own tricks (fake card decks, dinner plates with false bottoms, hollowed-out eggshells), practiced for hours in front of our bedroom mirror (which hung on the wall between the windows to our backyard, and in front of which Robert acted out his Robert Shalita Shows), and put on shows for friends and relatives. (One Saturday morning I waited until Robert and my father had left for synagogue—my mother was working—and tried a trick that involved flaming newspapers. Things got out of hand, and the next thing I knew I was furiously pouring saucepans of water everywhere, and stuffing charred bits of paper and dishtowel into the garbage can and the drain. That night—but how had they found out?— I was chastised and punished.)

In the cellar of our building, next to the storage bin, Robert and I had a radio station that consisted of a corrugated cardboard table on which we produced sound effects—wind and rain, locomotives, horses' hooves—and a microphone that, without electricity or batteries, could make us sound as if we were talking through an amplifier. While our mother slept above us, Robert and I made up our own stories based on characters from our favorite radio programs (*Captain Midnight, Baby Snooks, The Life of Riley, The Lone Ranger, The Shadow*) and acted them out.

We collected autographs by writing fan letters to favorite entertainers (to our surprise, we actually received glossy signed pictures in return—"To my pals, Jay and Bobby, with Best Wishes from Eddie Cantor"), we joined the Paul Winchell and Jerry Mahoney Fan Club, and practiced, for hours, trying to throw our voices so we could become ventriloquists.

"Dad once came in and grabbed the dummy from me and threw it on the floor," Robert recalls. "He said he didn't want me mimicking people. He spit at me. And mother once ripped the shirt off my back for mimicking her. She hated that most of all—if she thought people were mocking her." He laughs. "Mother hit us with a hanger, remember? And while she whacked us she always said, 'This is hurting me more than it's hurting you!'—but Carrie took her teeth out to eat."

Carrie was the black woman who, once every two weeks, cleaned our apartment. She cleaned for my mother and her four sisters, who traded her back and forth by phone ("Listen, you take her this week," our mother might say, "and I'll give her back to you next week").

"And I remember playing soccer with you in the backyard, using a tennis ball, and being able to kick you in the shins, and you using me as a backstop and making me warm you up so you could become a pitcher for the high school team. I remember how you threw your fastball as hard as you could so you could hurt me and I was scared, and I missed the ball, and it hit me in the throat, so I never played catch with you again."

Three other families rented apartments in our building, and in each apartment, as in ours, there were two brothers. Leo and Phil Rubensohn, elderly bachelors, lived in the three-room apartment next to ours, on the ground floor, their bedroom backing onto our kitchen.

Phil, the younger brother—studious, polite, quiet—worked as a bookkeeper, and he spent most of his free time reading novels; when I went to him once to ask for a recommendation for something to read for a book report, he opened up the *The New York Times Book Review* and advised me not to choose books from the best-seller lists, but to look below the best-seller lists, to the *other* books the editors recommended, which books, he said, were often more interesting. He told me that his favorite author was Willa Cather, and I recall how surprising it seemed to me that this man, who hardly ever said anything to anyone—his brother, Leo, was the great talker and kibitzer—could know so much about books while at the same time having no apparent need to tell others about them, or about the pleasures he took from them.

Leo, whom we were taught to address only and always as *Mr.* Rubensohn, had an independent income (the family owned a children's dress company, Tiny Tot Togs, in upstate New York), never worked at a job, and dressed impeccably; even on the most broiling summer days, he always wore suit, tie, and hat when he went outside. He was famous in our neighborhood for his daily walks—his "constitutionals"—during which he would make conversation with everyone he met, tease children who crossed his path (or waited for him), invite groups of children into his kitchen for milk and cookies—and for his sayings, some of which Robert and I still repeat to one another: "So what do you think this is, your birthday?" he might say to a child who took an extra cookie; or, if he wanted one of us to do something for him, he would clap his hands and ask: "So, young man, how would you like to do something for your country today?"

Leo was the benefactor of a Jewish orphanage, and he would receive calls, made to our apartment (he and Phil never had a telephone of their own), from the alumni of the orphanage—"my boys," he called them (including, most frequently, the comedian "Professor" Irwin Corey, and the harmonica player Leo Diamond)—and whenever he used our phone to make an outgoing call, he would leave a nickel (or dime) on our tele-phone table. Once each year he went on a cross-country trip by train, staying with alumni of the orphanage and their fami-lies, and arriving in California by New Year's Day, in time to attend the Rose Bowl.

He seemed to know everyone in the sports, entertainment, and newspaper worlds (Walter Winchell, Toots Shor, Ed Sullivan, Ned Irish, Leo Durocher, Leonard Lyons), and he spent most evenings going to sporting events—basketball games, track meets (he took me with him each year to the Millrose games at the old Madison Square Garden), and, at least once a week, boxing matches at Madison Square Garden or the St. Nick's Arena.

What I remember most about the Rubensohns' apartment is that it hardly seemed lived in, there was so little furniture in it, and because it was so spare (their kitchen, larger than our living room, contained only a small refrigerator, a metal-topped table, and two chairs), it seemed wonderfully *free* to me. The two brothers never cooked (except for soft-boiled eggs Phil made for himself), and would often send me or Robert to the German deli on Rogers Avenue to buy them suppers of baked macaroni, Limburger cheese, and rice pudding. I loved to go on errands for them, and to hang around in their apart-ment—talking with them about books, sports, and school, or drawing pictures for them—in rooms so unlike the rooms of our apartment, so without clutter and noise.

I loved, too, to watch Leo, in front of his mirror, attach his starched collars, put on his pince-nez glasses, and adjust the slope of his gray homburg, and to wonder what it would be like to grow up and have a life like his—a life in which one was seemingly free from the tumult and obligations of families like ours (from wife, from children, from jobs, from cooking, from fights, from financial need), and free *for* everything else—free to do whatever one wanted whenever one wanted to do it.

Their bedroom, without curtains, its single shade forever

drawn, was furnished with only a four-poster bed, a wooden armoire, a straight-backed chair, and a cherry-wood trunk. When, in their old age, each of the brothers became ill, my mother cared for them in this bedroom, and after they died she talked bitterly and often about how she had received nothing from them, or from their sister (who, she said, "never lifted a finger for her own brothers"), except for a pair of Czechoslovakian teacups and saucers, and the cherry-wood trunk.

"They were very generous to us, very generous," Robert says. "They gave me the most money of anyone for my Bar Mitzvah, and Phil liked the cold weather, and after he died I used to think he was still living in the back room. They had a set of the Harvard Classics in their living room, remember? And a framed photograph of Leo and his boys over the fireplace.

"I also remember when Leo got sick and his stomach went *way* up. He howled and he howled at night—oh boy, did he howl—and they took him to Methodist Hospital and he died the next day. And once, before that, his stomach swelled up, I remember, and I was the only one home. 'Don't look! Don't look!' he said. 'Get a doctor! Get a doctor!' So I ran around the corner to get a doctor and I went to Dr. Busky's house and he asked if Mr. Rubensohn had insurance, and I didn't know, so he wouldn't come. By the time I got back, a doctor was there, though.

"I remember meeting Leo in the hallway on my birthday—this was after Phil died—and he gave me an envelope, and I thanked him. But I didn't look in the envelope and he kept telling me to look—'You better look,' he kept saying. 'You better look.' So finally I looked. It was for half the amount."

When I say how curious it seems to me that Phil and Leo slept together in that one four-poster bed for so many years, Robert tells me I'm wrong, that they didn't sleep together there, that Leo slept in the living room on an iron daybed. He also says that I'm wrong about who died first: I say it was Leo—Robert says it was Phil.

(On a Sunday in October of 1991, when I visit Robert at South Beach, he is on "room restrictions"—lying on a sheetless bed, without his teeth, staring at the ceiling of his bare room and trembling uncontrollably. "Hi, Robert," I say. "I'm Mr. Rubensohn," he says.)

The Kleins, Hungarian Jews who owned a butcher shop around the corner, on Rogers Avenue, lived in the apartment above us, and they had two sons, Norman and Milton. Norman, five years older than Milton, died of cancer when he was twenty years old, and our mother nursed him in the bedroom he and Milton shared (directly above the bedroom Robert and I shared) during his long dying. (In the forty-four years that passed between Norman's death and his mother's death, Milton tells me, neither he nor his mother, in each other's presence, ever once spoke Norman's name aloud. A curious fact, since, when I visited with Milton's mother a year or so before her death— and after not having seen her for two decades—within a few minutes of our reunion she was talking about Norman, his death, and her lifelong grief.) With the money given to her by the Kleins for having cared for Norman, our mother took Robert, then seven years old, on a cross-country train trip aboard the Twentieth Century Limited and El Capitán, to visit with relatives in Los Angeles.

After my mother and Robert returned home, she raved endlessly about life in California—it was a land of milk and honey in which you could pick oranges and grapefruits right off trees, in which there was never snow or ice—and she tried to persuade my father to move there so we could all start a new life together. She had even secured the promise of a job for him, as an attendant in a parking lot owned by a cousin. To my surprise, our father refused to do what she begged him to do.

"What do people take me for, anyway?" he said. "God didn't

give me a brain so I should spend my life sitting in a tiny booth all day giving out tickets."

The Baldwins, an Irish family—a mother and two elderly bachelor sons (each of whom I would sometimes encounter in our hallway as they staggered home drunk; one of them, I was later told, went to jail for killing a man in a barroom fight)— lived in the front upstairs apartment, and from 1940 to 1960, in which year our parents moved with Robert to Queens, neither Robert nor I ever had a conversation with any of them. Once a year, though, at Christmas, we would go upstairs to admire Mrs. Baldwin's Christmas tree, to give and receive a kiss.

On Saturday mornings, Robert and I usually walked together to our synagogue, Congregation Shaare Torah, which was three blocks away (adjacent to our high school, Erasmus Hall), for Junior Congregation services. The services took place in the basement, in so-called vestry rooms, where sets of sliding walls transformed the open space, weekday afternoons, into our Hebrew school classrooms, and the services, and the Bar and Bat Mitzvah classes that followed the services, were conducted by Dr. Emanuel H. Baron, a small, learned man with a flamboyant sense of humor, a ferocious temper, and a penchant for eccentricity.

Like Mr. Rubensohn, Dr. Baron was legendary in our neighborhood. He gave rubber nipples to boys to suck on when, in class, they acted like babies; he mocked young men for coming to synagogue dressed casually ("You come to the House of God dressed like an iceman!"); he stopped High Holy Day services if a mother arrived late with her child (while a few hundred of us turned and stared at the mother and child, he would, arms crossed against his chest, glare at the woman and declare, "We'll wait, madame—we'll all just wait").

Yet of the thousands of children who passed through his life at Shaare Torah, he singled out Robert as his favorite, and declared him the synagogue's "official mascot." From the time

Robert was an infant, at the moment of the opening of the Holy Ark, Dr. Baron would stop services, lift Robert in his arms, and carry him around in the procession that followed the Torah. Then he would hold Robert up to the Torah so that Robert might kiss its silver breastplate and velvet covering. Without this kiss, Dr. Baron declared, the services could not properly proceed.

When our mother was working day shifts, my job, after school, was to pick up Robert from the woman my mother paid to take care of him (or from his nursery school), to make a snack for us, to go on errands (a list would be waiting), and to clean the house: to dust and vacuum all the rooms, do the kitchen and bathroom, wash the floors, sinks, bathtub, toilet, etc. (To cure her migraines, our mother was forever taking enemas, the dull, amber-colored bag and tubes hanging above the bathtub throughout our childhood.)

I resented having to clean the house each day (and not being able to go out and play with my friends), but I also took pride in being responsible for Robert. (In later years, especially when I was feeling anxious or depressed, few things would restore me to some calmer sense of self than domestic chores: cleaning, shopping, or cooking; washing, ironing, or mending.) I remember, when I was nine or ten years old, going to a new nursery school our mother had found for Robert, and being surprised, when I went to pick him up, to find one of my classmates there. Her name was Jean Skinner, and she was an intelligent and pretty black girl, a classmate of mine throughout elementary school. She was there to take her younger sister home, she said, and I remember how wonderfully grown-up it felt to sit beside her while we waited, and to talk with her about what it was like for each of us to care for our younger siblings. And I remember, especially, how proud I felt, when the door opened, and Robert came out into the waiting room, to have Jean watch me dress him in his winter clothing. I remember the warm, admiring light in her eyes, and how this friendly light seemed to be there through the years that followed, in elementary school, junior high, and high school, whenever we would meet—in class, or along school staircases or corridors, or on the streets of our neighborhood.

When my mother was working night shifts (and sleeping during the day), my major job was to take care of Robert, while also making sure the house remained completely silent—no radio, no friends, no noise (if Milton, who hoped to be a jazz musician, began practicing his saxophone, clarinet, guitar, flute, or piano, I would race up the stairs to tell him to stop). And if my mother was working double shifts—afternoon and evening—I would prepare supper for Robert, me, and my father. If I did not perform my duties in a way that pleased our mother, my father would slap me around (until the year of his death, if he merely moved his hand upward to smooth back his hair, I would flinch) and rail at me, shouting that our mother was right: I was selfish, mean, and inconsiderate—that the only person I ever thought about was myself.

Robert loved to do whatever he could to make our mother happy—collecting bouquets of flowers for her, cooking special concoctions to welcome her home, writing poems to her, putting cold washcloths on her forehead when she had migraines, performing household tasks without being asked. When he was about three years old, he tried to clean both the living-room rug (a Persian rug my mother would later trade for wall-to-wall carpeting) and the framed Dutch reproduction above the living-room couch (men in high white collars smoking long-stemmed pipes) by scrubbing them down with a mixture of Ajax and water, for which act, one that stained the picture forever, he was lavishly praised.

I tried to please our mother too—by bringing home good grades, by drawing pictures for her, by making fancy birthday and anniversary cards for her. When I was in the fourth grade, I saved up money for months and scouted all the local stores that sold greeting cards in order to find and buy for her the kind of fancy and expensive Valentine's card I thought she would love (it cost fifty cents, a huge sum in 1948, and had a plush, lace-embroidered, rose-scented, satin-covered heart). When I brought it to her and she opened the envelope, however, she shook her head disdainfully, sneered, and threw the card in my face. *"Anyone* can buy a card!" she declared. "If you *really* loved me, you would have *made* me one."

From the time Robert was born, our mother maintained that he was a sickly child, and she doted on him for his ailments. Robert was small at birth (under six pounds), and, in his infancy, subject to continual stomach and bowel problems, and to various rashes, fevers, and allergies. At ten months old, he had a bad case of chicken pox; at twenty months, he contracted Dukes's disease (a vaguely described viral condition that results in rising and falling fevers and rashes), and he was, soon after this, diagnosed as being a "celiac baby." For this disorder (characterized mostly by alternating cycles of diarrhea and constipation), treatment consisted largely of a special diet—long lists of foods he was not allowed to eat (cereals and breads), and others he had to eat often and in abundance (liver and bananas).

Robert was, also, throughout childhood, forever vomiting. He became nauseated before, during, and after meals, and during virtually all family trips—whether by car, train, bus, or trolley; he would sometimes throw up in our car before we had driven to the end of our street. What portion of these ailments and conditions was caused by viruses, allergies, or bacteria, and what portion by anxieties, feelings, and needs that were without any strict biochemical causes—who can tell? What seemed clear, though, was that my mother was most alive when others, like Robert (like her patients, like children at summer camp, like friends who came to her with their problems), needed her.

"What a love affair I'm having with this one!" she would exclaim, while she hugged, kissed, and caressed him. "What a lover boy this son is!" Her attentions to him filled Robert with joy, while they filled me with jealousy, and with disgust. Our mother seemed to thrive on adoration, and I tried to get Robert to be less adoring. I tried—for my sake as much as for his, surely—to get him to be more independent, less sickly (more mine and less hers?)—less attached to what seemed, even then, her insatiable need to have him need her. "You know, Jay, it was like this," Robert said to me, a week or so after his first breakdown in 1962, "I wanted Mother, but you were always in the way."

Summers, beginning when Robert was seven and I was twelve, our mother took us to Camp Winsoki, in Rensselaerville, New York, a camp owned by our cousin Shelley, a rabbi married to my father's niece Marilyn (one of Molly's three daughters). Some years at Camp Winsoki, our mother worked as the camp nurse, but more often she was something called Camp Mother, the woman who tended to the needs of several hundred Jewish children: their allergies, homesickness, bedwetting, fingernails, toenails, scalps, hair, diets.

Except that its staff and clientele were predominantly Orthodox Jews, Winsoki was a camp like most American summer camps. ("Camp Winsoki," the camp's brochure stated, "is dedicated to the spirit of youth, the love of nature, the development of good comradeship, and the fostering of the ideals of our American and Jewish heritage.") We played baseball, volleyball, basketball, and tennis; we made ashtrays, lanyards, and gifts for our parents in arts-and-crafts; we went on raids to the girls' bunks in the middle of the night; we swam, hiked, sang, made campfires, and put on productions of *Carousel, Oklahoma!,* and *South Pacific;* and at the end of each summer we divided ourselves into two teams and went at each other ferociously in four days of a fanatical quasi-military competition called Color War.

During the school year, Robert and I were the most observant of our Jewish friends: keeping kosher at home and away from home, going to synagogue each Saturday, observing all major Jewish holidays, putting on tallis and tefillin and praying in our living room six mornings a week. But at the end of each school year we journeyed north with our mother to Camp Winsoki, on Triangle Lake ("cradled in a mountain top, Triangle Lake is the second highest lake in the state of New York"), where we were among the few campers who did not come from Orthodox homes, or attend yeshivas.

All of our aunts and uncles on our father's side of the family were Orthodox: they observed the Sabbath and holidays faithfully, not only spending these days, all day (except for meals), in synagogue, but stopping all other work and activities: they did not ride, cook, write, draw, shop, turn on lights, play ball, or telephone. Some of our father's brothers and sisters had, in fact, objected to his marriage to our mother on the grounds that she did not come from a "good" Jewish family, or from an observant one (they knew her parents did not live together, while their own father had been the spiritual leader of their community, equal in authority and honor to the rabbi, both in the old country—Ryminov—and the new—East New York).

After our father and mother married, however, even our mother agreed that our father's family accepted her fully. Still, except for special family occasions (weddings, holidays, Bar Mitzvahs, graduations, funerals), and for those times when our father left my mother because they were going to get divorced, and for those times when our mother left our father (Robert's birth, summers, her trip with Robert to California, getaways to milk farms), Robert and I spent little time with relatives from our father's side of the family.

For eight weeks each summer, then, living among Jews who prayed three times each day and studied Torah and Talmud after softball and basketball games, Robert and I often felt as if we were outcasts—strangers in a strange land, living in exile among Jews. (The summer I was fourteen years old, I had a mad crush on a girl named Anita Frank, who seemed to like me as much as I liked her. Though she would dance with me at socials, she would not hold my hand, kiss me goodnight, or be my girlfriend, because, she said, I wasn't "Jewish enough.")

• • •

"I hated being there," Robert says. "It was awful, awful—it was very painful, Jay. It was like watching Mother lance the boils on your face. But I had friends, I had friends—and sometimes one of the Puerto Ricans who worked in the kitchen, Tony or the other guy whose name I forget, would come into our bunk at three in the morning, when Steve Mishkin and I were doing it—the first times I did it with boys were at Camp Winsoki, you know—and he would tell us to stop because it was a sin.

"I wanted to be there and I didn't want to be there. It was like my Bar Mitzvah. I had a hundred and four temperature that day, and *you* wanted me to tap dance. You did! You *did*! You came into the bathroom and told me everyone was waiting for me to tap-dance and that I should hurry up. Then our Uncle Hymie came in, watched me piss, and asked me if I said a *brocha* first.

"I remember pushing Shelley's jeep into the lake, and how Marilyn was always on the phone, so one day we called her to the office, and told her to stand by, and got all the phones to ring at once and she went crazy, not knowing which one to answer.

"But mostly I remember going off by myself and lying down and reading and relaxing. Sometimes Mike Samet and I went for a swim on the girls' side at night, when everyone was asleep, but we both had our Red Cross certificates, and he watched me. And sometimes we would row across the lake and pick flowers for the girls—and I remember on Saturday all the guests and staff members pushing Dad into the crib—into the beginners' area of the lake—and I remember there was a path near the new bunks, and on Saturdays I would take it through the woods to the baseball fields where the Spanish workers played softball. But I didn't play with them.

"And I remember the Pentecostal rites they had, and Nemo [the head cook] singing—'He's coming, he's coming, he's coming again—to gather his people to Je-ru-sa-lem!'—and sometimes I took evening walks with Irene Landau and we looked at the stars, and that was Camp Winsoki for me."

Throughout elementary school, Robert was a good student, often the favorite of his teachers, not only for his intelligence, but for his playfulness and his imagination—for his dancing and singing, for his poems, for the gifts he would bring them, for being able, most of all, to make them laugh.

But he was also interested in history, and starting at the age of six or seven, he prided himself—like our father—on reading *The New York Times* each day, and (also like our father) being able to retain an enormous number of facts. During the 1952 election campaign, when he was nine, he amazed everyone with how knowledgeably he could put forth the case for his hero, Adlai Stevenson, against Dwight Eisenhower. And when he was twelve, in seventh grade, he won his elementary school's History Prize, and, in a citywide ceremony, received a medal from the American Legion.

Shortly before he entered the seventh grade, he was chosen for the SP (Special Progress) Junior High School program on the basis of his IQ (above 130, the minimum required for SP) and his grades. In this program, in which students completed three years of schoolwork in two years of enriched curriculum, he thrived.

At the start of his second year in the program, however, the same semester in which I entered college, our mother took him out. He was already one of the youngest boys, even in the SP class, and he was also one of the smallest, and she didn't want him to become traumatized socially, she said—to arrive in college so much younger and smaller than all the other boys and girls. (She had, for similar reasons, kept me out of the SP program entirely: having been "skipped" ahead twice previously, I was already a year younger than most of my classmates.)

Robert was disappointed, especially because being removed from the SP class meant being separated from his closest friends. But he never protested openly to our parents, or to me. ("But every morning on the way to school, and every afternoon on the way home, he was angry," one of his friends from that time, Sue Havens, tells me. "I couldn't believe how angry he was at your parents. We really felt for him. There were three of us who used to spend all our time together—Robert, me, and Theresa O'Connor. Theresa was Robert's girlfriend, but we were both madly in love with him—he was *so* creative, so loving, so warm and funny—and we told him we wouldn't abandon him just because he was in a different class. But of course, after he was taken out of the SP class, things changed, and we drifted apart.")

"You were in the house," Robert often says to me, about our teenage years, "but you never really *lived* there, Jay."

And whenever he says this, I nod in agreement with him.

Before Robert was born (I recall saying this at one of our early family therapy sessions, and saying it with the pride—vanity—that came from being able to show the therapists I had figured out, and understood, what had been going on in our family), I had had my parents all to myself—and after he was born, when our father began failing in business, and our parents began battling daily, I moved out of the house anyway I could, physically and emotionally, and Robert became the target, as it were—often the willing target—for their sufferings, frustrations, and resentments.

While (overtly) I may have been pretending not to care about what happened at home (and coming to believe that no matter my anger or achievements—or because of them—somebody else would always be preferred to me; that the more I wanted something, the more certain it was that it would be denied me or taken from me), or about how much devastation our mother and father brought down upon one another, Robert was becoming their confidant and ally—in their fights, in their reconciliations, and, above all, in their determination to-keep-the-family-together-no-matter-what.

All through junior high and high school I worked after

school at odd jobs (traveling by subway to and from Manhattan three or four afternoons a week for several years, to work, for seventy-five cents an hour, in a dry cleaning store in the garment district), and when I wasn't working, I found any activity I could that would keep me away from our home: I stayed in schoolyards, playing ball with my friends, until everyone else was gone and it was dark; I walked my friends home and hung around their apartments hoping their mothers would invite me to stay for supper; I took any part-time after-school job I could find, and on weekends and in the evenings worked for the caterer at our synagogue; I joined dozens of after-school clubs at our high school, and, several afternoons a week for a year and a half, worked as an actor at the Board of Education's FM radio station (WNYE); I organized and became president of the teenage club at our synagogue (the Minyonaires), arranging for our weekly meetings, our dances, our basketball games and leagues; I became an officer in the city-wide Jewish youth organization of which we were members, etc.

Though I stayed away from our apartment as much as possible, I continued to bring home good grades, and to do my parents' bidding when it came to household responsibilities, and—usually—to do most things I thought would please them, and what they told me would please them. Though I weighed only about a hundred pounds when I entered high school, I made the baseball team; when the coach found out I was a thirteen-year-old freshman, however, and thus ineligible, he told me to sign up with one of the amateur leagues that played its games on the local ball fields at the Parade Grounds. As soon as my mother found out I was planning to play games on the Sabbath, though, she ordered me to quit the team; it would absolutely *kill* my father, she said, if he ever found out I was playing ball on the Sabbath. I stormed and I screamed . . . but I did what she said.

That same year, I joined the Boy Scouts, worked hard at my badges, was appointed a den chief, and was put in charge of a group of Cub Scouts; when our troop planned an overnight bivouac on Staten Island, however, my mother refused to give me permission to go. Several of the older boys from the troop, along with the scoutmaster, came to our apartment and begged my mother to let me go—but their presence only confirmed her in her decision, and in her suspicion: which was, she said, that some of the older boys wanted me there in order to take advantage of me sexually.

When my best friends and I arranged, at the time of our junior high school graduation, to celebrate by going to the movies with our girlfriends, my mother refused to let me join them. My friends' parents telephoned my mother and pleaded with her—I was president of our school, and it was only a movie, after all, and we would all be going together in a group—but my mother refused to give in, and my father backed her up, laughing at me, and asking (as he would often through my teenage years) how a *pipsqueak* like me was going to protect a girl if somebody attacked her while I was escorting her home at night.

I stormed and I screamed and finally (my mother would still, mockingly, be quoting my words back to me, and to others, five decades later) I turned on her and shouted, "What do you expect me to do—suck on your titties my whole life long?"

But, again, I did what she said. I did not go out with my friends to celebrate our graduation (and I obeyed her wishes and did not go on dates until three and a half years later, halfway through my senior year of high school).

In the spring of 1955, during my last semester of high school, when I was accepted at Columbia College, and said I intended to go there, my mother again fought against my decision, and with greater ferocity than she had previously fought me about anything. "Why," she kept arguing, "should you go to a difficult school like Columbia, where you'll be a small fish in a big pond, when with your brain you can go to

Brooklyn College, a few minutes away, and be a big fish in a little pond?" All she wanted in this life, she claimed, was to spare me *suffering*. Since she and my father could not give me any money toward college, why should I have to go out and work, and suffer, in order to attend Columbia, when I could go to Brooklyn College for free?

She wept and screamed and carried on so ceaselessly that my father (who initially approved of my choice, and was proud of me for having been accepted to an Ivy League school) began begging me to do what she wanted merely to prevent her—his repeated fear—from having a nervous breakdown.

This time, however, I defied her. Whether she liked it or not, or helped me or not, I was going to go to Columbia, I declared, which, though only an hour away by subway, seemed light-years away to me in everything else—a different world entirely from the one I was living in: more cultured, more demanding, and, in prospect, a world that would not be, or seem to be, merely an extension of high school, and of the Brooklyn-Jewish world that seemed, too often, narrow and suffocating.

By working summers, vacations, afternoons, and weekends (and by getting partial scholarships after my first year), I paid my way through Columbia (tuition, in 1955, was $750 a year), and I also tried, while going there, to draw Robert along with me.

I left our apartment early each morning (usually taking the subway with my father) and came home late each night (staying on campus to study, or to take part in extracurricular activities: teams, theater, glee club), and I often took Robert with me to classes, and to restaurants and bars, with my friends, after classes. Robert and I talked endlessly about my friends, and courses, and professors (long discussions, before sleep, and during walks, about Homer, Klee, Cervantes, Stravinsky, Prokofiev, Dostoevsky, Salinger, and—especially—Camus), and about Robert's friends, courses, and teachers; I loved how happy he was to be with me and my friends, and I took great pride in how impressed they were with him—with how smart, witty, and mature he was (at the West End Bar one night, he brilliantly held his own in a debate with the future valedictorian of our class); and I loved, too, being able to encourage him in his own interests: art, movies, politics, poetry.

In the spring of 1956, in his junior high autograph album (at the end of my first year at Columbia, and the end of his first year out of the SP class) he listed his favorite authors as Orwell, O. Henry, Shaw, Mencken, and Fadiman, his favorite sports as tennis and basketball, his hero as Jean Shepherd (we would lie in the darkness together, Sunday nights, listening to Shepherd's radio broadcasts), his motto as "Excelsior!" and his favorite college as Columbia.

During the Christmas season, my first year at Columbia, I worked long shifts at the post office. I was signed up to do the same for my sophomore year when my mother came to me and offered me a deal. Robert had not been doing well in school, and she was very worried about him: his grades were falling, he kept complaining about being bored, his attention span was terrible, the way he dressed was outrageous, his sleep and eating habits were bizarre. She was so worried that she was getting ready to hire somebody to tutor him—but why should she hire a stranger when I could stay at home during my vacation and earn money while at the same time helping my own brother?

I accepted her offer. But Robert hated learning from me as much as I hated tutoring him, and our study sessions rarely lasted five minutes before we were screaming, cursing, and driving each other crazy. After a few days I gave up, but when I did, I blasted Robert with every accusation and fear I had previously used in blasting myself. I was going to have my say, once and for all, I told him, and he had better listen, because if he didn't, he was the one who would suffer the consequences for the rest of his life.

I praised him to the skies for his gifts (his intelligence, his sense of humor, his generosity, his kindness, his talents as artist, dancer, athlete, musician, and actor), and then I buried him under an avalanche of words in which I tried to draw the most horrifying picture of his future I could conjure up: *Did he want to wind up with a life like our father's?*

Did he want to be condemned forever to be our mother's worshiping lackey? Did he want to wind up having to grovel and beg her for forgiveness, and for everyone else's charity? Didn't he remember how our Uncle Murray, refusing to give our father a loan, had reduced him to tears only a few months before? Did Robert want to be a nothing and a failure like our father his whole life long?

Now, I argued, was the time to practice scales: to develop those skills that would enable him to become a Somebody instead of a Nobody. But Robert seemed to believe, in the analogies I used then (which were not unlike the analogies our mother had been using), that he could get to the top of a staircase without using the stairs, that he could play instruments without having to practice them, that he could somehow acquire skills magically. I didn't like being the one to say so (though in the moment itself I doubtless loved nothing more; it felt wonderful to let the words pour forth—words that seemed to make so much obvious *sense*—and to be pouring them forth in order, as I believed, to save Robert by getting him—like me?—to save himself), but if he didn't begin to change—to take help when it was offered, and in the way I offered it—it was his funeral.

That evening, I told my mother off too: told her that no money in the world was worth going through what I'd just been through—having him resist me, mock me, tease me, and taunt me (endless stuff about me being his smart-aleck, phony, know-it-all, big-shot, Ivy League, snot-nosed big brother). As it turned out, I received no money. When I asked for my payment, my mother looked at me in astonishment. "You mean you'd actually take money from me to help your own brother?" she asked.

●   ●   ●

In January of 1957, midway through my second year at Columbia, I tried out for the role of George Gibbs in the Columbia Players' production of *Our Town*. I didn't get the lead, but I did get a part as an extra, and when the director, Sorrell Booke, said he needed someone to play Emily Webb's brother Wally, I recommended Robert.

Robert auditioned for and got the part, accompanied me several times a week to Columbia for rehearsals and performances, and did splendidly in the role. He was, everyone agreed, a natural. (In later years, our mother would often maintain that if only Robert could have spent his life on the stage—could have been an entertainer—everything might have been different: for by being in show business, she said, he might have received the endless praise that would have kept him from feeling so bad about himself, from feeling unappreciated and unloved.)

A month or so after our final performance, while we were visiting our Aunt Esther and Uncle Jack (our family's dentist; we joked about how our teeth always seemed in greater need of repair when college tuition bills for his two children were due) in their new Long Island home, I asked my cousin Leatrice—their daughter, recently graduated from medical school—to feel my neck: I had some swollen glands that hadn't gone down for a while. Leatrice felt my glands and told me to get myself checked out at Columbia's health services.

I went to the clinic a day or two later, and the young doctor who examined me told me to wait for a few minutes, that he wanted somebody else to look at me. An older doctor came in, probed a bit, told me he wanted me to check in to St. Luke's Hospital later that week, and to stay overnight, so they could perform a biopsy.

I took the subway home and told my mother that I wouldn't be home one night that week because I had to go into the hospital for a biopsy (I had no idea what the word meant— thought it was simply a lab test to find out if I had some kind of infection, like the kind that had caused boils in my nose and ears during my high school years), and within an hour or so, after my father arrived home from work, my parents were sobbing away in their bedroom.

I did not go to St. Luke's. Instead, my mother had the biopsy performed at a Brooklyn hospital where she worked, and by a surgeon she knew. A week or so after the operation, I was told that the results of the biopsy (the pathology was performed by Dr. Sidney Farber, who followed the course of my illness and recovery for several years) were what we'd hoped for: the cells were benign. Still, there were a few cells that were "suspicious," and because of these, the doctor had "stripped" all the glands he could get to during the operation, and now wanted me to have some radiation treatments as a "precaution."

For several months after that, I went to St. Luke's twice a week for cobalt radiation. Although my throat closed up completely for a while, I do not recall experiencing any other side effects. The medical director of the Columbia Health Services examined me every week for a while, and then every two weeks, and then, for my final two years of college, once a month.

As I learned many years later, when I sent for my medical records, I had had cancer—what was then termed giant follicular lymphoma (Hodgkin's disease). But that spring, and in all the years that followed, nobody in my family, and none of the doctors who treated me, ever told me this. They all corroborated my mother's story: that the cells were benign, and that I was given radiation, frequent blood tests, and regular examinations "just to play it safe."

And so I believed two things simultaneously: I believed that I had cancer (otherwise, why were they radiating me?) and that, therefore, I had about a year to live; and I believed what my mother and the doctors told me: that the cells that were removed were benign, and that there was nothing to worry about.

The previous summer, between my freshman and sophomore years, I had worked as a busboy at an upstate (borscht circuit) resort, the Pioneer Country Club, and had earned good money—enough to pay for most of my second year of college. I was planning to return the summer after my biopsy, but my mother begged me to go to Winsoki with her (where Shelley would give me a job as dramatics counselor), so she could "keep an eye" on me. I did what she asked. (When you're with a person who is manic-depressive, or has manic-depressive characteristics—as Robert and my mother did—and when you love this person and want this person's love, what seems most frustrating is that you find yourself, against all sense, acquiescing to his or her desires—endlessly holding back, endlessly changing your responses and behavior, and thus, through habit, your very self, in the hopes that you will not set off the beloved's rage or mania—in the hopes that you will somehow figure out how to please this person, how to make this person happy, how to somehow heal whatever it is in this person that causes the mania, the rage, the withdrawal, the depression.)

And that summer—before and after camp—believing I had a year or so to live, and wanting to leave something of me behind before I left this world, I also decided to do the thing I desired above all: I began and finished a two-hundred-page novel which I called *Joel Campus: College Prophet*. It was a satire about a young college student who, believing his death is imminent, discovers, *Reader's Digest* fashion, a Message for Humanity, and becomes a beloved national hero. When I returned to Columbia in the fall, I brought the novel to Charles Van Doren, who had been my Freshman English teacher a year and a half before, and who, since that time, had become a national hero (the subject of cover stories in *Time* and *Newsweek*) for the knowledge (and personality) he had demonstrated while winning large sums of money on a television quiz show.

Charles loved the book—told me he thought it was a young man's *Pilgrim's Progress*—and sent me, and the book, to his publisher. And so I dreamed of becoming, at the age of nineteen (and before my imagined and imminent demise, at twenty or twenty-one) the American Françoise Sagan. (Sagan, at the age of nineteen, had recently published her first novel, *Bonjour Tristesse.*)

Though the publishers I sent it to, with Charles's recommendation, sent glowing letters about the book and my talents, none of them bought it. (When I brought the first letter of rejection to Charles, and told him it didn't bother me, he looked at me with surprise. "Really? How can you *not* be upset? Why, it's as if somebody has just told you your child is ugly.") Nor did I die, or ever have a recurrence of the cancer.

But I was, in my new life as a young man who had actually completed a novel (and who, by this fact, along with the intimations of mortality that had been mine since the biopsy, was made—at least in my imaginings—an infinitely more attractive and romantic figure to women), much happier. For the first time since I was a child, I felt free—unafraid—to glory in my imagination, to live within it, and to take risks with it; for the first time since I was a child, I allowed myself to acknowledge the force of my deepest desire—to become that thing I had previously hardly let myself dream of becoming: a writer.

It was only when I was, for the first time, living away from home, as it were (attending Columbia, and showing up at Martense Street only to sleep, and, sometimes, to eat), that I recalled that I had, nearly a dozen years before, at the age of eight, written an entire novel. It was as if, I have often thought since, in order to keep my deepest desire alive—to save it during those years I had to live at home (when everything I did, felt, and valued seemed subject to aggrandizement, expropriation, humiliation, and destruction)—I had sent it so far underground that even I didn't remember it was there. For in my imagination—in those hours when I was making up stories and living lives other than the life I actually lived—I was a free and happy young man.

Yet all the while I was making use of my operation—my wound, and the drama and secrecy surrounding it—to somehow set me free, it was forcing Robert into hiding. He was ordered to keep the news of my actual state of health a secret from me (which he did), and to keep his feelings about my operation (and everything it engendered—in him, in me, in the family) to himself.

From the time he first broke down five years later, in 1962 (in February, the same month in which I was operated on), until our most recent phone call (I am writing this in February of 1996), he has repeatedly asked—dozens of times a year— how my cancer is, and if I am going to die soon. (When he does this, I sometimes wonder: Does he believe that if I suddenly become sick, he will become well, and that if I die, he will somehow be born anew—be granted a second chance, a new and different life?)

Six months or so after my radiation treatments, when Robert and I were arguing in bed one night, he suddenly jumped on top of me and started scratching and punching. I grabbed him by the wrists, kicked, and threw him off.

A day or two later he complained of pain in his groin area, and blamed me for it. Our mother had a doctor come to the house who was not our regular family physician, but, she said, a simply *wonderful* new young doctor she'd met at the hospital and wanted us to meet. The doctor examined Robert (Robert rested, during the day, in our parents' bed), found nothing wrong, said he should take it easy and go back to school the next week.

The doctor returned the next day, however, and the day after. On the third day—I can still see his face, pale and horror-stricken, when he emerged from the bedroom—he gave my mother the news that something *was* wrong—she was right to have been worried—and that Robert had to be rushed to a hospital for an emergency operation.

The operation, a partial orchiectomy, was successful, and Robert was assured of what was true: that it in no way affected his sexual development or potency. Still, the timing—an operation on his genitals at the onset of puberty (he was thirteen and a half), and a half year after my operation for cancer— was, at the least, a piece of dreadful bad luck.

"Listen," Robert said to me, when I visited him on the day after his surgery, "Aunt Ethel was already here, and you won't believe what she said." He imitated her: " 'So, darling, as long as I had to be in the neighborhood for a funeral this morning, I figured I'd visit you, too, and kill two birds with one stone.' "

Throughout high school, Robert performed well, if erratically: if he liked his courses and teachers, he did honors-level work—but if he didn't like them, he did poorly, sometimes failing courses. Then—and he would take pride in this ability to take intellectual vengeance upon teachers he disliked—he would study hard and get high grades on the statewide Regents exams so that his teachers, according to state educational policy, would be required to pass him. In his senior year, he won a New York State Regents Scholarship (something I had not achieved) and was accepted to CCNY.

Robert says that his high school English teacher, Miss Batchelor, once called our mother to tell her he was writing "crazy stories." (But Stephen Gillers, a professor of law at NYU, was in that English class with Robert, and remembers the stories differently. "They were wonderful," he says. "Not at all crazy, and not at all like the stories the rest of us wrote—certainly not like what Miss Batchelor wanted. I envied Robert at the time—to be so imaginative, and so unconventional. Miss Batchelor wanted happy stories with happy endings, and Robert's were very different—way beyond what the rest of us were doing. They were like Thurber's tales, I thought. But I also recall that Robert used to sit by himself, near the back of the room, and I remember vividly this one story he wrote, where, at the end, people just go off walking and walking into the snow.")

Until Robert left high school, the only person besides our mother who ever voiced fears about there being anything wrong with Robert was our Aunt Mary and Uncle Arnold's son, Richard. Richard, a year older than Robert, had been adopted by Mary and Arnold at birth. Three years later, in 1945, they discovered that he had muscular dystrophy. (When Mary told my mother the news, my mother urged her "to give Richard back.")

When Richard was eight years old, with the help of other parents of children with muscular dystrophy, Mary founded the Muscular Dystrophy Association of America. A few years later she would break with this organization (and found a new organization, the National Foundation for Muscular Dystrophy) for many reasons, among them the fact that the MDA was putting virtually all its money into the search for a cure and little into care for those afflicted with the disease, and because she was shocked by the way funds were being handled, with smaller and smaller percentages of donations actually being used either for research *or* for victims of the disease (for which disease, fifty years later, a cure has still not been found).

Mary—who later set up the first Independent Living Programs in the United States for the disabled (taking chronically ill patients out of Willowbrook, on Staten Island), and who was responsible for most of the early New York State legislation on behalf of handicapped people (curb cuts, access to public rest rooms and public transportation), and who, when her sister was paralyzed in a freak accident, took in her two infant nieces and raised them as if they were her daughters—was the most important person in the world to me when I was a child, the only person who, I felt, loved me completely and unconditionally. (I've often wondered about the life I might have had if Mary had not been there, regularly, in my life, during those early years—if, before Robert was born, I'd had nobody with whom I felt free to give and take affection.)

She was not a "real" aunt, my mother often reminded me: she and Arnold were my parents' friends. But Mary and Arnold lived on the same block my parents lived on when I was born (Ocean Avenue, between Lincoln and Parkside, across from Prospect Park, and a few blocks from Ebbets Field and the Brooklyn Botanic Gardens), and my parents left me with them whenever they went out, or during the day, when they were both working. (Mary's major aim, with muscular dystrophy patients and the other handicapped individuals she worked with, has remained simple and constant: to get them out of institutions, and to teach them, as much as possible, to learn to care for themselves—for those who can do this, she maintains, are the ones who have viable lives, and survive.)

When Robert was in high school and Richard became confined to his bed and wheelchair, Mary paid Robert to be a companion to him (something that embarrassed Robert), and several afternoons a week, over the course of a few years—until, Robert says, our mother made him stop—their friendship thrived.

But Richard was always concerned about Robert. "I worry about him," he would often say to Mary, after Robert left. "He's wonderful to me and we're great pals, but sometimes, in the middle of doing something together, he just seems to disappear for a while. Sometimes I just *lose* him. Then, a while later, he comes back. . . ."

In the summer of 1958, I returned to Winsoki for the last time (again as the camp's dramatics counselor; Robert was a camper-waiter that year), and in the fall, at the start of my final year of college, and while our father was filing for bankruptcy, I took an apartment near Columbia, at 107th Street and Broadway. My parents had promised that if I put myself through Columbia for the first three years, they would, my senior year, give me a hundred dollars a month toward living at school. I asked for the money now, but my mother claimed that because my father was going bankrupt, they didn't have anything to give me. I stuck to my demand—a promise was a promise— and they kept their word.

My mother kept telling me, too, how relieved she was that our father was finally doing what he should have done years before. "His business was always a sickness," she said. "A terrible sickness." But our father was humiliated and ashamed, especially at not being able to pay back relatives and friends who had been lending him money.

"I have a new best friend every week," he had bragged to me years before, about those from whom he borrowed money. A few years after this—when I was out of college—he would break down, sobbing away, after attending the funeral of his favorite nephew, Joey Leifer, who died in his early forties. "I never even paid him back," my father blubbered. "I never paid him back, I never paid him back . . . my own nephew, and I never paid him back . . ." (What I did not know then, and only learned from Mary many years after our father's death, was that our mother had hidden money with Mary and others so that she could, without my father's knowledge, and notwithstanding his bankruptcy, pay off his debts in full.)

Living away from home for the first time in my life, I also did something our mother had previously forbidden—a week or two into the fall semester of my senior year, I tried out for and made the Columbia (lightweight) football team.

"I don't know if you realize it," Robert wrote me at the end of October, "but your little football throw has raised a rucass around here.

Prolonged discussions go on for hours about their "Joe College." It may have to come to the time when all money out of Martense will stop. But I don't think that will come yet. I happen to think that joining the football team was the best thing you have done in a long time and would like to see my "big" brother play sometime.

Do you want me to notify the "folks" that you are short on cash? Do you want me to send you any more (I earn at least 10 a week of which only four are needed—the rest either gets spent on my delicate stomach or mind or just gets lost)

It would be advisable if you wanted money to drop in some time just for love, and then the next night call for the money. Or something like that—you know how to be lovable.

When our team played its final game against the University of Pennsylvania, Robert and my girlfriend came to the game together. My girlfriend—the first real girlfriend I'd had while at Columbia—had the same name as my mother, Anne, but not the same background (she was descended from the Mayflower Brewsters). She had had a mental breakdown two years earlier, while in her first year at Smith College, had dropped out of college for a while, and had now returned to school as a student at Columbia's School of General Studies.

When, on the evening after this final game (which we won), I brought Anne home to meet my parents, and when, during dinner, the situation became unbearably tense, Robert invited Anne to leave the table with him. They went to his bedroom.

He returned a while later, while our mother was carrying on loudly about how my dating a gentile girl was killing her. When Robert sat down between me and my mother, my mother lifted the breadknife and pointed its blade at me.

"Here," she cried. "Here! Why don't you just cut my heart out with this, and be done with it."

She handed the knife to me. I did not take it. She set it down on the table, in front of Robert. Robert looked at me. He looked at my mother. He looked at the knife. He picked it up and passed it to me.

6

AFTER I GRADUATED from Columbia in June 1959, I worked as a yeoman aboard a merchant marine ship for the summer, and in September I left Brooklyn and headed west— to live away from New York City for the first time in my life— to Indiana University, where I had been awarded a graduate fellowship in the English department, and where I intended to write my third novel. (Under the direction of Richard Chase, I had written a second novel during my senior year at Columbia.)

In all the years since, whenever Robert and I talk, and unless I pointedly bring up something that occurred during these years, he will talk, with few exceptions, always and only about things that happened and people we knew in the years before I left Brooklyn, and before he had his first breakdown.

Sometimes, then, when people ask why I think Robert broke down and why he has lived most of his life in mental hospitals—and sometimes when, as now, I reflect on why it is he has never been able to return in any sustained way to the world most of us live in—it occurs to me that one way of understanding what has happened is to note that Robert may simply have been trying to hold our family together in the way we were a family before I left home and before he became a mental patient.

Perhaps living forever in hospitals and halfway houses ("You put me here, Jay," he often says when I visit him on various wards. "You and Mother put me here") has merely been his way of never leaving us (of remaining dependent upon us), while trying to keep us from never leaving him (of making us take care of him). If it is true for Robert, as for most of us, that—emotionally, developmentally, physically—one can't go home again, and if this becomes too unpleasant and terrifying a prospect to endure, perhaps creating a life in which he never leaves home, as it were, is simply his way (willful or otherwise) of avoiding this possibility, and its consequences.

Thus, in his worst periods, when what he says—his streams of seemingly unrelated associations—seems incomprehensible, his language is filled almost entirely with references to things that happened, and people he knew, in the years before he broke down: to the fights between our parents, to the secrecy about money, to his operation and mine, to our aunts and uncles and cousins, to tap dancing, the Rubensohns, the Kleins, Mary, Richard, Dr. Baron, Camp Winsoki, *Our Town,* Erasmus, Columbia, Martense Street.

And his rages—he will, for example, scream at me for hitting him in the throat with a ball as if I did it two minutes ago—suggest not only that he is, during these times, apparently living, emotionally, in the world we lived in nearly fifty years ago, but that he seems to believe he can make us (me) somehow pay for whatever he feels we did to him during those years by making us move back into that world with him.

"Listen, Jay," he says to me, his voice racing, while we sit in Baltic's courtyard a few months after Eli's graduation, "Burton is here, and I'm worried about him—I think he's going to marry Theresa—but Joey's not doing well. And Aunt Pearl gave me a poem yesterday but I wouldn't read it, and Martin is here too—*he is, he is!*—but Aunt Evelyn and Uncle Paul are dead, *boruch hashem,* and I think Aunt Evelyn pushed him off the roof, and you're not leaving, you know. You're sick, Jay. Talk to Henry—maybe he can help you. Maybe he'll give you therapy by phone. And let's get a prayer book and say Kaddish for Mrs. Klein—for Mrs. Ilana Klein, who came down the stairs in her silk nightgown last night—and Saturday is Passover, so why didn't you bring me matzoh today? I asked you to, but you never listen to me—you *never* do!—only listen, Jay: what I'm really upset about is cousin Ronnie. He's been here for a while, and he doesn't look good—he lost his teeth, and he's on a lot of medications, and he's been drinking a lot again, and he's thin—he's very thin, Jay, and very lonely. . . ." Robert weeps, kisses me on the cheek, holds my hand, then suddenly laughs and talks in a more natural way, as if he too knows that what he has been saying is nonsense. "And listen, Jay, I think Mother is still angry with Dad." I smile—for he has said what he will say next before—and I ask him why he thinks our mother is still angry with our father. "Well," Robert says, "she hasn't spoken with him in fifteen years, you know. . . ."

When I hear Robert talk about people we knew when we were boys—people like Martin, Dr. Baron, Joey, Mary, Richard, Leatrice, and our father, who are all dead, but whom he talks about as if they were living with him at the hospital— and when it occurs to me that whatever the cause, organic or psychological—if single cause or causes (or *discernible* cause or causes) there are for his early breakdowns and the life he has led since—and when I try, as here, to conjure up the world we lived in and the persons we were in the years before he first broke down, I remind myself that I do so not in order to somehow prove there was any necessary cause and effect between, say, our family life back then and our lives since—his life as mental patient, mine as writer and father—but simply because this is the life we knew, and because, before our paths diverged, the life he lived and the person he was were full, rich, and complex, and because, however different our lives may seem now (and however different the particular neurobiological substrata in each of us, and however different our individual genetic predisposition and/or susceptibility to, say, schizophrenia, or manic depression), what we are *not* different in is this: that who we were and what we are were formed in the four rooms of our Martense Street apartment, and at Camp Winsoki, and at Erasmus, and at family gatherings, and in all the feelings and memories that persist in us—in all the mysterious, unknowable, infinite ways any childhood affects and creates the life that follows.

When I think, for example, of 221 Martense Street, I can summon up thousands of details—the thin stripes, dull green and orange, that ran waist-high, like a false railing, along the curved hallway of our building; the exact curve of the hallway itself, and the way I took comfort from being able to slide along its curve with my body the last few steps before entering our apartment; the lovely geometric patterns made by metal struts in the skylight on the second floor just above the door to the Kleins' apartment; the iron ladder, a few feet away, in a narrow closet (old newspapers stacked on the floor) that I used for climbing onto the roof when nobody knew I was doing so; Mrs. Klein's threadlike homemade noodles, which she set out on dish towels in her living room each Thursday night, in preparation for the Sabbath; the linoleum in our bedroom, crisscrossed with blue, red, and silver lines, upon which I invented a football game in which the players were plastic chesspieces stuffed with clay; the sound of coal clattering down the coal chute in the alleyway just below our kitchen window, and below the potato bin built into the wall there between our window and the floor; the slanted, red-painted wooden cellar doors, under our bedroom windows, against which I played games of modified stoop ball; the barbed wire that ran along the fence that separated our backyard from the yard to the apartment house next door, and which I tried to avoid when I climbed onto the garage roofs, or into the backyard next to ours, to retrieve balls . . .

I can still see every inch of every room and closet in our apartment; every inch of each classroom I attended, and of our synagogue, and of our summer bunks, and of the rooms of my friends' homes and of my cousins' homes—I can see them and conjure up their colors, smells, tastes, and sounds at will, and when I do, I wonder about what I can never know: what it is like for Robert, in his feelings and memories, when he sees and remembers rooms, places, objects, experiences, smells, colors, sounds, and tastes from his childhood. ("My most vivid memory," he says, when I ask him about Martense Street, "is waking one night and going into the kitchen and seeing Grandpa's teeth floating in a glass of water, on top of the washing machine. . . . And my happiest memories are the Robert Shalita Shows.") I wonder about what it is like for Robert, in his mind and heart, when he lives again in the richness of the life that was his and that may, or may not, have led in any inevitable or necessary way to the life that has been his in all the years that have passed since we were boys together.

When I read the current literature that proclaims that all mental illness is exclusively organic in origin, and amenable to organic cures; when I encounter, again and again, psychiatrists who prescribe for Robert yet know nothing about his history or his feelings, what drives *me* crazy is the sense that who Robert actually *is* is being ignored and denied; for whether or not (and to what extent) his condition is organic in origin or nature, the nonorganic part of his past and present, as it were— all those feelings, thoughts, memories, fears, and hopes that were born on Martense Street a half century ago—all those experiences which I have sketched here so summarily (from my perspective, my flawed memory)—Winsoki and our parents and the Rubensohns and Robert's friends and our schools and the Robert Shalita Shows—all these, along with feelings, thoughts, memories, hopes, and fears unknown—they formed and created Robert's character and his identity, which character and identity still exist (are still in the process of evolving and becoming), and in greater complexity than ever.

For paid professionals, then, to act as if Robert were merely a vessel of flesh in which (bad) chemicals somehow rose up once upon a time and made him ill, and in which other (good) chemicals must now be poured in order to either cure him or keep him quiet—this is not merely the dead end of a scientific materialism not so different from (ineffective) witchcraft, but it deprives Robert, to put it most simply, of what he still possesses in abundance: his humanity.

When, for example, in the fall of 1991, after Robert had been doing well in one of Beacon's supervised residences—getting along on his own, and with two roommates, for the better part of two and a half years—and when he then broke down, he was, during the first seven or eight days of his hospitalizations, passed through six different psychiatric wards, evaluated and treated in various ways by at least six different psychiatrists, and given at least three new medications, two of which he had never, to my knowledge, been given before.

When he finally arrived back at Baltic, and I spoke with Henry Grossman, and asked Henry why these new medications had been prescribed, he replied, "I don't think the doctors had the least clue as to how to treat Robert, so they just threw a bunch of drugs at him and hoped some of them would work."

What was my brother, I asked, some kind of national testing ground? I knew a little bit about the medications: could Henry explain why a doctor would prescribe an anti-Parkinsonism drug intended to be used primarily for rigid and catatonic side effects (of which Robert had none), when Robert was restless and manic? And why several antidepressants and antipsychotics in combination when combinations were almost never as useful as single drugs, and when all the literature I'd seen cautioned against excessive and frequent changes in medication?

Henry sighed, said that he couldn't justify what had been done by others, but added that sometimes, when the doctors didn't know what else to do, they used FDA-approved drugs for non-FDA purposes. . . .

And I thought, then as now, how different from witchcraft is this? There is more disagreement about basics in psychiatry—about etiology, diagnosis, treatment, prognosis—than there is in any other area of medicine, or, as far as I can tell, in any other science, whether human (social, behavioral, anthropological) or natural (neurological, biological, chemical).

(Though the existence of a genetic factor in most cases of schizophrenia, for example, now seems a given, and though there is little doubt that "the schizophrenic brain" is different, mostly with regard to neural networks, none of the changes so far reported—e.g., ventricular enlargement—are unique to schizophrenia, and no organic "marker" has yet been found with which to diagnose a schizophrenic person, as we can do with those, say, suffering diseases such as diabetes or cancer. Since no definitive differentiating organic findings have yet been found, then, and since most research suggests that the differences found—the qualitatively unique patterns of neural organization and function—seem to characterize *all* major differences in personality, including, for example, musical ability and gender, it makes as much sense, logically and medically, to believe that neurobiological findings are secondary effects of the illness or its treatment as that they are their primary causes.)

Since, then, we cannot always agree upon or know, as with Robert, what causes his mental illness (or what mental illness *is,* for that matter), and since we don't know why some medications work or don't work (though we do know that they often relieve symptoms), and since we don't yet understand the interactions of most of these medications with others, or their long-term effects, or why they work in some instances and not others, or even what they are actually *doing* while interacting with any individual limbic system or set of neurons, liver, heart, or kidneys—what kind of madness is it to throw a bunch of drugs at somebody and hope some of them will work?

And though some medications (whose workings remain a mystery)—like some incantations—do have salutary effects on afflicted human beings, and sometimes relieve suffering and enhance healing, what can it be like for Robert and for all those, like him, who have histories of chronic mental illness, to find themselves, again and again, under the care of new doctors (who don't know them), and on new drugs (whose effects, especially long-term, are largely unknown), and in locked wards?

How not, then, grow impatient when, following any of Robert's hospitalizations—thirty years ago as yesterday—everyone, in and out of the hospital, asks me what Robert's diagnosis is, and why I think it is Robert broke this time and what I think *precipitated* the break? The questions—with the years, and with the repeated breakdowns and hospitalizations—seem absurd. Whatever the immediate causes, the ultimate causes (and answers) seem obvious: because of his *life*. Because of the past three-decades-plus of his history. Why do you *think* he got this way? I want to shout. Because of how terrified he must get when once he begins to fall, that free fall into the darkest, craziest, most terrifying and most drug-filled worlds is sure to follow. Because even when Robert is wildest and most confused, part of him seems to understand fully what has been lost, and what continues to be lost. Because he has been here before and he is, literally, frightened to death of what might happen next. If you'd been where he's been, wouldn't you be?

Robert's life remains rich and complex—at least as rich in misery and fear as he and others might wish it to be rich in happiness—yet the richness and complexity of his feelings and identity at times like these (when he breaks)—the most *intense* periods of his adult life—are consistently denied and ignored (as if his illness were not a part of him, but were a kind of neurobiologically alien enemy—an intrinsically meaningless genetic anomaly—that has infiltrated an otherwise "normal" being), while those who have control over Robert's life treat him with pharmaceutical restraints, kindergarten-style rewards and punishments, and isolation.

Whether the Martense Street battles over money, college, or divorce caused or didn't cause some "predisposition" to schizophrenia in Robert to self-activate, or whether his operation or mine did likewise—or whether some schizophrenic or manic-depressive gene caused the bedtime fight between us that may or may not have caused the operation that led to the orchiectomy that may or may not have combined with hormonal or biochemical changes that may or may not have interacted with his particular neurobiological essence in such a way as to cause him to hallucinate and try to strangle our father . . . and whether or not we can ever know (or would want to know) of all the curious, sad, miraculous, bewildering, unpredictable, and mysterious ways in which the body does or does not interact with the mind (with what in other times and places we have called the soul); whether or not we ever have a science of the kind so many psychiatrists and mental health advocates yearn for (in which there will be "magic bullets" for schizophrenia—medications that will do for mental illness what, say, insulin does for diabetes), how not cry out against any and all attempts, when it comes to human beings with lives like Robert's, to reduce their humanity to their biology?

When dealing with a condition that arises from, affects, and shows itself forth in behavior, feeling, choice, and action—that brings joy, sorrow, grief, and tragedies that, daily and long-term, are distinctly human—and while trying by whatever means to ameliorate the horrors that accompany these lives, how not pay attention and listen to the stories of these lives from those who have led them, however confusingly and crazily they are told, when it is by this very telling—in the mad behavior and language we call mental illness—that some essential part of the human beings in possession of these lives is expressing itself, and doing so, often, as a means of survival? (For it seems to me that the behavior we call mad often comes into being in individuals in order to avoid, deny, and defend against feelings and actions even more unendurable, crazed, and deadly than the madness these individuals show forth.) Why such sustained efforts to ignore and deny the individual and unique selves—the very identities of those with lives that are sad in the extreme, yet which, with the slightest variation—in genes, or in luck—might be ours?

Or is it the very mystery of what we call madness (insanity, mental illness, craziness, lunacy), and the ways in which it feels too close to what we think of as our normal lives—too threatening to thoughts, feelings, fears, behavior, and impulses that are with us more often (and in more threatening ways) than most of us care to acknowledge—that seems to cause us, again and again, to condemn those afflicted with this condition to some *non*human category of life?

Thus, for example, though many members of our family still live in and around New York City, when in the spring of 1992 I asked a cousin—a psychologist—about the possibility of inviting Robert to his home for a family gathering that was to include the celebration of Aaron's high school graduation, the cousin became angry. He would, he stated, be the one to choose an appropriate time and place for a visit from Robert (this has not happened yet). And also, he noted, his future in-laws would be visiting that day. How, he asked, would he explain Robert to them?

When my sons overheard the conversation, they became incensed. "But Robert's *fine!*" Eli declared. "When he's with us and we're with him, he's really just like anybody else. . . ."

"And anyway," Aaron added, "he's *family.*"

In February 1960, six months after I arrived in Bloomington, Indiana, my parents telephoned one night and pleaded with me to come home. Robert had moved out of the house, and had stopped attending high school. Would I please fly home for a few days—they would pay my plane fare—and do what I could to persuade him to move back into the apartment, and return to school?

Robert was sixteen years old at the time, in his senior year at Forest Hills High School. When I left Brooklyn for Indiana the previous September, Robert had left Brooklyn (and Erasmus) for Queens. My mother, determined to find a new home there, had sent Robert on ahead (so he would not have to transfer schools mid-semester), to live with our Aunt Evelyn and Uncle Paul and their four children.

In early December, our mother found a four-and-a-half-room apartment in Kew Garden Hills, at the corner of Main Street and Union Turnpike—a five-minute walk from Evelyn and Paul's house—and in late December, she and my father moved in. Now, less than two months later, Robert had moved out, to an apartment on the West Side of Manhattan.

I was hardly surprised. My mother had been writing me about what she called "the battles royal" between her and Robert, and about "how very, very mixed up" he was. He was so mixed up, she wrote, that she only prayed he wouldn't mix her up too. Sometimes I received three or four lengthy letters a week from her, letters that detailed her fights with Robert, along with the glories of the new apartment. Even Robert and my father, she wrote, against whom she'd had to battle for years in order to move out of Brooklyn, now agreed that the new apartment was "a dream come true."

"I can't get over it!!" she wrote. "It's just the best thing I could have decided. How did I stay on Martense St.? How did I live there? How did I manage to run a home? How did I manage to go to work? How did I stay sane there?"

Robert was the best of sons and the worst of sons; often his behavior was exemplary, but mostly it was disturbing: his room was a mess, he came in at all hours, he slept in his clothes, he painted murals on his walls, he created elaborate and weird feasts. On some days he was "sweet as sugar" and on others it was "bombs away," she wrote, and just as she had been proved right before, when everybody fought her about the move from Brooklyn, so she would be proved right now: something was "definitely wrong" with Robert.

Through the Jewish Child Care Agency, she made arrangements for Robert to see a social worker, which he was doing, both by himself, and with our parents. In each letter she repeated the same messages: she wished me and Robert well in our strivings toward independence (as far as she was concerned we were "100% emancipated"), and at the same time she refused to make any summer plans for herself until Robert made his plans, for she would *never* leave him alone in the apartment with our father.

Much of this seemed, at the time, familiar, predictable, even comic: no more than the particular way our family had of playing out dramas I assumed were being played out in other families (especially in the middle-class Jewish families I knew well) whenever and wherever children were leaving home and/ or rebelling against their parents' wishes and ways. Now, though, Robert had gone beyond the familiar—he was working as a dishwasher at the newly opened Guggenheim Museum, and he had rented a room in an apartment with several older men who, my mother said, were a "dangerous influence" on him.

Through the previous summer, and into the fall and winter, Robert and I had been writing to one another regularly. His letters (typed without much attention to punctuation and spelling) seemed to me at the time not at all the writings of a deranged sixteen-year-old, but those of an enchanting and precocious brother whose very idiosyncrasies—his freedom *from* convention and conventionality—were his strongest qualities, qualities which (since I saw my own life as being excessively conventional) I admired, envied, and delighted in.

He wrote me about his love life:

Salutations from brooklyn,

Ah the world is wonderful the very air i brethe tastes. That lovely girl A is no longer my true and only love. But don't feel bad cheer up. It was my decision and glad I am for it. . . . i thank her for a year spent nicely and an adolescence that I grew up in and learnt about a lot of things but as of now we ain't compatible. So there goes A. She was a beautiful girl.

He wrote about life at Camp Winsoki, where he had returned, again, as a waiter:

the girls aren't even looking for sex/ O they laff and listen ardently to off coloured jokes and they look you over once or twice so that you are proud that you are masculin and they sing songs and raise their chests or breasts and they don't talk or they talk talk but they don't say anything like one of those old flickers where charlie chaplin runs madly about and the girls lips tremble with speech but one can't hear a thing.

He wrote about our parents, and his ongoing battles with them:

And comes the time to pick apart someone and as vultures who rrrip apart the dead carcass of a once uponatime living animule the people rrrrip apart the life from a livingdead object. there must have been a time way back when these people were people or children and they must have laffed just because it was raining or because it was fun to laff. . . .

And he wrote, too, of his worries about himself:

Our parents are so helpless poor mother father was bankrupt in business and she was bankrupt as a mother. They threaten everything imaginable but since there is nothing to threaten they pretend heartrending sobs and rages and psychiatrists and it looks like life will always be the same for some people. Right now I don't really know what my philosophy of life is and I don't really care. I live and improve and learn. I just hope my ego doesn't split in two or something. . . .

We wrote to one another about everything, really—our dreams, our desires, our doubts:

Tomorrow (it seems that our missles to each other are bravadoes "i can yell louder than you can, i can be more blase, i can make cherry pie—right in the eye?)

I go back to the Guggenheim and I fear the world of realité (as the french would say). It seems I quit around the second of January to taste life. To draw within myself to live all the hundred and one ways all alone and with companions if they would improve the taste. Well anyway I have found that I am truly independent but am only sixteen. . . . au revoir and you know that everynight that i puked i did so so i could get attention and wake you up it was my way of getting of loving you after all sometimes i spent two shifts a day at play.

I loved his letters—loved the flair and originality with which he seemed to be living, and with which he wrote about the way he was living—and while I gloried in his life and eccentricity, in the outward habits of my own life (I dressed plainly, had a crew cut, was always on time, tried not to offend or outrage; I wanted, I told myself, to save my flights of madness and fancy for the written page), I continued to minimize eccentricity and difference.

I flew east—the first airplane trip of my life—and spent four or five days with Robert. He was trying desperately to assert himself, but his struggle to set himself free seemed, literally, to be destroying him. (Or—as my mother and doctors in the years to come would contend—something wrong *in* him had been set free and was destroying him.) Whatever the cause or causes of his condition, he looked awful—pale, tired, unhealthy:

his eyes were glazed, his manner jittery and insecure, his talk often confused and confusing. Even his jokes—the sure sign that all was not well—seemed labored.

His apartment, on the Upper West Side of Manhattan, was filthy—dirty clothes, unwashed dishes, half-consumed meals lying everywhere; the first time I met his roommates, one of them stepped forward and, shouting as if he were addressing a rally, declared, "We all believe that your brother has performed a heroic act!"

Well, I thought at the time, maybe he has, maybe he has—but he is surely paying dearly for his heroism. As difficult as things were for Robert at home, they seemed worse in his new situation. Though I disagreed with those, like our mother, who equated ordinary teenage rebellion (unconventional or "inappropriate" styles of hair, clothing, politics, and/or prose) with mental illness—and though I was proud of Robert for having actually gone and done what most teenagers fantasized but few risked, I found myself working to persuade him to move back to Queens, and to our parents' apartment, at least until he could, in four months, graduate from high school.

I remember trying to get him to understand that I was on *his* side—that it was his best interests, and self-interest, that motivated my concern. Thus, I argued, a move back home would be good mainly because it would make life *easier* for him: by using our parents for what they could and should still be providing for him (food, clothing, shelter, education, medical care), and by allowing him to be free of the guilt and anxiety that defying them produced. So much of his energy was going into the act of liberation that he seemed to have little left over to do the things *he* truly wanted to do. When it came to our parents, why not simply disengage, and ignore them? Why not, I argued (though not in these words), do what I'd done and what seemed to work for me? Why not just accept room and board from them, and *then,* after he had graduated, go his own way and do what he wanted? Why not get on with his life without showing our parents everything he did, thought, and felt—and without inviting their never-ending opinions about what he was doing: the approval and disapproval, the love and the withdrawal of love it was so hard not to be affected by? He should move back home not in order to please our parents, I suggested, but simply because it might be useful to him to do so.

Sometimes I found myself agreeing with him that moving out was the best thing he'd ever done, and sometimes I told him I thought he was, by his move, protesting *too* much, thereby revealing a vulnerability that was easily exploited, and sometimes—when he railed at me as if *I* were his enemy—I railed back at him and told him that I didn't give a shit: he could do what he wanted with his life, and I would get back on a plane and return to Indiana and do what I wanted with mine.

Yet, on my fourth day in New York, when he told me he had made the decision to move back home, I had the sickening feeling I had won a battle I did not want to be part of—that I had done my parents' dirty work (again?), pressuring him into being somebody he didn't want to be, and into doing something that, no matter my sensible rationalizations, he doubtless felt (toward me as well as toward them) as submission and defeat.

When less than a decade later I described this period of our lives (in *Parentheses: An Autobiographical Journey*), I remembered all this. I also remembered how happy I was simply to be with Robert—how wonderfully *grown-up* it felt to return to New York, and to be taking walks along Broadway with my brother—to be eating out together, to be going to movies, museums, and bookstores, to be trading stories, jokes, confidences. (I was in love with a graduate student at Indiana University, Virginia Ann Turner, from Smithfield, Virginia—a bright, warm, delightful woman—a gifted and accomplished pianist working toward a master's degree in music.) Our coming together after having been apart, and at a time when Robert and I were both, for the first time, living away from home, seemed to bring with it a renewed sense not only of how close we were—of how much we cared about one another, relied upon one another, trusted one another—but of the new, separate, adventurous, and different lives we might yet have.

What I had forgotten, though, when I was writing *Parentheses,* was something else: that I had been attending classes at Indiana University until the day I flew to New York, and that when I returned to Indiana, I stopped attending classes. When I returned to Bloomington, I stayed in my dormitory room most days, all day, and, as if my life depended upon it, I worked on a new novel.

What I had forgotten for many years was that it was my trip to New York—to somehow save Robert by persuading him not to take risks with his life (not to drop out of high school)—that led me to my decision to take risks with my own life: to drop out of graduate school and to risk what seemed my safe (and predictable) prospects there for the sake of what seemed inseparable from myself: my writing.

A few months later, while Robert was living again in the Queens apartment, during his last weeks at Forest Hills High, I was officially dropping out of graduate school—leaving Bloomington to take a job in Indianapolis at a Chevrolet plant (I had spent the spring semester working on my novel and applying for jobs in the Midwest) as a junior executive trainee with the General Motors Corporation, a job I thought would enable me, by removing me from a world devoted to the study and criticism of literature, to become a maker of literature itself.

My parents now began to worry about me too—my mother about my sanity, my father about my judgment. In a special delivery letter he sent me that spring, he wrote that he "hoped and prayed" I would stay in school and finish what I started, after which he talked to me in a way that (still) surprises by its directness and tenderness, and in a voice that seems so different from the one I usually recall as his. (He wrote to me from work, and without showing the letter to my mother; whenever I visited him at work, I came in later years to recall,

I was surprised to see how happy he was to see me—how his face would light up—how confident and witty he was, how different he seemed from the father I knew at home.)

"You should know your Dad by this time," he wrote (the heading: "Monday Lunch Time"), "and I never spill salt on wounds by saying you should have done this or that and so on and so on.

However Jay my son, why don't you stop floundering so much—it should be clear to you that your parents are still, always were and always will be the ones who no matter what you did or do or will do in the future will stick by you—for you and Robert are ours and to the end we'll always try—if you would only permit us to be at your side with the love that we have.

. . . Jay dear—do not rush into an interview in Chicago—Indiana etc—because it will only lead to a job in a big organization and one job will lead to another job so what—With the brain that you have been endowed with—no flattery intended—or as you would bluntly say—stop the s—t—I honestly and sincerely mean it—do not settle just for a job. You are meant for better things . . . if things do not work out now in Indiana come Home—Yes I mean it come Home—and let us talk things over and permit us—I say yes permit us finally to try try and with you to try and steer yourself on the proper road.

Again you know me—I am not avaricous or in the vernacu-lar—money mad—But it would really be a shame for you to settle into a rut in an organization where you will just be a number.

I hope my fears are baseless and that you will rite back immediately that you have come to an understanding with your professors and are continuing your studies.

These few lines were just written as I went to lunch. They come from the depths of my heart and only want the best for you.

Love

Dad

He asked me to write back special delivery airmail, and enclosed a thirty-seven-cent special delivery airmail stamp.

"I have been doing next to nothing," Robert wrote me in June 1960, at the time of his graduation. "I have alienated almost all friends—including reading and writing. . . . So sorry the progress report for what ever the heck the date is would have to report—chronic bewilderment and sence of wonder setting in, occasional periods of intense desire slackening off into long periods of apparent nothingness."

He wished me good luck in my job at GM, asked my advice on a long list of questions (How much should he ask for from our parents for college expenses? What is love? Would it be silly to return to Winsoki?), and added, "I had some real questions, like am I really sane and really talented and some other unimportant things, but we can't remember everything."

"I didn't feel like moving to Queens," Robert says. "I didn't see what we gained by going there. First of all, you had to pay two fares to get there—and then the apartment was actually smaller than the apartment in Brooklyn. My room was smaller, that's for sure. I wouldn't go in the car with them in Queens, but I was going up on the roof of the house a lot, and mother didn't want me to. She was always afraid I would jump.

"I loved Madeline"—Evelyn and Paul's daughter—"but Uncle Paul scared me the way he looked at her and touched her, and the way he and his son—Stephen, not Martin—always lifted weights to see who was stronger. And oh yes, I loved Doxie too—their dog—and I once tried to make it with her, and I thought she would be upset with me, but forever after when I visited she always slobbered me with kisses.

"And I liked working at the Guggenheim—one of the other dishwashers had been with the Ink Spots—and maybe if I stayed there I could have worked in the gallery some day, but you *made* me leave and go back home, even if you were right. Those guys I was living with were nuts, Jay, and believe me,

I know about these things. But you were gone, and all my friends were back in Brooklyn, and I just had to get *out,* can you understand that? *Can* you—?

"You thought I was okay, but I wasn't. Mother was right all along, Jay. It was chemical—it was all chemical." We are eating breakfast at a diner on Staten Island, and Robert leans toward me.

"Listen, Jay," he whispers. "Do you ever run screaming out of the house? Do you ever just start going up and down the stairs and you can't stop, and from room to room, and first turning on every light and then going back and turning them off, and then just turning them on and off, and faster and faster and you can't stop?

"It's like the world turns into black and white for me sometimes. I get jittery and on edge—angry and anxious—and then I begin to panic about everything. I get suspicious and I don't sleep, and when I don't sleep I stop eating or I eat too much. I just keep eating and eating, or not at all. I can't work well or do anything. I remember things from years back, and they seem to be happening *now*—and I can't figure out what's now and what's then.

"When I'm in the house by myself I get very scared—every noise scares me, even the smallest sound from the refrigerator— low! low!—gives me goose bumps. I think the people on the TV are watching me and that I'm watching them. If I look outside and cars are parked I think people are waiting in the cars and I wonder who they are."

Robert pauses, rolls his eyes. "Now I don't *think* they have anything against me, but . . ."

"He was just a year or two ahead of everyone else," our cousin Madeline, who was also a senior at Forest Hills High the year Robert lived with her family, writes.

He just dropped out sooner than the rest of us did. But there was nothing at all wrong or disturbed with the way he thought and felt. We were the same age, but I admired him fiercely, and only wished I could have had the courage to have been as open about my feelings and thoughts as he was.

We constantly hatched plans, Robert always more outrageous than I could be. Best of all was the way he dressed. He was really terrific, and my parents used to go nuts, seeing the combinations he wore, but I loved them. I was a good student of his, but I was conservative in my outrageousness. He did the plaids that didn't match, topped by a bowtie. I could only pierce my ears and wear sunglasses in class.

I remember long discussions—soul-searching in the subterranean levels—Robert's assigned place in our houseHOLD—holding tank—the BASEment, the two of us always planning the Great Escape. . . . [He wrote me] poems on the occasion of my college graduation, eventual Peace Corps tour, and the Get-Away. I got away; he didn't. We planned my escape together. Maybe I needed his energy too and he didn't have enough for himself. I've always felt guilty about leaving him behind. He was taken away in a straitjacket. Martin jumped out a window. . . .

(When Martin asked for psychiatric help, his parents refused. Did he want to end up in Creedmoor like Robert? they asked. Did he want that kind of stigma attached to him for the rest of his life?)

That summer Robert found, to his surprise, that he was enjoying Camp Winsoki, where, in addition to being a waiter, he ran the camp's newspaper. "I met a nice Jewish girl and if I am not in love (which is debateable)," he wrote, "I am at least having fun discovering all sorts of things that one discovers when he starts out to learn some new territory.

Her name is Irene Landau and you probably remember her as having one, two or three slightly crazy older brothers. Well out of that same enviroment came a young woman sometimes crazy, sometimes beautiful and all the time herself. At first we both sort of hopped around and smelt each other but now well today, this dawn is a new day. . . . As to the parents. They sit around waiting for a letter from you, counting the hours between letters and counting the "i miss you's." . . .

In September 1960, Robert entered CCNY, and in October he sent me a long letter in which he said he was planning to move out of the Queens apartment, to Manhattan. He wrote that he was "tired of acting nicely I should like to be good," and he wondered why he had telephoned me earlier that week.

> Probably I called just to hear if you were alive, alive as you always have been to me. Probably and maybe not. Next time I use Mr. Bell's system of hari-kari it shall be after seven if I can remember. . . .
>
> Life is now something which seems part of me. And Henry Miller and N. West and Bill shakespeare and Picasso, Modigliani, Shahn, arp, Brancusi, Freud, Faulkner, Castro, Nixon, Stevenson, Chaucer, bread, The ancient Greeks, $f(x)$ = me.

In December, depressed both by my job at GM and by the fact that I was getting little writing done, I quit GM and began work on another novel (I had finished a third before dropping out of graduate school). And not long after Robert moved out of our parents' apartment in Queens and into an apartment in Manhattan (during his first semester at CCNY, and following his summer romance with Irene Landau, he had an affair with a fellow student, Samuel R. Delany, about which Delany has written in a volume of his memoirs, *The Motion of Light in Water*), I left my apartment in Indianapolis and, in order, I told myself, to make my GM savings last, and to finish the new novel, I moved back to Queens, into the bedroom Robert had just vacated.

A month later, in January 1961, one of my father's brothers—Hymie, who was fifty-nine years old at the time—died. On the night before he was buried, I stayed with my father while the *Chevrah Kaddisha* ("holy brotherhood") washed and cleaned my uncle on his kitchen table, wrapped him in draperies torn down from the living-room window, and then placed him on the floor in a corner of the dining room, after which, all night long, they chanted prayers.

By this time Robert had made two additional decisions: to drop out of CCNY, and to take a cross-country trip to California. The more idiosyncratic and bohemian his appearance in those months, the more certain our mother was, not only that he was sick, but that he had to be institutionalized. When he arrived at my uncle's house late that evening, she laid into him for how he looked. One of the mourners looked at him, and looked at me. "Your mother's right. Why do you come here dressed like this?" he said to Robert, and then added what others sometimes said: "Why can't you be more like your brother?"

A few weeks later our mother took Robert with her for a consultation with a psychiatrist, Dr. Oppenheimer, director of Adolescent Services at Kings County Hospital, who, after interviewing and testing Robert, urged our mother to hospitalize him immediately.

"Mrs. Neugeboren," our mother quoted him as warning her, "don't waste your time and money on private therapy. This boy is very sick and needs to be put away at once."

Robert reacted by saying it was the doctor who was crazy. Our mother begged Robert to cooperate before it was too late—to agree to go to Hillside, a teaching hospital sponsored by the Federation of Jewish Philanthropies (and noted, then, for its treatment of mentally ill adolescents), at which hospital, through friends, she had been able to secure a place for him.

At the time, I recall, I felt that hospitalization and psychiatric treatment of the kind our mother kept urging would be akin to sterilization for Robert—to minimizing risk and maximizing normality: to exorcising from him those unique qualities that made him who he was. I argued passionately on Robert's behalf, saying that what the family and the doctors really wanted was to make Robert into someone who was just like everyone else. They didn't care if he was well or not—they just didn't want him to be *different*. (My mother would counter my arguments by telling me that my writing was "a sickness worse than Robert's.")

What I had seen of Robert's social workers, and the conversations I had with friends and relatives who were studying to become therapists, did little to change my mind: their basic mission, vaguely disguised in pseudoscientific jargon, and filtered through the values and language of middle-class Jewish life, seemed to have little to do with what human nature or madness or true mental illness might or might not be.

Not only were homosexuality and use of marijuana, for example, deemed aberrant behavior and proof of insanity, but any straying from the straight-and-narrow road that led from a college degree to job, marriage, children, home, and a family life in which one was "a credit to one's parents" seemed cause, not merely for disapproval and disappointment, but for psychiatric treatment and/or ostracism. I remember having heated arguments with therapists, and with friends who were studying to be therapists, because they seemed to agree with my parents that the function of a therapist was to cure men and women of homosexuality, to get college dropouts to return to school, to get college students to find suitable mates, and to enable married mates to stay married. (I recall one friend—he had been voted "Most Likely to Succeed" in high school—telling me, after he received his doctorate and had been in practice for several years, that he had thrown away most of what he'd learned in graduate school, and had taken to listening to his patients and then "giving them some good old-fashioned advice.")

The mission of most therapists, I argued with my parents and friends, was simply to get Robert, and others like him, to act *appropriately*—which meant, back then, acting in ways society and those in power defined as appropriate. There was nothing biochemically or genetically abnormal about keeping one's room in chaos, loving poetry, wearing berets and bow ties, dropping out of school, hating and rebelling against corrupt systems, being gay, smoking pot, or not wanting to wind up in a suburban home with a spouse and two children.

What the doctors wanted to do to Robert, one way or the other, whether surgically or emotionally, I argued, was to lobotomize him—to use a radical surgical procedure to remove from him the very uniqueness and radicalism that was at the core of his strength and self. (The fear, and analogy, were not, in 1961, all that far-fetched. In 1961, lobotomy was a routine and medically praised procedure; only a dozen years before, in 1949, Egas Moniz, for having developed the operation of prefrontal lobotomy, had been awarded the Nobel Prize in Physiology and Medicine.)

One night a few weeks after Robert's interview with Dr. Oppenheimer, my mother announced that Robert had finally agreed to be institutionalized, and that she was making arrangements so he could be admitted to Hillside, probably within a week. I asked Robert to go for a walk with me. We wound up at a pizza parlor a few blocks away, near the Main Street Theater (Robert says it was the Parsons), where Robert told me he had "cheated" on the tests Dr. Oppenheimer had given him. He said he wanted to see what the inside of a mental hospital was like, and so had given answers he assumed would get him into one.

"I guess I passed the admissions test," he said.

I told him he was crazy to want to go into a mental hospital, that he didn't need to be hospitalized, that maybe he had a few problems—who didn't?—but that there was absolutely no need for him to be institutionalized. Robert listened, shook his head, and said that he just couldn't deal with the pressures anymore—the pressures from the parents to be somebody he wasn't. (In encouraging him to be more like me—to use my survival skills, my ways of leaving home and getting on with my life—was I, too, I wondered, trying to get him to be less like himself?) Maybe if he gave in this time and went into the hospital for a while, he said, things would get better.

It might be easy enough to get in, I said. But once you're in, how do you know you'll be able to get out? Dr. Oppenheimer had already declared, with certainty, that hospitalization would not be short-term. If Robert had really cheated on the tests, I suggested, why not take them again, with another doctor, and prove he wasn't sick?

Robert agreed to the new plan. The following week he was interviewed by a therapist recommended by Milton Klein (who was completing his doctorate in psychology), Dr. Robert Gould, who was then senior psychiatrist for Adolescent Services at Bellevue Hospital. A few days later Dr. Gould telephoned and said it was his conclusion that "there was absolutely no need for Robert to be hospitalized"—that he found him an interesting, imaginative young man who might benefit from some individual psychotherapy, but would probably not have much need for that either.

Before the end of the fall semester—while he was going through these tests and interviews—Robert took a leave of absence from CCNY. He returned for the spring term, and completed it successfully, passing his four courses with a C+ average. As soon as the semester ended, though, in June of 1961, he followed through on his original plan and set off across the country with a friend.

A few weeks later, he sent me a special delivery letter, from the Washington, D.C., area (a "Hello Joe," to our mailman, written on the envelope), about his trip, and his plans. "I am having myself and that is a joy," he wrote. "When I left you whenever that was you said some philosophical stuff about no matter where I go I'll always be me—well, yeah, only there are better more beautiful places to be me than downtown east village or Queens."

In Ohio, he stopped at Antioch College, and at the home of cousins, after which he drove out to California (stopping to

visit our cousin Ronnie, who was working in avalanche control
and rescue at the Alta Ranger Station in Salt Lake City), and
journeyed up and down the coast, staying for varying periods
of time in Los Angeles, San Francisco, Palo Alto, and Berkeley,
but settling for the longest stretch in the Monterey-Carmel
area, where he became part of a community that gathered
around a new, small, self-supporting experimental school, Emerson College.

In late June, after a stay in Los Angeles, and visits with our
mother's cousins (the cousins he had stayed with when he was
seven years old), and with friends, he sent my parents a long
letter that alarmed them in the extreme. He began by stating
that "dr. oppenheimer and his sicknesses aside i doubt i shall
ever be knowing what i am, or what i am doing," then told
our parents *they* were the ones who were sick ("gosh mommy
your friends must think I have nothing to do in the world
besides go crazy"), and he ended by telling them that one of
our cousins was having a first birthday party and he "might
bring the baby a reptile."

In a postscript, addressed to me, he asked me to send his
love to Aunt Mary and to tell her he was wearing Richard's
sweater—Richard had died two years before, at the age of seventeen—"and meeting some wonderful people thereby. I also
really remembered him and sort of traced some of my good
character traits to his remarkably optimistic always attitude."

"We left for California from East Houston Street," Robert says,
"in Steve Cantor's VW minivan. You were crying, I remember.
I was living with twins, but I didn't know it, and I woke up
once and saw them standing over me—*two* of them—and I
said, 'What's going on here?'

"Steve's parents gave him the VW bus instead of college. It
took us two weeks to go across country, and we picked up
people on the way. I went to St. John's of Annapolis, and
stopped at the cousins, Murray and Jackie, in Ohio. I was very
happy at Emerson—I thought everyone should go there. I never

was a regular student, though. I never registered and I didn't pay them any money—I had no money!—so I sold books at the Monterey Jazz Festival.

"I sat in on a comp lit class—poetry mostly—and some political science class where we read the newspaper every day, and studied Kierkegaard. It was like Summerhill, I thought then. Ben Saltman and Roger Stewart ran it. Mother was out there for the wedding of one of Esther Circle's daughters, but I didn't see her when she was there.

"I spent six months in California, and when I boarded the plane to come home I gave my flight insurance to the stewardess. And when I got off the plane in New York, with a bag full of vomit, I gave it to mother." He smiles. "She was a nurse," he explains.

Why did he come back?

"The parents pleaded with me to come home. They thought I was sick."

Was he?

"Yeah. I was pretty sick in California. I was living in Haight-Ashbury and sleeping on floors and not doing much—one day would lead to another—and they sent me a ticket by Western Union. I slept in co-ops in Berkeley, and went to the Free University of Berkeley sometimes, and smoked a lot of pot"—he raises his voice—"but it didn't do *nuthin'* for me!" He leans toward me and whispers: "Got any?"

When I say that I didn't think he was sick back then, he cuts me off.

"*You were wrong!*" he shouts.

I mention Dr. Gould, whom he remembers as being Milton's friend, but when I remind him that Dr. Gould interviewed him and said he wasn't sick, Robert says that Dr. Gould was wrong too.

"The first girl I ever fucked was at Emerson," Robert offers. "I put up a sign—'Young Man Needs Room Will Share It with Anybody'—and Mel Ratner, who founded the college with Al

Duskin, said, 'I have just the girl for you: my sister.' I was sleeping out in the living room, and she invited me in.

"I also worked at the Highland Carmel Inn and served Kim Novak—whom I did *not* fuck—and I got five dollars a night and steak and wine. . . . It was the highlight of my life, that trip across-country to California. I stayed away from medicines the whole time. I smoked pot and I drank, but no medicines.

"But I wouldn't get dressed, or I forgot to get dressed, or I got dressed bizarrely, and I wasn't eating or sleeping a lot of the time, and I felt awful—really awful sometimes—and then I wouldn't leave the house, and . . ."

He stops. "What was so great about the sixties?" he asks.

In the fall of 1961, while Robert was in California, I took a position as a teacher at the Saddle River Country Day School, a private school in New Jersey, in its second year of existence, where I *was* the English department, teaching seventh-, eighth-, ninth-, tenth-, eleventh-, and twelfth-grade English, bringing in my guitar and leading folk singing one afternoon a week, and coaching the (six-man) football team.

I moved out of the Queens apartment (despite our mother's objections: she didn't see why I wouldn't live at home and commute back and forth to the school—at least an hour-and-a-half drive each way across Queens, Manhattan, and New Jersey), and into a room the school's headmaster gave me in the old servants' quarters of the mansion in which the school was housed.

By this time I was twenty-three years old, had finished another novel (my fourth), and was still receiving encouragement, but no contracts, from publishers. For the first month at Saddle River, after the students and teachers had left for the day, the only other person on the grounds with me was a man named Stiney, who was part Native American, and who, when it bought the estate, the school had agreed to keep on, as gardener and caretaker, for the rest of his life.

Stiney had long hair he kept tied back with a bandanna. He talked with birds and animals (and they seemed to listen). He kept rocks on the wires in his room so that the electricity would not jump out when it had to navigate turns, and he never let anybody stay in the same room with him while he ate. He spent his afternoons moving savings accounts from one bank to another because the FBI, he told me, for deadly purposes, was trailing him.

He owned a trunk that was filled with rocks he had collected, and he invited me into his room one night and explained to me at length how the markings on the various rocks told of all past and future history. The room he slept in was about ten feet away from the (unlocked) room I slept in.

In early October, parents of a student located an attic apartment for me in Teaneck, about twenty miles away, so that I could drive their son to and from school each day, and I moved out of the servants' quarters. At the end of the month—on October 25—I made my parents a surprise party for their twenty-fifth wedding anniversary, to which about a hundred friends and relatives came.

A few weeks after this, Robert returned east, by plane, and moved back into his bedroom in Queens. He seemed very angry, tired, and confused, with little sense of what he wanted to do next other than to sleep, visit museums, go to movies, write poetry, and fight with our parents about how much he slept, how he dressed, how he ate, where he went, and who his friends were.

In early February, a year after his brother's death, our father and I went to the cemetery for the unveiling of the gravestone. Robert and our mother (who avoided all funerals, even those of her sisters, nieces, and nephews) did not come. The following weekend, while returning with me to my apartment after having dinner with a friend—Gladys Matthews, an elderly woman with whom I taught at Saddle River—and while we were going about seventy miles an hour on the highway, Robert became furious with me (for telling him I was worried about him), suddenly opened the car door, stuck out a leg, and threatened to jump.

I drove him back to our parents' apartment that evening, and was sitting in the living room when Robert suddenly appeared in the doorway, his eyes bulging. He began shrieking at me for having told our parents about what had happened in the car, came at me in a rage, and leaped on top of me, his hands clawing at my throat.

I threw him off, and, a short while later, after I'd calmed him down, I left for New Jersey. A week later our parents telephoned to tell me they had just returned from Elmhurst Hospital—that Robert had been taken there by ambulance and had been admitted to the hospital's inpatient psychiatric ward.

They told me that on the way to the hospital Robert had claimed that spiders were crawling across his body, and that he was being lied to: he was not being taken to a hospital, but to my funeral. My mother said that while she had been working the night shift, Robert had gone into the bedroom and tried to kill our father, and that when she arrived home he had begun fondling her breasts and trying to make love to her.

My parents telephoned Evelyn and Paul, and then got Robert into a taxi—where he immediately puked—and took him to the office of Dr. Becker, the psychologist Robert had been seeing. Although my mother had been telephoning Dr. Becker regularly during the previous few weeks, to tell him how bad Robert was getting (Dr. Becker, she said, kept telling her she was "an alarmist"), Dr. Becker was surprised by what had happened and astonished by Robert's appearance and behavior. When Dr. Becker tried to talk with Robert, Robert unzipped his fly and pissed on him.

Dr. Becker called for an ambulance. Robert was tied into a straitjacket and taken to Elmhurst, where he was medicated, and where, my mother said, the doctors told her he had had an acute psychotic breakdown, and that they were diagnosing him, initially, as a paranoid schizophrenic.

"I told them that if he had really wanted to kill me, he could have taken a knife from the kitchen drawer, right?" my father said to me. "So he must not have really wanted to kill me. That's the way I look at it."

Our father was fifty-eight years old, totally blind in one eye and legally blind in the other—a slightly built man, about the same size as Robert: five feet five inches tall, 140 pounds. He wept while he talked, as my mother had, and after I hung up, I walked around my attic room, in circles, weeping too, and dry-heaving—tearing at my hair, pounding my fists against walls and furniture, screaming at the universe, and believing that nothing made sense and that nothing ever would make sense again. If this could happen, what *couldn't* happen?

"What I remember is that I wasn't sleeping much, and I was staying up all night some nights," Robert says. "And Mother was working again and Dad was sleeping alone, and I was having hallucinations, only I don't remember what they were. I've never hallucinated much in my life, even on drugs, but I remember going into the bedroom when it was almost morning and Dad was snoring away as usual, and there was an invitation on Mother's vanity table below the mirror, on that glass thing where she kept her perfumes, and it was for a Bar Mitzvah, and I remember staring at it for a long time.

"It was for Bruce Stein, but I thought it said *Frank*enstein. I'd been reading this book about a Paris cult from the twenties that had to do with rays of the sun, and . . ." Robert stops, shrugs. "That's all I remember. And then I was strangling Dad, and he was saying, 'What is it, Robert? I'm an old man. I'm an old man. Leave me alone and we'll play gin rummy, all right?'

"So I stopped strangling him and he got dressed and said, 'Let's go for a walk.' So we went walking. We walked and we walked—oh boy, did we walk. And then Mother came home and I said some things to her and she got very crazy—but I never tried to make love to her the way she said—and the parents called Evelyn and Paul and they came over and things got crazier, with whether we should go in their car, or ours, or a taxi, and finally I got in a taxi and they took me to Dr. Becker's office, where I opened my fly and pissed all over his waiting room, I think.

"But he was a *bad* man. During our sessions he'd turn on his machine whenever I smoked—his air transformer—so loud that he couldn't hear me. And he kept telling the parents not to worry about me." Robert looks away. "He was wrong too.

"And I remember trying to get the spiders off me, and thinking you were sick again and they were taking me to the cemetery to say Kaddish, and I remember you coming to Elmhurst and playing your guitar for us and being my big brother. That was very nice of you, Jay . . . even though you weren't very good at it. And I don't remember trying to chew away my tongue, but I remember waking up and I was talking in French and nobody could understand me because I had a thick accent and I didn't have any tongue."

I visited Robert the evening after he was hospitalized, and for the rest of that winter, and into early spring, I drove, Saturdays, Sundays, and two evenings a week, over the George Washington Bridge, across Manhattan Island, then over either the Triborough or Queensboro Bridge and into Queens, to visit him on the ward at Elmhurst, where he was heavily medicated, and often straitjacketed or tied down to his bed.

He asked me to bring my guitar to the ward, and on nights when he was not immobile, or had not had catatonic seizures and been carried away, I would stay on after the visitors had left and, my back to the high barred windows, I would lead the patients and their aides in folk-singing (mostly the same songs I sang with my Saddle River students: "Show Me the Way to Go Home," "You Are My Sunshine," "Oh Freedom," "We Shall Overcome," etc.). Robert would sometimes pay attention, or sometimes leave the dayroom, or scream at me or about me—"That's my brother—my *big* brother, Jacob Mordecai, you know!"—or he would pace this way and that with other patients, or stand in one spot and bob back and forth as if in prayer. Once, when I asked the patients if they had any requests, Robert shouted from the far corridor, "Yes—can you play 'Far, Far Away'?"

When the singing was done and I would head toward the exit, Robert would shuffle along at my side, listing the things he wanted me to bring him the next time I visited (his tennis racket, his tefillin, tobacco, a watch, our Jerry Mahoney doll, our grandfather's false teeth), and while we waited for an aide to unlock the thick metal door, his eyes would brighten momentarily and he would ask if I *really* thought they were going to let me out.

He seemed suddenly a young boy in an old man's body. His shoulders were stooped, his neck stiff, his eyes nearly closed, his gait slow and shuffling, his speech slurred and stuttering, his skin pasty, his lips parched; when he was not rigidly silent or maniacally enraged, he trembled so uncontrollably that he could not hold even a cup or fork or spoon.

While he lay on his bed, in a ward with about two dozen other patients—some sleeping, some wailing and screaming—I would feed him, talk with him, tell him jokes, and I would think: The Robert I know and love lies dead somewhere inside this body, and nothing will ever be the same again. It was as if the world had come to an end, and the fact that I continued to eat, teach, drive, talk, sleep, and type as if I were alive—as if I existed—seemed an illusion not unlike Robert's delusions.

I wanted, most of all, to trade places with him. That first winter, and for years afterward, I felt, too, that I *was* the heartless killer my mother had always told me I was—for if I had a heart, I believed, surely I would have been—*should* have been—where Robert was.

In the Queens apartment, my parents and I spent hour after hour going over each detail of our visits with Robert—all our thoughts and feelings about him, most of which seem, in retrospect, to have been expressions of ordinary guilt—ordinary attempts to justify those things we had or had not done that had somehow caused or not caused Robert's breakdown and hospitalization. *All* information about Robert's condition was given to my mother, who filtered the data to me and my father, informing us of what the doctors told her we should or shouldn't do, and of what we should or shouldn't say in order to help get Robert well.

After I left Queens and drove back to New Jersey, and especially late at night, when I drove on narrow back roads near Saddle River, I would find myself weeping and screaming maniacally, "Oh you bastards, you bastards! . . . You fuckers!"— and I would also find that I had sometimes turned off my headlights to see how far I might go before I turned them back on, or, during heavy rainstorms, blinded by rain and tears, I would see how far I dared drive before turning on my windshield wipers.

How much of Robert's condition—his fate—was due to me? What had I done to cause his break, and what could I have done to prevent it? Though, afterward, I knew (and was told) that his illness was not my "fault," in my feelings then, and for years to come, I believed (a belief Robert consistently encouraged) that we were bound to each other in this: that any success or happiness I achieved had been earned, somehow, at the price of his failure and misery.

I continued, that winter and spring, to receive rejections of my novels and stories, did no writing of fiction, and found myself talking compulsively with friends, and with several of my former professors—Richard Chase (who lived in nearby Tenafly, and who had been encouraging me, and sending my books to his publishers), F. W. Dupee, and Charles Van Doren. During those months, I came to believe, as I would for years to come, that the one truly interesting thing about me—my only redeeming quality—was my brother's life. I talked with whoever would listen—friends, relatives, therapists—and when I talked about Robert, I felt always—the words I began using that winter—as if I were wearing his heart on my sleeve.

I felt as if being sick and locked up was somehow more

real—and certainly more honorable—than being well and in this world, and though I thought and talked about writing Robert's story—about starting a novel that would be based on his life—I wondered: if I succeeded, wouldn't I only be hurting him yet again in order (yet again) to serve *my* needs? By putting his heart on my sleeve—his private life into my public words—wouldn't I merely be using *his* life to fulfill *my* ambitions?

Friends listened patiently to the flood of questions that poured from me: What had made Robert break down, and had he always been crazy, and if he wasn't crazy before, what made him so now, and had I somehow made him crazy, or had my parents, and what effect would the drugs have on him, and would he ever recover, and what could I do to help, and had I done the right or wrong thing in saying or doing this or that—and *was* there a right or wrong thing—and why was he shut away in a lunatic asylum when people far crazier (and more mean- and evil-spirited)—the shits of the world—were getting on with their lives, enjoying the fruits of their evil and hypocrisy by preying on those less powerful (but far worthier) than they were . . . ?

I received few answers, but I did, by talking with others, discover that I was not alone. Virtually everyone I talked to had somebody—brother, sister, husband, wife, lover, aunt, uncle, son, daughter, grandmother, grandfather—who was or had been mad, who was or had been hidden away by the family—who had been locked away in a state institution for years, or who had committed suicide, or who had been hospitalized for one or more breakdowns.

Though part of me clearly subscribed to Romantic notions of the-artist-as-inspired-and-misunderstood-madman, and though part of me feared I would never be a real writer because I didn't have the courage to break down, to let my dreams and feelings rise up from within so they could literally burn themselves onto the page, my fear of going mad, just as clearly, remained greater than my desire to be mad. For on an hourly and daily basis, I soon came to see, there was nothing Romantic or attractive about being mentally ill. (To those who, in the years to come, would talk about the mentally ill as if they were the heroes and visionaries of our time—the truly sane people in an insane world—I would say what I once heard Joanne Greenberg say to someone who espoused this view. "Oh, if you'd ever been mentally ill," she said, softly, "you'd know it was a distinctly unpleasant experience.")

I visited with Charles Van Doren and his wife often that winter and spring, and when we met we did not talk about his fall from grace for having been implicated in the quiz show scandals. We talked, instead, and mostly, of how concerned we were about our brothers—he for his brother John, and I for Robert. (When we met for an afternoon some twenty years later, he suddenly turned to me and said, "You know, I was quite worried about you back then—you seemed very fragile, and on the edge of leaving us all." I smiled. "Well," I said. "I was pretty worried about you back then too.")

After hearing Robert's story, Charles told me of a psychiatrist he knew, John Rosen, and of a longtime friend and benefactor they had in common, Arthur Rubin. At the time, Rosen was considered something of a radical genius in the psychiatric world, his theories and programs much talked about. Partly because his approach contained within it a radical critique of the system in which Robert was caught, but more because he seemed actually to be getting results—to be curing those people called schizophrenic or psychotic, including many previously diagnosed as chronic and/or beyond help—his appeal for me was enormous.

Rosen had done his psychiatric training in the forties and fifties, at a time when, he noted (in the introduction to his book *Direct Psychoanalytical Psychiatry*), Brooklyn State Hospital, where Dr. Oppenheimer worked, prided itself on doing "more shock than any hospital in the East." Rosen described the abysmal conditions then prevalent in most institutions (where treatment proceeded "as if the etiology of psychosis had been discovered"), wrote of our ignorance of the causes and cures of psychosis, and, especially, of the increasing variety of psychiatric approaches that were then emerging ("a jumble of unrelated procedures, some of them brutal . . . a few of them seemingly harmless to the psychotic, if not humane").

What impressed me about Rosen (aside from the fact that he had been recommended by Charles, and that there was a possibility he might take Robert on as a patient) was the clear way he cut through jargon ("I avoid using the term schizophrenia altogether. Frequently it is used loosely as a synonym for 'psychosis.' . . . We define 'normal' as getting along in society, and being 'abnormal' as failing . . ."); his emphasis on the pragmatic, in which he kept his eye always on the object: paying attention to and healing the individual patient; his conviction that "the psychotic, like the neurotic, is not 'sick' in a medical sense"; and his method, which involved having the psychiatrist and a team of trained assistants commit themselves unconditionally, on a round-the-clock basis, to caring for the psychotic individual.

His program did "not confer immunity from psychosis," he wrote. Nor could it "be recommended on grounds of its simplicity, speed, or economy." The "governing principle" of direct psychoanalysis, in which the psychiatrist entered the patient's delusional world in active and imaginative ways (holding the patient, feeding the patient, responding directly to the patient's psychotic language or acts), was that "the psychiatrist must be a loving, omnipotent protector and provider for the psychotic individual." He must be "a foster parent to the psychotic individual who has regressed to infancy, and who must be brought up all over again."

Although Rosen's successes were later called into question, his approach seemed effective, sane, and humane to me in 1962—heroically so—especially when compared to the treatment Robert was getting at Elmhurst, and it served to reinforce my own often fearful, half-formed, and self-serving notions about what had happened to Robert, and what might be done to help him.

The only way Robert was going to get well, I began saying to friends, was if he could be removed from the environment (home and family) in which he had become ill, for this environment would, as long as he lived in it, continue to keep his wound open and to aggravate it. The only way Robert was going to get well was if he could be cared for constantly and unconditionally by others, until the time came when he had restored himself sufficiently to be able (if and when he chose) to return to the world most of us lived in.

Rosen also emphasized what seemed a revelation to me: that psychotic behavior might best be understood as a way—a desperately ingenious way—an individual had found not merely to leave reality for a time, but, more important, to survive.

("I'm all right because I'm insane, do you understand, Jay?" Robert would shout when I visited him at Elmhurst. "I'm *in* sane, do you understand? That's why I'm here!")

"As painful as it is," Rosen wrote, "psychosis is not as painful as that which it attempts to circumvent." Thus, "the administration of chemical tranquillizers," he maintained, "may suppress symptoms and produce the semblance of comfort, and so impede treatment." I.e., if the symptoms are gone, how know and deal with the problems that brought them into being, and that will remain if and when the drugs, however beneficent (which they were not at the time), are withdrawn?

I remember, too, that winter, telling Charles of the scene I constantly imagined—a waking dream in which I was racing through a dark tunnel where all around me rabid and snarling animals—dogs, wolves, tigers—were howling, drooling, snapping their jaws. I was trying desperately to get to the end of the tunnel (if there was an end), running along railroad tracks, in and out of caves, through sewers (like Jean Valjean in *Les Misérables,* in the pictures I recalled from the Classic Comic I'd read as a boy), and as I ran I kept turning back and reaching for Robert's hand. "Hurry up, Robert!" I cried. "Hurry! Please hurry! Please! Here—take my hand! Grab on and I'll pull you through. Please hurry . . . Please . . . !" I was running for my life and screaming at Robert that I wanted to save his life too but that I couldn't wait forever—that he should stop dawdling and clowning and teasing—that I didn't want to leave him behind, but if he didn't hurry and grab onto my hand, I would have to go on by myself. "Please hurry, Robert. Come on! Please . . . run, Robert. Run! Please . . . !"

When I met with Arthur Rubin (who wanted me to do writing and editing for him of the kind Charles was doing), and talked with him about Robert, he told me that Dr. Rosen had a long waiting list, but there was a good possibility we might get him to take Robert on as a patient.

Before this could happen, however, Robert was discharged from Elmhurst. During the last week of March 1962, he traveled a few miles east, in Queens, to the infinitely more pleasant surroundings of Hillside Hospital (with its low buildings, its lawns, its young people everwhere, it looked more like a college campus than a mental hospital), where—for the next nineteen months—he would remain.

7

IN OCTOBER 1973, when our parents retired and moved
to Florida, they shipped about twenty cartons of Robert's belongings to me in Massachusetts—books mostly, but also clothing, records, framed prints and drawings, his stamp collection,
his 16mm Bell and Howell Model 70 movie camera, his chess
set (a gift from me for his Bar Mitzvah), and personal items
Robert referred to as his "rememorabilia." They asked me to
store them for him against the day when, they hoped, he would
be well again, and would have a life and home of his own.

Among the items they sent north, along with the cartons,
was the cherry-wood trunk that had belonged to the Rubensohns. When, in the spring of 1991, I began work on this

book, I opened the trunk and went through its contents. I found framed pictures, oil paintings, an American eagle ceramic bank, small wooden African sculptures, Robert's *tefillin,* supplies for making oriental drawings and prints, a pipe rack, overdue library books, underwear, a 35mm camera lens, film for Robert's movie camera, a box of campaign-style buttons (MAILER FOR MAYOR, KOCH—CONGRESS, HARRIMAN*DELUCA*HO-GAN, POOR PEOPLE'S CAMPAIGN 1968, WALT WHITMAN CLASS OF 1957, CAMP WINSOKI), U.S. Post Office flash cards for Pennsylvania (Sec. A), photos from Emerson College, report cards, letters, ashtrays made at Hillside (because they were "cracked," Robert called them "psycho-ceramics"), and a thick pale-green binder, which I assumed contained Robert's poems.

When I opened the binder, however, I found, not the poems, but a neatly typed manuscript of more than one hundred pages, and on the title page, the following:

From the diary of a nineteen year old
mental patient named
robert gary neugeboren
p.o. box 38
glen oaks, n.y.

The diary begins on April 3, 1962, less than a week after Robert had been transferred to Hillside. "I shall go through the day trying to remember what has happened and how it happened this wednesday in april," Robert writes in the opening sentence.

> I awoke at eight after dreaming of a circus but i don't remember who i was in the circus or what i was doing—associated it with the contest that the activities committee is sponsoring on night activities. I changed my linen (they have a thing called linen exchange where you bring last weeks dreamed in and creamed in sheets in exchange for nice soft white new sheets, pillowcases and towels.) Then I rushed to breakfast. . . .

172

JAY
NEUGEBOREN

A few pages later, he describes his first morning appointment with his doctor ("I think I am happier in the morning because I have faith that a new day has just dawned and there are going to be new things that i can learn and see and be with"), in the course of which he says that she told him he "would have to stop seeing [his] friends that they were interfering with [his] therapy."

"I got sulky and resentful," Robert writes, "—the weekend was what i looked forward to and here she was taking my friends away. But she said that i made these friends when i was sick and that therefore they were mixed up and would only mess me up further. I understood what she was saying and she will allow me to see relatives so things are not too bad. I can have a friend if she agrees.

"Then she tried to wring out of me why and what happened just before i got hospitalized," Robert continues. "I quickly tried to communicate how depressed and apathetic and like a child i was. Some of my fears. She didn't seem to get what she wanted and i guess it will take a while before either of us understand exactly what was going on."

A few pages later, Robert has an afterthought:

Oh yes, during the session i wanted to know why everyone was so interested in me and said that she must enjoy seeing people get better and then stuck in that I saw Arnie S. last night and he was going to school and looked happy and maybe someday i could be like that. She asked me what i wanted and i said to have a girl and be happy to understand the world around me and to love those who love me.

Each time I go through Robert's diary, I find myself wanting to read it aloud to everyone I know—and to publish it entire, not only because it gives such a vivid, moving, and often delightful account of his daily life at Hillside, and of the way this kind of private institution cared for the mentally ill thirty years ago, but—more important—because it gives a sense of

Robert in Robert's own words: of who he was at nineteen, and of what a full and idiosyncratic life, imagination, mind, and identity he had.

The diary, along with the letters he wrote while at Hillside, remind me, also, of what the rules were back then, and of why Robert was often so frightened. The doctors at Hillside made it clear that were Robert not to respond within a year to their treatment program (medication plus psychosocial therapies), he would be sent to Creedmoor, a state hospital a few miles from Hillside (for anyone growing up in Queens in those years, "You belong in Creedmoor!" was the most common of curses), and that if, before the year ended, he did not improve substantially, or if he regressed, they would resort to what they referred to as "other means." In 1962, this meant utilizing the treatment that most terrified Robert: ECT—electroconvulsive (electroshock) therapy. (Dr. Max Fink's *Convulsive Therapy: Theory and Practice,* a text that champions electroshock and other forms of convulsive therapy, "is derived," Fink writes, "from the studies of convulsive therapy from 1954 to 1962 at the Hillside Hospital in New York.")

Robert kept the diary, which he showed to his therapists, for about six weeks, and for each entry he went through his day, noting what he ate, wore, did, thought, and felt. The diary is filled with lists and data, and filled, too, with accounts of his therapy sessions. In addition to recounting regular meetings with his doctors and social workers, he writes about taking part in a large array of other therapies and activities: art therapy, creative therapy, dance therapy, group therapy, music therapy, occupational therapy, music appreciation classes, poetry classes, pottery classes, bridge classes, UN classes, sketching classes, science classes, current events classes, et al. He participates in athletics (biking, tennis, Ping-Pong, a doctor-patient softball game), a talent show, work groups, a photography club, folk singing, sight singing, play reading, dances, choral club, picnics, KP duty, a communal Seder, government meetings, and a sleepaway camping trip to Bear Mountain.

His diary is filled with impressions of people at Hillside, and of his feelings about them ("That Millie is so talented, beautiful and winning that i want to love her, but in my present condition who knows if i can really love another human being humanly"), even while he fears that the doctors and our parents are conspiring to steal from him the individuality and the friends he loves ("Forgot to mention that we continued our argument about my having friends, the parents still trying to choose my friends for me and telling me to break off relations with my friends").

His diary also contains some of his poems. As prologue to his second entry, for example, he composes three haikus:

> little chips of diamonds
> dandruff for my hair
> melting in april

> black on green
> do you grow like seeds
> and what makes you fly when i come near?

> green webs on gray, today
> tomorrow waving webs with blue
> mixed with yellow bolts

When Millie is put on restrictions and must have an aide accompany her wherever she goes, Robert writes a poem for her:

> the love between us
> grows like ivy
> poisonous and itchy
> it goes up and down my skin-shell
> goosing me into pimples
> and all i know
> blows away before your asking heart

That same week he also writes a poem to our mother, one which (like Kafka's letter to his father?) he never gives her:

mother mother mother dear
why when you are always near
do I feel so absolutely un me
why by now can't you see
that the whole wide world is not just you and me?

He describes visits from relatives (Aunt Esther and Uncle Jack "ask three times if they have to tip the chef for giving us coffee. Just like 'outsiders'—they always have to pay for everything: nothing for nothing is their motto"), and from friends ("Then A. said she saw Linda, and she thought she was mainlining and I asked what was that, she said taking H. Shit! So I cross off Linda from my list of friends, just like that you say goodby to a beautiful friend so maybe it isn't so"), but mostly he writes about his life and friends at Hillside, and his hopes for the life he will have when he leaves:

I relax and tell David that I am learning how to relax. He approves no end and says there is no reason to be miserable. We talk about the people who come to visit me being sick, and how I am getting better. That when I was in california I had nothing in my head but now that wouldn't frighten me. . . . Well, I've got another chance now and I'll go to berkeley to get an education, a scientific one, and then I can be free again after analysis. We talked about being strong and independent and art, and I was glowing because once again I was in touch with a human being.

On April 17, 1962, his nineteenth birthday, he meets with Dr. Steiner, who gives him a battery of tests that last more than three hours, and include Rorschach tests ("I kept insisting that they were only ink-blots and that it was a crime to make them anything else. I found about five things however which he never heard or saw before which made me quite proud"), and a thematic aperception test, where he is shown pictures for which he is asked to make up stories, which stories he remembers clearly ("A girl on a bridge. 'She is about to jump when the longshoremen down below invite her in for a game of bridge. She plays with them and realizes that she has what to live for. When she leaves Lennie follows her, rapes her, then stabs her. Her friend Jim Steel writes her story and wins a pulitzer prize. He drinks himself to death however since he has lost the only thing or being he has ever loved' ").

He also writes, at length, about our family. "First I called mother," he writes, on the first day of Passover, "to wish her a happy Pesach and she decided to give me a lecture. Said the doctors said I was very sick and that I had too many friends on the week end. I told her to stop it and we both hung up." Then he adds this:

I know i'm sick probably better than anyone—it is me who feels un free and depressed and inferior and slightly paranoid, nobody else, it is me who finds it hard to sit still and concentrate. It is I who haven't been able to communicate with people what the hell is she complaining about. I am perfectly honest with the doctors and my parents. What do they want—it takes time and more time. It took how many millions of years to produce me and my enviroment—I can't get well over night.

From the evidence of the diary, it appears Robert talked openly about everything with his doctors—his operation, his homosexuality, his taking of drugs (pot, poppers), his friendships, his shame, his trying to make it with Evelyn and Paul's dog, his envy, his guilt, and his ordinary, daily fears and desires ("Why do i always want to know if these people are married— why my fixation?" he asks, and answers: "Naturally i am afraid of getting married and becoming like dad"):

listening to henry miller on the phonograph and hearing another man say that man is lonely, i recognized the shadow of myself seeking and reeking from aloneness. And every so often i remember that call it whatever you may but i am in a mad house. Cheerful, no?

In late April, after he has gone through a staff screening during which he is interviewed by eight staff members, including three doctors, his psychiatrist suggests he may soon be ready for discharge. When this occurs, she asks, what would he think of moving into a foster home?

> For three minutes I was speechless, then i said it was what i have always asked for but how would my parents take it, and i guess i still feel dependent on them and need them.
>
> She said alright, i didn't have to decide now, it was something that we could talk over some other time. Then she said the social worker, Mrs. Leader would be seeing my brother and father, and i said good—jay was sicker than me.

On May 15, he writes in his diary for the last time, a two-page entry about dance therapy ("had to sit on the sidelines a lot, think that has to do with the thorazine"), group therapy, individual therapy, bridge class, lunch, Ping-Pong, movies, and a four-page letter he sends to a friend who has been transferred to Creedmoor ("I included some of my better poems and a hope that he will get better").

"Wanted to hear segovia," the diary ends, "but the old men on the ward were listening to some western. Heard the last half hour. It moved me so that there were tears in my eyes at one point. Played tickle the tummy with alan and then we came back to my room and exchanged poems. He has some imagemaker within him. He really liked my stuff and i was proud, that is about it."

Robert seemed increasingly happy that spring and into the summer, especially about the freedoms he continued to gain— freedom from heavy doses of Thorazine, freedom to leave the hospital more often and to have overnights at home, freedom to see friends he wanted to see when he wanted to see them. He participated enthusiastically in Hillside's wide range of programs, becoming, among other things, editor-in-chief of the Hillside newspaper, and president of his living unit.

As part of a research grant, he was one of two patients chosen to meet with both a psychiatrist and a psychoanalyst, and for a few months met regularly for psychoanalytically oriented therapy sessions. Repeatedly, his doctors expressed their pleasure with his progress, said they would probably discharge him before the end of summer; and so, with their approval, Robert began planning his return to college.

"The thing I remember most about Hillside," Robert says, "is that there was always a lot to do. There were good meals too. It was a pastoral hospital because it was in a country setting, and the people seemed with it. I had a lot of friends there, and the staff was good.

"First of all, you were constantly in therapy—three times a week—and I had Drs. Zitrin and Glick, for my psychiatrists. It was a teaching hospital, so I had Dr. Schiff too, for my psychologist. In the morning there was art therapy, and then . . ."

Robert stops. "It was so luxurious and beautiful, Jay. . . ." Again, Robert doesn't say anything for a while. Then: "It was the best hospital I was ever at, by far. It was like Camp Winsoki, only without relatives, and with lots of drugs. I became editor of the hospital newspaper, the *Hillside Herald*, the same way I did at Winsoki.

"Donald was my first roommate at Hillside—they put us together by ages—so I got to have other roommates too. There was this guy Mike I played Ping-Pong with a lot, who was very withdrawn—he would walk around the room as if he were hiding from the FBI. He wore sunglasses and a suit jacket all the time, no matter the weather, and would just walk back and forth and back and forth. He graduated from Princeton, I remember, and that was all I knew about him. But I was with Donald for six months, and then I got sick again."

Was there anything about Hillside he didn't like?

"I hated the Thorazine. It was awful. You don't know. You don't *want* to know. You can't do *anything* when you're on it. My mouth was always dry. The sun makes you itch and burn. I think it ruined my teeth too. It made me want sweets all the time. Then it constipates too, and gives you this big belly—remember the belly I had then, like an old man? And do you remember when we went to Jones Beach, to pitch-and-putt together, just the two of us, and you didn't believe how the sun reacted to me and made me sick?

"But then—I don't know—things went wrong at about six months, and I got sick again. I was getting better and started going to Queens College, from Hillside—there were two of us who enrolled at college while we were still patients, and Dr. Glick sent me home one weekend without my medicine. They were reducing it. He was going on vacation, and maybe he forgot or was too busy—I don't know—I mean, I don't remember exactly what happened. Afterwards they said they made a mistake, that they *rushed* me out too fast. So they agreed to let me stay on for an extra six months. I think they felt guilty.

"So that weekend, I was acting inappropriately, I guess. Maybe I was. Maybe I *am*! But first they would up my medication, and they they would reduce it. It was crazy. Up and down and down and up, the way they still do."

Does he recall how much Thorazine he was getting?

"Oh yes!" he says. "Eight hundred units of Thorazine at night and six hundred in the morning, and some other medications—Stelazine and something called Kemadrin, I think. Other things too, maybe. But I went home and I was pacing a lot, and screaming, and going back and forth and I couldn't do anything. The Thorazine made me crazy! I felt so awful, like I couldn't *do* anything, and I kept screaming 'No!' I remember that. 'No! No! No!' And at the hospital, Charles Fried, who was my friend, and later my roommate—he and a bunch of other patients started a petition, to give to the doctors. They thought I was going to die, that the drugs were killing me. I thought so too."

Does he have any idea of what made the difference—of why, as at other times, things changed the way they did?

"I don't *know*! Nobody knows, Jay—I told you before!" he shouts. "I don't know what made the difference and why things suddenly changed," he continues, calmly, a few moments later. "I don't think it's any one thing or another, really. I mean, I think it has its own rhythm—like a life of its own—that it's just something in me that comes and goes, about every year now, or maybe every eighteen months. That's all. I don't think there are any reasons."

Is he interested in knowing what I remember and felt about those times?

"Who gives a shit what you felt?" he says. "You felt guilty, right? Well, you shouldn't. It was all chemical."

In late June, when my teaching at Saddle River was done, I, too, decided to return to school—to go back, on a trial basis, to Indiana University for its summer session.

I was twenty-four years old, and had now completed seven books, none of them published. Though I went for what seemed to me impossibly long stretches during which I did no writing at all, and feared I would never write again, I did complete two short books that year: a young adult novel, and a book about nuclear disarmament. But I longed to see my books in print, I longed for readers, and I longed, too, to be somewhere else. I longed, that is, to do for myself what I kept urging for Robert: to get out of New York, and away from home and family. (One evening, after a visit to Hillside, and while I was working on a novel in Robert's room, my mother walked by, looked in, and laughed at me. "Mark my words," she said. "You keep doing that, and you'll wind up in a straitjacket like your brother.")

When, through the years, I have thought about my visits

with Robert at Elmhurst and Hillside that year, what I recall more vividly than the visits themselves are the times spent afterward. For the visits with Robert during the winter and spring of 1962 were never as excruciating as the hours spent with my mother and father after visits.

What usually happened (and would happen again two years later, when Robert was hospitalized at Creedmoor) was that after screaming and recriminations about who-did-what-right and who-did-what-wrong—about who was to blame for what, and why, and when, and where, and how, and how often—all discussions would quickly turn, not to Robert and to what we might do to help him, but to my mother, and of how we could best show our love for her.

All visits—even (or especially) those that lasted only a few minutes—would usually result in a four-or-five-hour session in the Queens apartment, during which most of my father's energy and mine were spent trying to convince my mother that it was not, for example, her *fault* that Robert had yelled at us and refused to see us. Hour after hour, my mother would pace the floor, howling and weeping, accusing me and my father of criticizing her, of blaming her for Robert's illness, of not loving her.

The mildest suggestion—that, for example, she not comment first thing on the way Robert was dressed—would bring about tears, wailing, and venom: Why were we criticizing her when all she wanted was for Robert to be well? Why did we insist on torturing her? And who the hell were *we,* anyway, to be telling *her* how to treat her son? What the hell had *we* ever done for him? If not for her . . .

Sometimes while she ranted she would bang her head against walls or doors. What had she done to deserve a life like this? Why was the world filled with so much hate and violence when all she wanted was for people to love one another? "Oh, I know how you despise me, Jay," she would say. "Don't think I don't. I know how much you hate listening to the sound of my voice. . . ."

Once, when I begged her to calm down, and when—a first—
I finally said she was right, that I *was* tired of listening to her
talk about *her* suffering—could we, instead, please try to talk
about what would be best for Robert?—she left the room and
returned a minute or two later, a wide strip of adhesive bandag-
ing taped across her mouth.

When I tried to sympathize with her, she told me that
nobody would *ever* know what she felt; and when my father
and I suggested she get help for herself, she became even more
enraged: "Don't you tell *me* I need help!" she would declare.
"I'm not the crazy one in this family," she would say, and then
she would go on familiar tirades in which she warned us never
to tell her to get help, because she was *never* going to change,
because the whole world would have to change before she would,
because someday she would be proved right about *everything*. . . .

The family therapy sessions at Hillside (once a week that
spring) seemed to me grotesque replays of scenes from our
apartments on Martense Street and Union Turnpike, and I
began to believe more and more that as long as Robert was
asked to get well within the context of the family, he was
doomed. To enter a therapy session was to enter a war zone
where no possibility of understanding or healing existed, and
where, I explained to friends, Robert would never win, since he
was, for starters, simply no match for my mother, and since—a
theory I'd long held to—despite her words to the contrary, my
mother loved nothing so much as the fighting itself; she was,
and had always been, most truly alive when embattled against
real or imagined enemies—when engaged in confrontations
with my father, Robert, me, her parents, or her sisters.

But I did not feel this with anything like conviction, consis-
tency, or clarity. There was an enormous emphasis at Hillside
at that time on family therapy—explanations from doctors and
social workers at virtually every session about how if one person
in a family was sick, then the sickness and problems were
endemic to the family itself, in which family the sick child
had somehow become the "carrier" or "target" of some general

familial malady. Therefore, they explained, the way to mental and emotional health was for the family to work its problems through *with* the sick child, so that the family could understand and heal its wounds, and the child take its (proper) place, once again, within the family. (Compare, in 1996, the way in which such beliefs have come full circle. Mental illness is now a "no-fault" brain disease of adult onset, and the organically afflicted child is usually seen as the pathogenic force in an otherwise normal family—a belief that seems to defy common sense, suggesting as it does that the disturbed child can induce pathological behavior in otherwise normal adults, but not vice versa.)

I disagreed, but though I argued about this and other things with my parents and with Robert's therapists, I don't recall doing so with much conviction or intensity. Mostly, I wanted to avoid being blamed for Robert's illness. Mostly, I wanted to be somewhere else. To have gone against the prevailing wisdom—of either my parents or the doctors—would, I feared, have brought down upon me the accusation I could least tolerate: that I was making things worse for Robert, and keeping him from getting well.

Mostly, too, until I left New York City that summer, I was unaware of how frightened I was—of never writing again, of never loving or being loved, of going crazy and winding up where Robert was—and I cannot say that I felt then what I like to think I knew then: that what was going on was a fight to the death in which Robert was going to lose, and during which no doctor or therapist, it seemed to me, had the courage, or good sense, to say to my parents: If you truly love this child, stay out of his life until (if ever) he is strong enough and well enough to deal with you, and with life, again.

I do remember feeling *battered*—feeling an enormous fatigue, a deep desire to be away from it all, from everything and everyone I knew—along with an insatiable hunger for some peace and quiet: for a few days—a few moments!—that might be free of rage and guilt, of exhaustion, frustration, madness, doubt, and family.

I recall, one Saturday or Sunday afternoon in late spring, watching—and envying—Robert and his friends, from a distance, as they danced together across one of Hillside's immense lawns. How wonderful it must be to be free of all responsibility! I recall thinking. How wonderful it must be to be so defined by the world that others see to all your needs. How wonderful it must be to be taken out of the workaday world for a while and set down in a peaceful, idyllic setting where most decisions are made for you by others.

And how wonderful it must be, above all, I felt, to be taken care of by others.

Back in Bloomington, I was happier than I'd been in a long time. I went to classes, played ball, wrote papers, spent time with old friends, made new friends, and even wrote several new short stories. Robert and I sent letters back and forth regularly.

"Dear jay the student," Robert wrote (a drawing of a kite on the front of the envelope, with the notation: "via floatation—go fly a kite buddy"), "i like to receive your letters but would rather have you here of course. I want you to get your masters and if you want your phd, whatever the heck that is. I guess that is what my doctor has because i just found out today that he is a psychologist and not a psychiatrist." The doctor, he noted, at the end of this first letter, was "trying to get [him] to tell things again—i hope he is successful."

Until I saw how happy I was to be among people my own age again, I did not fully realize how lonely and isolated I had felt during the previous year. And until I began receiving long letters from my mother—handwritten, usually, edge to edge across several pages of green hospital "Order Sheets"—I did not realize just how relieved I was to be far from home.

Her first letter that summer was filled mostly—six dense pages—with news of Robert, and was typical of the letters that would arrive several times a week for the next year. After some perfunctory remarks about my new life and the weather, she embarked on a lengthy narrative about her nephew and niece,

Herb and Sue, who wanted to visit Robert. My mother had called Sue and tried "tactfully and pleasantly" to tell her about the kind of "understanding" Robert needed from visitors, yet Sue, it seemed, had not only rejected my mother's advice, but had rejected her "plea to withhold from Robt the fact that I did call." My mother then went on a long tirade (the word "reject" often emphasized with six or seven underlines) about those who, like Herb and Sue, "*Reject* their parents, their gifts, *reject,* reject, etc. will even reject a plea from a mother, humbly asking a simple favor to safeguard (aid in health) their child (a sick pt.)."

"Let's face it," my mother wrote, Sue "hated my guts as a meddling parent—& that Herbert feels his mother ruined his life or didn't help him properly (do the rt things)—I really feel only the *deepest sympathy for them,* their *hates,* their rejections. . . ." A few sentences later, and after asking me to please give her "English lessons" so she might learn to "better express" herself, she was comparing Herb and Sue to the followers of Hitler and Mussolini:

You know what I really think of them & the generation they represent? Well, after World War I, Hitler and Mussolini seemed to be heroic in uplifting a down-trodden people via socialism and at the beginning I felt these innocent people didn't forever have to suffer defeat because of wars—and socialism, radicalism and isms seemed oke to me—But they didn't know when to stop. . . . And so on and on went Hitler—you know the rest—

And so with the Sue's and Herbs . . . they will do more destruction, and unhappiness—in their teachings—they are going too far—& don't know where & when to stop & not have a revolution, because they will cause *more turmoil* & strife in young rich minds—too radical—I counted on them to bring a better health—but you will see—they are going to cause more mental illness.

"Enuf of that," she continued. "Dad really objects to my writing like this—do you? Is my opinion (or analogy) wrong in your judgment? I'm really expecting an answer from you."

Her letter went on for three more pages, after which my father added a brief note in which he did not mention Herb and Sue, their visit with Robert, or my mother's letter.

After I discovered Robert's 1962 diary, I began going through cartons stored in the attic of my Northampton home, many of which I had been transporting from place to place, unopened, for more than thirty years. I found thousands of letters—from friends, editors, writers, relatives, and others, and, mixed in with them, hundreds of letters from Robert, and from my parents. And while, for several months, I read through these letters, I was sent back in time to the years in which Robert and I grew up—to a time when airmail and special delivery letters were reserved for emergencies, and long-distance calls and airplane trips for the wealthy; a time when letters and manuscripts were written longhand, or on manual typewriters, and copied with carbon paper. I was sent back to a time when one could begin to reconstruct one's own and one's family's history from a family's storehouse of documents, photos, diaries, and letters—to a time when news traveled more slowly and variously, and, always, on paper—a time when letters, like diaries in their way, and novels in theirs, were the principal means by which we recorded what we thought, felt, remembered, and desired, and the means by which we communicated to one another all those ordinary and extraordinary moments that were the way we lived then.

During these years, too, primarily as a product of family interaction theories, mothers were often being focused upon as "primary pathogenic cause agents" of schizophrenia (Robert's diagnosis at the time), and were labeled, as my mother was, "schizophrenogenic mothers." But as Dr. E. Fuller Torrey, former special assistant to the director of the National Institute of

Mental Health, points out (in *Surviving Schizophrenia: A Family Manual*), such concepts, along with family interaction theories, and psychoanalytic theories, have long since been "discarded" by all mental health professionals except "for a hopelessly out-of-date few."

Torrey and others often claim that "there is as yet no evidence to support the view that parents bring about, in the formative years, the tendency for their children to become schizophrenic in later life" (thus, in all the literature put out by NAMI, et al., the repeated emphasis on mental illness being a "*no-fault* brain disease"); still, given a condition whose origins and course remain so refractory to understanding *and* treatment, and for which, in the medical literature, concepts such as a "predisposition," "susceptibility," and "tendency" continue, in their vague way, to abound, one wonders. Although it would be hard, scientifically, to *prove* that any human being literally drives any other human being mad, common sense indicates that if you keep hitting a child in the same sensitive place, over and over again—consistently or inconsistently—your blows will have effect. (Or, to put it another way, as Dr. Michael Robbins does in *Experiences of Schizophrenia,* "while pathological parenting alone may not be sufficient to produce schizophrenia—contrary to what is implied in Fromm-Reichmann's [1948] unwittingly inflammatory concept of the schizophrenogenic mother—dedicated parenting, in many instances, can probably abort it." I.e., if "bad" parenting cannot harm a child indelibly, one wants to ask those who believe all mental illnesses are exclusively no-fault organic diseases, does it follow that "good" parenting is without significant issue? "The evidence," Dr. Robbins writes, "particularly from studies of monozygotic twins, suggests that there is a constitutional vulnerability to schizophrenia, a differently organized brain, and that, unless this is compensated for by exceptional parenting very early in life, it will lead, by a series of recursive transformations, to the qualitatively differently organized psyche we call schizophrenia.")

"There are no porcupines here and I miss their quills," Robert wrote me after I had written him, in July, of my decision to stay on in Bloomington and complete my master's degree, "so I use my typewriter knowing fully well that working with machines slowly and surely makes one himself into a sense-less machine.

But i am lazy like so many other Americans who live in the age of anxiety, but i am not anxious because i have the pleasure every evening of wiping away my feelings with the taking of some drugs. So your favorite brother is not only an emotionally disturbed mental patient but also a drug addict. I have been born a jew but of late have become a catholic going to confession twice a week.

In September, while I was enrolling for classes in Indiana, Robert was enrolling for classes at Queens College. Four weeks later, in early October, my father wrote that Robert had broken down again.

Son:
    We wrote you that last weekend Robert was home and off drugs completely. . . . Well it seems that the combination of taking away the drugs completely—the thought of being re-leased from Hillside was a little too premature—Do not get alarmed Robert has had a slight setback—
    We saw Robert yesterday and had a roundtable discussion with Dr. Glick and Robert—Dr. Glick assures us Robert will be all right—Robert said it was all too much and all in all—it will just take a little longer and perhaps on a much more solid ground.
    Jay—do *not* pick up the phone & call us—We will rite you and keep you informed—We have another roundtable confer-ence set for a week from Monday. In the meantime he is in good or I shall say the best hands, and Robert knows it. He

is not bedridden—dressed—going to activities, meals etc—No school (I think that was too much also). So be patient and we will keep in touch with you.

Robert was put on private nursing care around the clock, his medications were increased, and although he was as sick some days as he had been at Elmhurst, my father and mother remained optimistic.

"Now 'tachlis' or what makes us feel Robert is getting better," my father wrote a few weeks later.

> Well this week he went ice-skating & to a NY Show with the group and enjoyed himself and acted very normal—Yes he gets upset now and then—but the Dr. says he comes out of that very quickly and definitely is on the upgrade. I put the question right to him. Will Robert get better? Will you have to resort to shock or other things? Dr. Glick's answer—"Of course one can never be 100% sure—but I feel that we will bring Robert around without resorting to other means & we feel that Robert is going to be alright."

My mother provided minute-by-minute accounts of therapy sessions ("robt brought out that I used to get migraines and sometimes he felt the cause of it—but more than that he used to wish that he could take the pain and suffering for me and there were actual tears flowing from him when he was remembering how he couldn't take the pain away from me to himself"), along with family and local news (Evelyn and Paul bought a new dishwasher, the rabbi was recovering from a hernia operation, and so on).

I wrote Robert frequently (my mother advising me as to what the doctors said I should and should not say to him), attended classes, and found myself becoming more and more depressed. I began running in front of cars and trucks to see if I could get to the other side of streets before being hit. And at Thanksgiving, after an unhappy end to a romance with a woman I had fallen in love with in New Jersey the previous years, I decided to stay in Indiana by myself during the holiday. (In 1961, shortly before Robert's first breakdown, I had made an emergency trip back to Indiana to try to save my relationship with Virginia; now, alone in Bloomington again, I recalled how I had sat in Virginia's car with her a year or so before—knowing I had discovered too late just how much I loved her, and fearing I would never again find a good and true woman who would love me in return—heaving, sobbing, and repeating, over and over again: *"What's wrong with me? What's wrong with me? What's wrong with me?"*)

On Thanksgiving weekend, after skidding in front of an oncoming car on a dark, wet street one night, and cracking my shin open against curbstone, I became frightened that I might actually succeed in doing myself permanent harm; the games I'd been playing, I decided, were more dangerous than was absolutely necessary, and I stopped them. And at Christmas, when things were going better—Robert was making gains (his medications were reduced, he was awarded more passes out of the hospital), and my writing was going well (and I was falling in love again, and with a woman I would, a year and a half later, marry)—I felt ready to return to New York.

Before I did, though, I called ahead and asked for a conference at Hillside with Robert and his doctors. And when we were all assembled there (Robert, our parents, two doctors, a nurse, and a social worker), I told the group that I was thinking of starting a new novel, one that would be set in a mental hospital not unlike Hillside, and that I had a few questions. Most important, I wanted to know whether writing the novel could *harm* Robert in any way. If the book was published someday, what effect would it have on him? How did *he* feel about my writing the book, and would it, perhaps, be better to put it aside until he was out of the hospital, or better not to write it at all?

My father responded by asking why *anyone* should ever have to know about Robert and his hospitalizations. Why couldn't

I write about something else? My mother said what she often said: All she wanted was to spare me and Robert suffering— so why should I put myself through more rejections? Why couldn't I face reality, stay in graduate school, get my Ph.D., and *then* write novels if I still wanted to? For their part, the doctors and social worker (from whom I actually seemed to expect yes-or-no answers) did what they usually did: they nodded a lot, and returned my questions to me: How did *I* feel about writing the book? Why was I asking them if I should write it? What effect did *I* think it would have on Robert?

Robert smiled through all the talk, made jokes about his-brother-the-novelist (and himself-the-poet)—and added that he thought everyone in the world could benefit from knowing about Hillside.

I returned to Indiana after a week at home, and, without dropping out of classes this time, began work on the novel. (When I told my father I was thinking of submitting an earlier novel—about a wildcat strike at an automobile plant in the Midwest—for my thesis, he wrote back: "Is it possible a wrong choice to submit as a thesis to Indiana University—if I recall the book, it is quite critical of Indiana.")

My mother's first letter to me, after my return to Bloomington, announced the "good news" (arrows drawn around her words, the key words underlined four and five times each) that Robert was "recovering to *total* recovery & *probably permanently*." She also wrote that she had asked about electric shock and was told that "those are referrals to State pts like Creedmore—Robt is NOT one of those and according to hillside attitude it is used too promiscuously, and only IF & WHEN they couldn't help a pt—then they would consider it before sending the pt to a state institution."

A month or so later, in early February, after I had received a letter in which she wrote that Robert was "just miraculously better," she telephoned to tell me that my father had had a massive heart attack, and that the doctors advised me to fly home immediately.

I flew home that night, and when I visited my father in a Queens hospital—Booth Memorial, where my mother often worked as a nurse—he was in an oxygen tent. He smiled at me and reached for my hand. I put my hand into the tent. "Be good to your mother," he said.

Against all prognoses, however, he began to recover, and a week or so later, when he was out of danger, I flew back to Indiana.

"It was really wonderful to see you yesterday looking in such great shape," Robert wrote our father, after he visited him in the hospital (the letter written in February 1963, exactly one year after Robert's own hospitalization at Elmhurst). "I'm sure you do not like to stay in the hospital as much and probably more than I. But we both have been overtaken by a sickness that we both know so little about.

I trust however that the doctors and staff at each one of our hospitals knows exactly how to treat us. Perhaps I sound clinical. But I know now as never before in my entire life that medical science is really as great as mother always told us. With each day here at the hospital I am getting stronger and healthier. I am enjoying things and understanding more about myself and the world that surrounds me with each hour. I am much less frightened now than I have ever been in a long time. The family conferences along with the rest of my therapy has helped me immensely. Yours and Mothers' patience and good ready-to-learn attitude has told me time and time again how glad I am to be your son.

. . . I know how much Jay would, like me, want to be near home and able to see the family. But that shall come in time. One thing I am learning through therapy is that things take time. And for the first time in a long time I am not [in a] rush about anything. Except of course getting well. I think all of us patients would like to get out of the old hospitals and back in the world that we enjoy so much.

My mother wrote me about the intensity with which Robert was identifying with our father—fearing blindness and impotence while trying to help him recover:

At the conference, the drs discussed this and it was brought out that he could have impaired vision like his father, also some pt was transferred to a state hospital, and that too he didn't want to see. Also, he was resting several mornings to help conserve his father's strength. Get it—he was resting for dad— now you know why I said they are moving him real slowly— but the drs explained how robt got over this by being able to talk it out—whereas the pt who went to creedmore could not. In other words, while robt seems much improved, he is able to recognize that he gets psychotic symptoms and can overcome them after talking and explanations from the drs—it seems this is good health in the mental hospital—can't you bust?

Robert wrote several times a week from his hospital to my father's, and in his letters, as in those from my mother and father, the news that he was, in his own words, "learning how to have appropriate behavior" and "learning to accept *discipline*" is repeated so many times that it often seems the hospital is a mere extension of the extended Jewish family, and that love of one's family and socialization to middle-class norms are the equivalent of sanity.

"I often think of you dear dad," he writes, a week after our father is discharged to his Queens apartment. "Of your sense of humor, of your warmness and feeling for people, of your quickness of wit and the incisive way that you have with ideas. I think of your gentleness and the love that you have for the entire family.

Even with all the fighting that I put up I want you to know that both mother and you are among the best parents that a child could ever ask for. Numerous times when I have needed you you have always been ready to help even at times that it was very difficult for you practically. When I look around me and see children who grew up without knowing what the term LOVE meant I consider myself more than lucky to have two parents who care a great deal as to my stability and good health.

Robert's compliments—to our father, to our family, to Hillside, and to the healing powers of psychotherapy and discipline—now multiply and abound. "I'm sure Jay has told you how much he was impressed with Dr. Schiff," Robert writes. "I feel very lucky that I have such a great doctor. He will make me or rather with his help I will really get very well.

I was glad to see you in good shape Sunday and gladder still to hear the progress that you are making generally. I'm sure you know how much I think of you and want to be with you and see you get better so that we can carry on on the firm foundation that we are cementing with the help of the whole family and my doctors. I really feel good and am enjoying myself and the activities here. I have full confidence in my self and my doctors and know that I am with each day getting better and better.

Robert's language is suddenly, as here, without its usual flair. What he writes reads as if it might have been written by *any* patient at Hillside. For all the generosity, love, and goodwill in the letters, their tone is now flat and lifeless, while the sentiments seem as perfunctory as they are sincere. Robert, that is, no longer sounds like Robert:

I am really quite lucky that I have such doctors and that they are so patient and ready and able to help me lead the best of all possible lives. I only should have come earlier when it was first indicated that I could use the hospital but enough for spilt milk.

We are planning to have two Seders here. This week makes it a year that I have been at Hillside. I am glad that I came here and found out all I did about myself and my feelings. I am not so glad that I had to come here, I'm sure I could have had more fun going to college but it is not something that I am going to cry over. I think I have gotten an awful lot out of my stay here.

Nor is Robert unaware of the changes going on within him. "I do not know if some of the sparkle has been taken out of my life by psycho-therapy," he writes, a week before Passover, "but I do know that I am much more realistic and much happier."

That spring and summer, our father recovered, quit smoking (he had been going through three packs of Chesterfields a day until his heart attack), and returned to work; our mother finalized her plans to leave private-duty nursing and take a position with the city as a caseworker; I made some progress on the novel, wrote a half-dozen new short stories, and completed my master's degree; and Robert recovered from his breakdown, was accepted for a vocational rehabilitation program (at Altro), and then, at the start of the new school year in September, eighteen months after his transfer from Elmhurst, was discharged from Hillside.

Shortly after our father's heart attack, I had decided to accept a graduate fellowship to Columbia University, and to return to New York. Since one did not, in Columbia's graduate school, have to attend classes, I intended to use the fellowship, not toward a doctorate, but toward financing the time I needed to work on a new novel. And so, at about the same time I was returning to New York and moving into a single-room fifth-floor walk-up apartment on Manhattan's Upper West Side,

Robert was leaving Hillside Hospital and moving into a single room in downtown Manhattan, at Fellowship House, a halfway house on East 20th Street sponsored by the Federation of Jewish Philanthropies.

While Robert was at Fellowship House, he held down various part-time jobs, worked as a messenger for our Uncle Arnold, and saw a psychologist once a week (and a Marxist therapist, Dr. Harry K. Wells, occasionally). In addition, he and our parents met regularly for a few months with Abe Schwartz, a social worker from the Federation of Jewish Philanthropies. I attended several of the sessions, and they seemed generally friendlier and less tense (less mad!) than those we had been through at Hillside. And now that we were both living in the city again, and away from home, Robert and I—sometimes with his friends, sometimes with mine, but usually by ourselves—spent lots of time together, going to movies and museums, taking long walks, trading stories, jokes, and memories, sitting in coffee shops or restaurants or our apartments, and talking about the kinds of things we had always talked about.

In June of 1964—after a year in which I completed the novel set in a mental hospital, and Robert successfully completed a year out of the mental hospital, at Fellowship House—I was married, to Betsey Jean Bendorf, the woman I had met a week or so after my last semi-suicide dash (and crash) in front of oncoming cars. Robert was best man at the wedding, and a group of his friends from Hillside and Fellowship House, along with Abe Schwartz, came to the wedding. A few weeks later, while I was moving nine blocks south—from West 85th Street to West 76th Street—Robert was, with the approval of Abe and his doctors, moving out of Fellowship House, setting himself up in his own apartment, and registering for classes at Queens College.

Once again, all seemed well . . . and then, once again, about a year to the day following his release from Hillside, Robert broke. (I was, surely, absorbed by my new life as a married man: by my new apartment, by a new job as an instructor at Columbia, by a newly completed novel, etc.; still, I saw Robert often, spoke with him almost every day, and can recall no warning signs, no significant precipitating events.) The staff at Fellowship House tried to get Robert into Hillside Hospital, but Hillside refused to take him back, and so Robert was taken, by ambulance, to Creedmoor.

I was surprised that he had broken, and, especially after my first visit to him at Creedmoor, more upset and discouraged than ever. How not? This was Robert's third breakdown within less than two years, and it was his worst. And whether it was brought on by (his feelings about) my marriage, or our father's heart attack, or his discharge from Fellowship House, or the prospect (and pressures) of being a college student again—or by chemicals in him, or chemicals put into him—by medications taken or not taken—or by combinations of these, and/or by things in him and in our family and in the city and in the times and in things known and unknown and unknowable— by timing and luck and who knows what else—what I sensed then, and what surely seems clear now, thirty years later, is that once he had broken for a third time, and was hospitalized and heavily medicated yet again, and locked away in a state institution famed for its cruel and nightmarish conditions, the very fact of this breakdown and institutionalization had as much to do with his condition at that time, and of the condition and life that would be his in the years to come, as whatever it was that may, until this moment in his twenty-second year on earth, have brought on the condition that led to this breakdown, and to the two preceding it.

From this point in time, and through the next fifteen years, Robert would have so many breakdowns, releases, and readmissions—would wander through so many hospitals, wards, welfare hotels, and halfway houses—and would have so many different drugs, and in enormous doses and combinations, poured into him—that their order is a blur, and neither of us can ever determine with certainty the precise sequence of events, or recall which events, episodes, doctors, and medications coincided with which hospitalizations.

Once he was incarcerated, a half year past his twenty-first birthday, in Creedmoor, how ever again make sense of his life and history in anything like a simple, linear cause-and-effect manner? Once he was incarcerated in Creedmoor, how ever again be hopeful in the ways we had previously been hopeful?

In those years, Creedmoor, whose first sizable buildings were opened to patients in 1926, was called Creedmoor State Hospital (it changed its name, in 1974, to Creedmoor Psychiatric Center; it drew its name, as far as I can discover, from the Creedmoor rifle, and from a private rifle club which held its shooting camps, at the time of the Civil War, on what would become the hospital's grounds). Set on over three hundred acres at the easternmost edge of New York City, a mile or so short of the Nassau County border, it comprised seventy buildings, the tallest of which, Building 40, a wide seventeen-story yellow-stucco building with heavily barred windows, rose like a giant tombstone from the green parks and low suburban sprawl of Queens.

In 1956, just before the introduction at Creedmoor of the new range of antipsychotic and antidepressant drugs (the majority of which Robert would eventually be given: Thorazine, Mellaril, Trilafon, Stelazine, Navane, and Haldol), Creedmoor had more than six thousand patients lodged in facilities certified to hold slightly more than four thousand. Straitjackets, continuous-flow tubs, sedative packs (patients tied to tables in moist sheets), various kinds of shock treatment (electric and insulin-coma), and lobotomies were the prevailing forms of treatment.

(In *Is There No Place on Earth for Me?*, a book set for the most part at Creedmoor Hospital in the sixties and seventies, Susan Sheehan notes that the introduction of lobotomy in 1952 constituted "further evidence," the hospital's annual report stated, "of the desire to keep up with the modern trend in the care of patients.")

In 1962, nearly 65 percent of New York State's more than eighty thousand institutionalized mental patients had been hospitalized for five years or more, and almost 30 percent for twenty years or more. Robert entered Creedmoor in the fall of 1964. He would, during three separate hospitalizations, spend four and a half of his next nine years there.

8

ON SUNDAY AFTERNOONS at Creedmoor I attended mass
meetings on Robert's unit, at which meetings patients and their
parents (and/or spouses) would, one after another, rise from their
chairs, go to a lectern, and take turns telling us their life stories,
or giving speeches, or babbling, or giggling, or simply standing
and staring. Those who were able to speak coherently usually told
of how they (or their family member) had become sick, of how
long they had been sick, of when and how and where they had
been diagnosed and treated (or misdiagnosed and mistreated), and
of how, until they discovered Dr. Laqueur and his insulin unit at
Creedmoor, they had despaired. Their stories all had the same
moral: They had been lost . . . now they were saved.

The meetings were held in an enormous room that seems, in memory, the size of two high school gymnasiums. It was bright and airy—by all accounts, Laqueur's ward was the most (if not the only) pleasant ward at Creedmoor—with high, barred windows on three sides and, about midway down the longer side, in front of windows from which one could look out at people picnicking and playing baseball across the road in Alley Pond Park, dozens of folding chairs set out in rows that faced the lectern. The parents who ran the family organization that raised funds for the unit (my mother sold knickknacks from the trunk of her car) sat at a long table behind the lectern with Dr. Laqueur, and with those patients and staff members he had chosen for giving that afternoon's presentations.

Dr. Laqueur was a Belgian-born psychiatrist who had taken charge of Creedmoor's insulin unit in 1951, the year he completed his residency there. He was a genial, rosy-cheeked, cherubic-looking man—forever smiling, forever voicing encouragement and making jokes. He seemed to me, generally, to make sense, and—what also appealed—rarely to equivocate. In the section of her book that deals with Sylvia Frumkin's time on his unit, Sheehan quotes him saying to a suicidal young man who had threatened to jump out a window, "It's up to you, but if you decide you don't want to live, for God's sake don't jump out the window. You might fail and end up a cripple, and then you'd be worse. Just take pills and do a good job." The following year, Sheehan reports, the patient took an overdose of barbiturates and died.

Our mother had worked hard to get Robert accepted into Laqueur's unit. "It's better than Hillside," she said. "The *richest* patients, who couldn't get well at the fanciest private hospitals, get well here. Why? Because this doctor who runs it is a genius, that's why!"

When Dr. Laqueur entered the unit on Sunday afternoons, it was as if a holy man had appeared. All eyes would turn to the far end of the room, from which he would stride forward, five or ten patients and family members clinging to him—

pawing him, shouting at him, grabbing at his clothes, pleading with him—while he moved forward serenely, smiling to one and all, waving, sometimes turning to speak to someone. The attendants would come to his aid, to lift patients from his arms and shoulders, to push away others who were crowding him, to clear his path to the lectern.

Dr. Laqueur believed that the secret to curing schizophrenia (and other mental illnesses) lay in a combination of insulin-coma therapy (also called insulin shock) and multifamily group therapy. In an entry on insulin-coma therapy in the 1975 edition of *The Comprehensive Textbook of Psychiatry*, Dr. Lothar B. Kalinowsky discusses Laqueur and his work at Creedmoor, and describes Laqueur's technique, one that consisted of injecting increasing amounts of insulin into a patient, at fifteen-minute intervals, until the patient fell into a hypoglycemic coma. Dr. Kalinowsky notes that after the introduction of pharmacotherapy in the 1950s, insulin was abolished in most hospitals. Its elimination, he states, "is very much regretted by everyone who has had experience with this treatment." (When Creedmoor shut down its insulin unit in 1969, it was the last state psychiatric hospital in the United States to do so.)

Kalinowsky's lengthy (and chilling) description of what happens to a patient who receives insulin-coma therapy coincides with descriptions Laqueur gave at Sunday-afternoon sessions:

Approximately 1 hour after the injection of insulin . . . the patient shows the first signs of hypoglycemia—feelings of tiredness and somnolence and perspiration. During the second hour, the patient's sensorium becomes clouded, and he falls asleep. Some may become restless, toss around, and yell. Others are disoriented or show hallucinations, which are often different from those due to their illness. Patients who never hallucinated before may develop hallucinations during the state of hypoglycemia. The speech becomes dysarthric. Aphasia and apraxia may be noticed. The motor phenomena during the second hour consist of automatic movements, forced grasping, myoclonic twitchings, and various dystonic manifestations. Different schemes have been developed to show the disintegration of brain functioning according to various levels. . . .

A not infrequent occurrence is convulsions, mostly observed during the second hour of hypoglycemia. . . . During the third hour, the patient can go into a true coma. The coma stage is reached when the patient is unable to respond to stimuli of various kinds. The deepest coma is reached when the patient no longer responds to painful stimuli with a needle or to supra-orbital pressure. At this stage, spasms similar to those of decere-brate rigidity may occur, the pupils do not react to light, and the deepest or so-called midbrain stage is characterized by a change of the pupils from dilation to miosis, absence of the corneal reflex, and disappearance of tendon reflexes. It is this stage that is considered most effective but also a definite danger sign, one to be avoided by less experienced workers. At first the patient is usually left in coma not longer than 15 minutes; in subsequent treatments the coma can be slowly prolonged up to 1 hour.

The 1961 edition of *The Merck Manual* (my mother's copy, in which she marked up sections dealing with mental illness) is more wary. "Provided the total period of hypoglycemia does not exceed 6 hours, an uncomplicated shock may be continued for 2 to 3 hours," it states, but warns: "Insulin shock therapy is attended by many dangers, among which are after-shock (a relapse into unconsciousness, perhaps many hours later), pro-longed coma, severe convulsions, and extreme vasomotor or circulatory collapse. It is contraindicated in pregnancy (it is lethal to the fetus)."

Patients were roused from their comas by the administration of either a sugar solution through nasal-tube feeding, intrave-nous (or intramuscular) glucose or glucagon, or adrenaline and thiamine. Laqueur, along with his carefully selected staff of nurses and attendants (Sheehan notes that "all his nurses were pretty"), monitored patients through a series of bedside lights:

green (safe coma), yellow (medium-deep coma), and red (dangerously deep coma, requiring immediate termination of the coma).

Laqueur's aim, he stated at every meeting, was simple: to restore the patient to the family and community, and to do so by whatever worked. Sometimes insulin coma worked; sometimes electroshock worked; sometimes drugs worked; and sometimes combinations of the three worked. Laqueur prescribed electroshock and drugs liberally, but the fact that he repeatedly said he did not believe that any of these treatments could truly "cure" mental illness made his advocacy of their use seem measured and credible.

The hallucinations, delusions, and mad behavior we saw on the outside, he explained, were mild compared to what festered within and produced the overt symptoms. It might take a lifetime to deal with underlying causes and pathology, and the chances of success were slim. Since, too, nobody really knew what caused mental illness, he argued, or to what degree and in what proportions its origins were in nature or in nurture, it behooved us to be practical. In dealing with chronic mental illness, therefore, his objective was modest and workable: to enable the patient to return to the world, and since in most cases this meant, first, returning the patient to his or her family, that was where the important work had to be done.

Despite what seemed to me his sanely skeptical attitudes toward mental illness, and his admirable admissions of ignorance, Laqueur was passionate and unequivocal in his advocacy of insulin-coma therapy. Each Sunday he produced patients and parents who provided testimonials, celebrated his successes, and explained his technique, its rationale, and its effects: how the comas would be induced, and how the length of the coma would gradually be increased until, deep in sleep (near death, in fact), the patient would experience "total peace"—freedom from all anxiety, fear, and psychosis.

Being repeatedly plunged into an unconscious state where forgetfulness reigned—a state like that of the fetus—would somehow, he claimed, act to free the patient temporarily from the fear of the unconscious itself—that is, from those fears, phobias, delusions, and traumas that had until then kept the patient from functioning in the world. Awakening from a coma, the patient would be unusually peaceful and symptom-free, and it was during this period of time—this calm in the psychotic storm—that the patient was most capable of being healed: of tolerating psychotherapy, and of restructuring his or her inner and outer life.

Although in his early years at Creedmoor Laqueur had advocated a course of treatment that consisted of up to ninety comas, at the time Robert was on his unit, he was talking about maximum gains being made when the patient had been immersed, generally, in between forty and sixty comas. Still, patients and their needs varied; sometimes a hundred comas might be necessary to achieve success.

Insulin-coma therapy alone, however, could only provide temporary relief, not full remission. While the patient was receiving shock treatment and/or drugs, the patient would also be part of multifamily group therapy, where, once a week for an hour-and-a-quarter, three, four, or five families would meet with a single therapist. Laqueur made elaborate claims for this system of group family therapy while mocking traditional one-on-one (Freudian) therapy as having proved useless: Had it helped those who were here, who had received countless hours of individual therapy at the most celebrated and, he would emphasize, the most *expensive* private sanitariums?

In theory, much of what Laqueur said about multifamily group therapy sounded reasonable. The actuality, however, was different. Nothing Robert said or did during his years at Creedmoor ever seemed to me as purely deranged as these multifamily group therapy sessions. To put three, four, or five psychotics and their families in a bare prisonlike room, with only an inexperienced intern as guide, was itself the maddest of enterprises. Kafka, I used to say to Robert during sessions, when something particularly bizarre had occurred, didn't know the half of it.

During the sessions, anywhere from a dozen to two dozen of us would sit in a circle, the therapist asking us—shouting to be heard usually—what we wanted to talk about, or how we felt, or what we thought of what somebody had just said or done. Meanwhile, patients would wander around the room, or hallucinate, or shout incomprehensibly, or assault a member of their family or of someone else's family. Often, when the situation became dangerous, the therapist would ask an aide—the presence of one aide, like a prison guard, was required at each session—to restrain a patient, or to return a patient to the ward.

My own guess at the time was that the reason Laqueur promoted multifamily group therapy had little to do with the rationales he set forth, but—budgetary and custodial priorities, as ever, leading to budgetary and custodial solutions—with something simpler: neither he nor the state had the funds or staff for anything else—for individual therapy, or for therapy that could take place in smaller, more manageable groups.

I objected to insulin shock as strongly as I had to electroshock, and when Robert said he did not want to be put into an insulin coma, I fought with my parents on his behalf. At home, after Sunday meetings, my mother would carry on about how it was hard enough to have a son who was mentally ill and to have to fight against that, but to have to fight against me too—because I didn't see that insulin coma was the only thing that would save Robert—this was more than she could bear.

I countered by saying that it was simply barbaric to burn out people's brain cells or to send them into comas, and to pray that when and if they survived, they would somehow have been shocked back into health, or sanity, or—precious, mysterious condition—*normality.*

If you held people from windows by the ankles, I remember

saying, and dropped them several stories into ice-cold freezing water, and then hauled them out, and then did this to them again, and again, and again, they might get well too. Holocaust victims went white-haired overnight; accident and amnesia victims sometimes recovered early memories or lost incapacitating fears; priests, shamans, and con artists had often cured people of incurable diseases by having them touch cow dung and cow bones that were proffered as holy relics; patients often responded better to placebos than to medications. If faith could move mountains, and belief could save, who knew what faith and belief in the magical and healing properties of *anything* or *anyone* might do for *anybody,* especially in a realm where the very interaction of mind and body was central?

But Robert was not anybody, and he did not seem so far gone to me that we had to resort to such ill-founded, dangerous, and utterly terrifying methods. The comas induced a frightening sense of helplessness in its victims, yet this very feeling—of being unbearably frightened and helpless—had often been central to inducing the emotional disturbance and breakdown in the first place; how then, I argued, cure the disease with its cause? If, as even Laqueur admitted, nobody knew what caused schizophrenia, or what exactly the shock and drugs did to it, and if . . . The arguments and fights, like the meetings and the therapy sessions, went on and on.

(Everything I have read about insulin-coma therapy in the years since indicates not only that there was no basis for cure in the treatment—like drugs, it had a sedative effect; like electricity, it had a shocking effect—but that many who suffered the comas also suffered lasting neurological and psychological damage. It was, according to the *Comprehensive Textbook of Psychiatry* [1990], "the treatment of choice in all cases of schizophrenia" in the 1940s; in practice, however, electroshock was usually used because it was cheaper and simpler. In 1992, while visiting Robert at South Beach, I happened to meet his new psychiatrist; we spoke briefly, and when I tried to give him a sense of Robert's history—he seemed to know nothing—and the history of his treatment, and said something about electro-shock and insulin shock indiscriminately burning out brain cells, he shrugged, dismissing my concern. "There are lots of brain cells," he said.)

Still, though I argued against insulin shock—Robert submit-ted to several treatments, and then refused to endure any more—and though I found the multifamily group therapy ses-sions absurd, I did not always argue strongly against Laqueur himself, since I was, often, as entranced by him as my parents were, especially when he spoke at meetings of how the family, and not the patient, was "the locus of the illness." I, too, hoped for sudden cures. I, too, had my fantasies about what would happen if and when Robert recovered—how we would visit each other's home, take pleasure from one another's children; how he would become a distinguished and beloved poet, and the critics and essayists would come around, to try to account for the lives and work of the Brothers Neugeboren. . . .

When Laqueur spoke of the ways in which families (and not patients) *created* illness in one of their members, he made sense to me. When he spoke of the ways families tried to deny their true problems, so as to ignore the reality of their victimized member, he made sense. When he spoke of the ways families tried to force their victimized member to conform to behavior the family demanded, he made sense. When he spoke of all the overt and covert ways messages, accusations, and punish-ments were inflicted upon the person the world designated as mentally ill, and when he spoke of the ways in which families themselves somehow *needed,* if unconsciously, to keep the vic-timized member from getting well, he made sense.

Like my parents, I wanted to believe that Robert could be cured, and could resume the life he was living before his break-downs; but unlike my parents—thus the appeal of much of what Laqueur said, especially his more psychoanalytically fla-vored explanations and hypotheses—I wanted to believe that there was nothing *innately* wrong or sick in him: that Robert's pathology was an acquired one, and acquired in and because of our family, and that it could, thus, with enough understanding and working through, be exorcised.

Then too, by this point in time, what were our alternatives? Robert had now passed his twenty-first birthday, had been out of high school for four years, had proved unable to sustain work, or school, or to be able to care for himself, and had just suffered a third major breakdown. He had already received megadoses of a wide range of new, highly touted antipsychotic drugs (Thorazine, Stelazine, Mellaril); he had received hundreds of hours of family therapy, group therapy, individual therapy (and psychoanalytically oriented individual therapy). Nor could we afford any kind of sustained private psychiatric treatment in those clinics (Chestnut Lodge, McClean, Austin Riggs) noted for working with schizophrenics and, especially, with young schizophrenics.

(While Robert was at Creedmoor, I wrote long letters to several of these institutions, telling them about Robert—giving his history, sketching his character, and trying, in my appeals, to make him sound as fascinating and unique as he was. They all wrote back thanking me for my "moving letter," and saying pretty much the same thing: they were sympathetic to Robert and to our situation and felt they could help, but they could not begin to undertake treatment unless the family could guarantee minimum lengths of stay of at least two years, at minimum annual fees that amounted to five or six times the amount of my father's yearly salary, and more than triple my parents' combined yearly income. "Chestnut Lodge"—the setting for Joanne Greenberg's *I Never Promised You a Rose Garden*—"is a small, private psychiatric hospital entirely dependent for survival upon patients' fees," its clinical director wrote. "There are no 'angels,' direct or indirect, no government agencies to pick up deficits. Each patient simply has to pay his way. There are no 'scholarships' or 'research patients' or whatever of that order.")

If Robert was not allowed to stay on Laqueur's unit, where would he go? Hillside, which had a staff-to-patient ratio ten times that of Creedmoor, refused to take him back (my mother made valiant attempts), and the other units at Creedmoor to which Robert might be sent were, simply, godawful: they confirmed and surpassed every stereotype then current about state mental hospitals. (Sheehan's book gives a detailed and horrifying description of just how awful front *and* back wards at Creedmoor were during the sixties and seventies, where errors, incompetence, and physical abuse were rampant, and the breaking of rules intended to protect patients routine.)

One evening, at the start of a multifamily group therapy session, the young therapist, Kate Greenbaum, came in a few minutes late, looking pale. She said she had been walking across the grounds of the hospital when she was stopped by a woman who identified herself as a patient, and who, seeing Kate's ID tag, asked if Kate would help her. The woman wanted to get out of the hospital. Could Kate look her up in the hospital's records and arrange for an exit interview? The woman said she had not been seen by a doctor for seventeen years. Kate was wary and noncommittal, but she wrote down the patient's name.

A week later, on our way to Manhattan (Kate lived there and, to save me the train and bus ride back to the city, often drove me home after weekly sessions; I felt nervous and unsure of myself during these drives—judged, and found wanting, for my opinions and reactions, my nervousness given edge by what seemed to me our attraction to each other), Kate told me she had looked up the woman's history, and discovered that the woman was telling the truth: she had not been seen by a doctor for seventeen years.

The great and not unreasonable fear, then, was that Robert might prove so uncooperative that Laqueur would ship him to one of Creedmoor's back wards and that once there, Robert would become even angrier and more uncooperative, would be given more drugs and less care (more shock, more abuse), and would never again emerge.

•　　•　　•

There were usually about eighty to a hundred people in the assembly hall on Sundays (the wards were segregated by sex, but female patients and their families came to Sunday meetings with male patients, and Laqueur encouraged socialization between the wards: dances, get-togethers, group therapy, outings). While people spoke from the lectern, and while Laqueur lectured—handling questions and heckling with the ease of a night club comedian—the hall itself was a true madhouse: patients would be running around, screaming and howling, or taking off or exchanging clothes, or standing in grotesque, frozen poses, or repeating single phrases endlessly; family members would be arguing with one another; aides would be chasing patients, restraining them, dragging them away.

At some point during each Sunday-afternoon meeting, the same extremely depressed man would step to the lectern and, like a football coach shouting to his players at halftime, start working himself up into greater and greater frenzies, praising Laqueur as if Laqueur were God, exhorting us all to work and to work, and then to work harder—harder! harder! harder!— for the benefit of Laqueur!—and for our children!—and for the unit's Family Organization, of which he was the president.

Sometimes Robert sat with us in the lecture area, and sometimes he wandered around the room with other patients. Often he would take me with him and introduce me (by my various names and titles: Yakov Mordechai, Michael, My-Brother-the-Writer, My-Brother-Who-*shhhhh!*-Had-Cancer, My-Brother-the-Big-Schmuck) to patients and staff, telling me about each of them, and which items of clothing and food he had traded with them. Often, the instant we gave Robert something—a watch or book or pack of cigarettes—he would turn and hand it to the first patient he saw, at which point our mother would begin scolding him. . . .

Robert would tell me about the different staff members— about which ones were kind, and about which ones beat him up. He would also, during virtually every visit, shout that when I died, he would get to marry my wife. Sometimes he said this jokingly, but if I made even the mildest response to his assertion, he would begin screaming: "It's true! It's true! When you die, I marry your wife! It's in the Bible, Jay—ask Dr. Baron! When you die, I get your wife!"

I spent several Sundays talking with a young intern, Stephen Mirsky, who told me how much he liked Robert, and how he was going to cure him. He sometimes invited me on walking tours of the meeting room, and while we walked he told me about the patients and why each was there. Sometimes patients would stop him, and sometimes he would go up to a patient, ask a leading question, listen to the answer, give some advice, make a joke, then motion to me to follow him to the next patient. He seemed able to talk with the patients in their languages, entering their fantasies briefly in bizarre dialogues, after which he would chuckle to himself.

The patient who fascinated him most was a thin, elderly man who sat, like an aged schoolboy, at a small desk, writing nonstop in notebooks. The man was dressed in a somewhat shabby suit, and Stephen kept asking the man questions. The man would look up, smile, and would reply in sentences that were, to me, incomprehensible, after which he would return to his writing. He wrote and he wrote, filling up notebook after notebook. "Amazing, amazing," Stephen said, each time. "That man has twenty-seven separate and different personalities. Twenty-seven. He's been written up! Twenty-seven distinct personalities. Amazing."

When, after asking Stephen specific questions about things Robert had done and said, I asked him the question that was with me most of all—what could I do to help Robert, and how?—he shrugged. "Just be yourself," he said, and walked away. I stood and watched him continue on his tour—he walked in a slight Groucho Marx crouch, his hands clasped behind him—and I felt more bewildered than ever. *Just be myself?* It seemed the most impossible task in the world. How, given Robert, given this ward—given life!—could I ever *just* be myself . . . ?

Sometimes, on Sunday afternoons, Robert was enraged and/or impossibly manic, but at other times he was totally calm, and the two of us would walk around together as if we were anywhere but in a hospital, talking about the things we usually talked about, or we would joke about Dr. Laqueur and the meetings, which we referred to as Bund Rallies, and which, we agreed, could not compare with the Robert Shalita Shows.

In order to remain on Laqueur's unit and not be shipped to another ward, Robert signed papers agreeing to undergo a series of insulin-shock comas, but when he refused to endure any more, and after he had been acting up on the unit—breaking a TV set, attacking and biting an aide—he telephoned me one day, in a panic. They were, he said, going to send him to Building S, the building where the most deteriorated of Creedmoor's patients were housed—a building that, according to Kate Greenbaum, had one doctor assigned to six hundred patients. Robert asked me to please, please call Dr. Laqueur, to arrange a meeting, to do *something*.

I called Laqueur, asked if he could give Robert a second chance. Would he delay the transfer and meet with me and Robert first, to talk things over? We set up a meeting for the next afternoon, at one o'clock. When I arrived shortly before one, however, and told the attendants I had an appointment with Dr. Laqueur, they checked their schedules, found nothing, told me to leave the ward.

I insisted they find Laqueur, and told them I would wait. I waited, and eventually caught Laqueur as he was hurrying by. I reminded him of our conversation. I got Robert, and he and I followed Laqueur down a corridor. Laqueur found a small, empty room—a desk and three chairs, nothing else—and invited us in.

I made my appeal, and Robert promised to be cooperative. He said he didn't like the comas, but he was taking his other medicines and didn't want to go to a different ward. Could Dr. Laqueur please give him another chance? Though Laqueur seemed quite focused while he listened to us, I had the distinct impression he did not know who Robert was. (Robert's regular psychiatrist was an elderly man named Lebovic, who spoke with a heavy Eastern European accent, but so softly that I could neither place the accent, nor, for that matter, ever understand anything he said. He seemed woefully forgetful and inept and, in my memory, looks very much like the man who wrote in notebooks.)

"What I notice most of all," Laqueur said to me, when he announced that our time was up, "is that your brother keeps interrupting you all the time." He turned to Robert. "Why won't you let your brother ever finish what he is saying?" he asked.

Robert said it was the medications—they made him nervous and sent him on talking jags, like our mother. Robert and I made some jokes about her, Laqueur laughed, said he would delay Robert's transfer for a week or two. As he opened the door for us—our conference had lasted no more than ten minutes—Robert told him that I was a great writer, that I was going to have stories published soon. Laqueur asked me a few questions, shook my hand, and winked at me. "And you, young man," he said. "Stop being so concerned about your brother. You should get on with your own life."

One evening, a week or so later, during a rare lull in a multifamily group therapy session—we were all sitting quietly in a circle, waiting for something to happen—Robert stood and walked across the room, to where our mother was sitting. He told her that he really loved her and would prove it. She beamed with pleasure. Robert bent over to kiss her. "I love you, Mommy," he said. He kissed her on the mouth. She screamed. Robert stood up, smiled, returned to his chair.

"He bit me," my mother stated, even as she began trying to stop the flow of blood from her lip. "Look, David," she said to my father, showing him the blood. "He bit me."

Nobody said anything, and so my mother spoke again, directing her words to Kate. She spoke with exceptional calm, as if she were asking what time it was. "Now, Doctor," she said (though Kate kept telling her she had not received her doctorate, my mother insisted on calling her Doctor), "could you please explain to me why my son does things like this? I just want to understand. I'd really appreciate your opinion on this."

I remember, also, three of the regular patients from these groups. One was Irene, a thin, haggard woman, perhaps thirty years old, who, no matter what was said to her or about her, never spoke, but, eyes forever downcast, picked away at herself: at her fingernails, her legs, her cheeks, her lips, her neck, her ears, her scalp.

Then there was Joel, an effeminate man in his thirties, who constantly yelled in a shrill voice at Kate and at his parents because, he said, they didn't treat him the way Dr. Brothers did. (Dr. Joyce Brothers had become famous at the same time as Charles Van Doren, for winning a large sum of money on a TV quiz show.) Joel watched her on his ward's television set regularly—she had a show where she dispensed psychological advice—because Dr. Brothers, he maintained, was the only person in the world who *truly* understood and loved him.

Whenever he mentioned Dr. Brothers, Joel's father—a short, balding fat man—would giggle, while Joel's mother (who looked exactly like his father, except that she wore a dress and had more hair) would clutch at her purse and ask Kate to help them: What were you supposed to do? What were you supposed to do if you had a son who was born like Joel?

Then Joel would rise—would sometimes stand on his chair—and start screaming at his parents and at Kate even more angrily, because, he said, all they wanted to do was to be mean to him and destroy him—to tear him apart and cut him up and belittle him.

"Dr. Brothers understands me—Dr. Brothers is kind and good to me, not like *you*!" Joel would shout. "Dr. Brothers isn't always attacking me and ripping me apart. Why can't you be kind and loving to me the way Dr. Brothers is . . . ?"

And I recall, especially, a young man who attended sessions intermittently, often without his parents. He usually stood by the door and leaned against the wall as if waiting for the session to end; he only attended because he was required to, he said. He seemed to me the most normal and articulate of teenagers: bright, handsome, athletic-looking. He laughed at the aburdities of the sessions, said what he had to say with confidence (including his opinion that these sessions were useless, and that Dr. Laqueur wasn't as great as people cracked him up to be), and he did so without any gestures or behavior that seemed to me in the least unusual, much less crazy.

On rides back to the city, I told Kate I couldn't understand why this young man was a patient—he never said or did anything that seemed out of the ordinary, and he always expressed his feelings clearly, and with animation. Kate rolled her eyes (in the same way she did when I said that Dr. Laqueur made sense to me), and I recall her suggesting to me that it was, in fact, this young man's seeming normality that was the eeriest thing about him.

That spring, while out on a pass from the hospital, the young man sat down in front of the United Nations, set himself on fire, and died.

Sometime in February or March, about six months into Robert's stay at Creedmoor, I announced to our group what I had already told Robert—that I had decided not to attend any more sessions.

I felt, I said, my words carefully rehearsed, that there was nothing I could say to Robert or that he could say to me that we couldn't say to each another without the sessions. I said I thought the sessions, by dredging up old resentments and problems, only served to keep problems alive, and were therefore counterproductive. I said I didn't think Robert was crazy or sick, but that being immersed in all the stuff we were immersed in during these sessions might make *anyone* sick.

I ended by saying that I preferred to have a relationship with

Robert that existed as much as possible *outside* the hospital, and *outside* therapy sessions, and didn't feel we needed the protection or anything else the sessions provided in order for us to be, simply, brothers.

Robert beamed. Kate approved. My parents said I was betraying and abandoning the family. Still, I stuck to my decision. And though I couched my statements, and reasons, in terms that emphasized the good my getting out of the group would do for Robert—how it might help him—mostly I wanted out simply because I wanted to help myself.

I was tired of commuting back and forth to the hospital three or four times a week. I was tired of the sessions at the hospital and of the sessions at my parents' apartment, and I was scared that if I kept spending time at Creedmoor, *I* might never get out. I was trying to get on with my own life— marriage and friendships, teaching (at Columbia), writing (a new novel), politics (civil rights and antiwar activities)—and I was scared, once again, that if I didn't get away from my family—if I didn't physically remove myself from its madness, and from Creedmoor (I didn't always laugh when Joel talked about others wanting to tear him apart)—I would fall apart too. When I stood in Creedmoor's dingy lobby three or four times a week, waiting in long lines with hundreds of others (most of us carrying shopping bags full of food and clothing that would have to pass through a security inspection) so we could visit our mad relatives, I used to wonder how it was that any of us, away from Creedmoor, could do anything *but* talk, wonder, worry, obsess, weep, and scream about Creedmoor, and about all that led to it and away from it. How have time in one's mind or soul for *anything* else? How not be forever consumed and exhausted by grief, rage, and despair?

In late spring of that year, 1965, Robert was discharged from Creedmoor, and began working part-time as a messenger for Arnold. Through the Federation of Jewish Philanthropies, he saw a psychologist for individual therapy once a week, and he may—neither of us can remember for sure (and even when we think we remember something clearly—memory being ever ingenious, self serving, and unreliable—we sometimes disagree in large ways)—have been in one of the federation's halfway houses briefly. (Creedmoor itself had no halfway houses in Queens to which it could refer its patients.)

A month or so after his discharge, he and Charles Fried, a friend from Hillside, arrived at my apartment on West 76th Street and announced that they had good news: they had found an apartment together. "Guess where?" Robert asked, smiling broadly.

The apartment they had found, and rented, was on the fifth floor of the brownstone next to mine on West 76th Street.

"I remember wandering around the city," Robert says, about his first admission to Creedmoor. "I think it was that time— I wandered and I wandered, and I wound up at Fellowship House, and even though I wasn't supposed to be there, Bill Kraus, who worked there as a social worker, put me up for half a week. But then he had to call the parents, and since Hillside wouldn't take me back, they took me to Creedmoor."

I tell Robert of the reading I've done in several books (Sheehan's, and James Wechsler's *In a Darkness*) about Laqueur and his unit. Robert nods, but offers nothing. I ask if he remembers the name of the young man who killed himself, and he says his name was Kenneth Delia. Ken's suicide is mentioned in both books, I say, but neither book says how he killed himself.

"Oh, he immolated himself—he set himself ablaze in front of the UN," Robert says, and he looks away. "He had a nice family."

Does Robert recall how many insulin comas he himself had?

"Only one or two, I think—I got infections from them— from the injections. They were painting the rooms, and the paint contaminated the needles and everybody was getting infected." (In another conversation, Robert claims he *never* submitted to insulin therapy.) "I didn't want them. Dr. Laqueur was a very pompous man, you know. The ward was monopolized by his insulin-therapy crap."

And Lebovic?

"He was a tired old man. Dad said he should retire, and he was right." Robert closes his eyes, pretends to fall asleep. Then he speaks very softly and slowly: "What I remember most about Creedmoor is that Dad came every Saturday and Sunday, and brought me tobacco, and the paper, and the news." Robert begins crying. "He came all by himself sometimes, every Saturday and Sunday, no matter what."

Robert says he remembers Kate Greenbaum well, and that he would be able to draw a picture of her. He remembers that she married, gained a lot of weight, and changed her name to Schwartz. I ask if he recalls the time Kate said she was going to write a book about Creedmoor someday and call it *The Helpless Dictator,* because that's what the patients seemed like to her: helpless dictators. When parents complained about how their lives were controlled and ruined by their mentally ill child, Kate would ask them how it could be—since their child was helpless, locked up, and drugged up—that this sick, helpless child had such extraordinary power to dictate and control so many aspects of its family's life.

Robert nods. "That was me," he says. Then: "Mother worked for the Family Organization, you see. Every Friday two families were in charge of bringing in special meals. There were food orgies—Cokes, hot dogs, sodas, potato salad, the works. And she used to take stuff to her cabana club, and try to sell it all there. The cabana"—a fenced-in swimming pool and snack bar in Bayside, Queens—"was full of sun lotion and screaming children and Jewish parents who weren't rich enough to live out on Long Island. I went there a few times, but mother wouldn't let me go out into the neighborhood when I lived at home."

To sell stuff for the organization?

He smiles. "No. Just to go. It was none of their business, she said."

Who you were?

"Yes."

We start to talk about the therapy sessions at Creedmoor, and Robert laughs.

"I bit mother's nose once," he says. "Remember?"

I say yes, but I thought he bit her lip.

"It was her nose, Jay. It was her nose. Don't you remember how she had one of those early off-center nose bobs when she was in nursing school? And how she used to always push our noses up so they would stay small?

" 'But look at the way he's eating,' she said about me. 'Just look at the way he eats,' she kept saying, and she wanted to know why I ate that way. So I went over and ate some of her nose." He shrugs. "I did it because it was funny. I wasn't hallucinating or anything. I was just imagining. I had a *huge* imagination in those days."

He says he thought the family sessions at Creedmoor were the best he ever had, because you could see how other people reacted: "If one person said, 'That's terrible—what are you doing?' maybe they would stop and change."

Did Robert know that our father would always run to the bathroom before and after visits, and that sometimes he didn't make it in time, and would wet his pants?

"He wasn't there," Robert says.

He stares off into space for a while, then shrugs, and continues: "He was always quiet. Our ward—Laqueur's—was the good ward, but they beat us up there the way they did everywhere else at Creedmoor. Listen, Jay—do you remember Mr. Stingley?" he asks. "Well, Dad used to slip him five dollars every time he came. He was good to me. He was good to me mostly—but he liked to polish his shoes on me too, you know."

He recalls the man who wrote in notebooks all the time— "That was Old Man Loewinger," he says—and he recalls the numbers of the various buildings he was housed in: 40, 25, 28.

"At Creedmoor I used to talk to the buildings. I remember one time I was in Building 28, and I thought I was making a movie. I was probably hallucinating, but I thought it *was* a movie—Creedmoor itself—and that I was in it. The Thorazine did it. I hated it. And I used to get passes to go out on the grounds and I would escape into town and go to movies—I saw *Deep Throat* and the Ibsen play with Nora in it.

"Then there were the conferences." He rolls his eyes. "Oh brother," he says. "I hated the conferences too—screenings, they called them—when decisions were made about transfers or discharge. There was always a whole bunch of people on the other side, and it was scary, and they kept asking me why I'd gotten sick and if I was gonna do it again. 'Will you do it again? Will you do it again?' It was ridiculous."

Did he really attack people?

"I hit a nurse in the face once. I bit somebody's finger off," he says. "I think I swallowed it. Eleven aides were trying to get a straitjacket on me. I got into fights all the time."

In January 1966, about a half year after he was released from Creedmoor, Robert enrolled for two courses at CCNY (Principles of Art, Sociology), attended classes all semester, and received B's in both courses. He enrolled in two more courses (Composition and Literature) for the summer session, and again completed them, again receiving grades of B in each.

Sometimes, living next door to each other, we would see each other five or six days in a row, and sometimes a few days would go by when we didn't see each other at all. We went on peace marches together, ate meals together (in my apartment, in restaurants), went to movies, shows, concerts.

The previous fall, shortly after Robert was discharged from Creedmoor, I had completed a ninth book, *Big Man,* which became, in the summer of 1966—nine years after I'd written my first novel—my first published book. (*Big Man* tells the story of Mack Davis, a black All-American basketball player caught in the basketball scandals of the early fifties. "I work at the Minit-Wash, washing down cars," Mack says, early on. "That's how come I got such clean hands. Yeah, me, I got the cleanest hands of any fixer around.")

On July 6, I received a special delivery letter from Robert, sent from 152 West 76th Street to 150 West 76th Street. "I'm about half way through Big Man," his letter began,

it's been one of the important readings in my life—which has been filled with words. At first of course I started searching thru the book for references of me—after all if I'm going to be immortalized in one of the truer tales of the twentieth century the fucken author better get it right. . . . Well I found some resemblance and a whole lot of other familiar amalgamations and alternated between fury, worse tears, which was broken by just laffs for those of the prehistoric era—they're here alright but so is Mack, and Willa [Mack's girlfriend]—they live louder than those murmurings of jealousy. . . .

I'm glad I didn't get to see this novel before. Until little ago I wasn't really ready for any new or novel. Somehow at this time in this place this day and some after the anniversary of what was once an american holiday I managed to start reading something by my big brother. Feeling free i now disown you of that title—you're no longer my big brother. Jay Neugeboren will do.

There are things to be said but they will be or won't. There are going to be plenty of monday morning foul shooters so why bother. You somehow got it down, and its there bound for who knows whom or what gee—excelsior.

Me—there's no shit on me I got the dirtiest hands this side of Queens but these bitten down fingers are going to pound out something or other—brother, through all the hallways and wanderings I have always felt and known your love and no matter how hard I'd try defaithing you'd like plastic man manage to stretch. If there ever appears on the american scene something by robert gary you know if nobody else cares to who his big man is.

I want to return and then go on to the world which is scheduled for this wednesday. i just had to take a break from one of the most exciting and angering morning watches i have been priveleged to make in this so short and (un) happy life i live.

While I was away for a few days, and Robert was looking after my apartment (feeding the cat, watering the plants), he took a message from my friend Jerry Charyn, who called from California to ask if I was interested in teaching at Stanford for a year. I already had plans to go to Europe, but a few days later I changed my plans and accepted an offer from Stanford.

In late August, while I was preparing to leave for California, Robert started throwing tantrums, and nothing anyone—I, Charles, his therapist, friends—said or did could calm him down. Every time I phoned, he screamed, cursed, and hung up. On the day before I started out across country for California (repeating the trip Robert had taken five years before), I went next door and rang his doorbell. He came downstairs, and the instant he saw me, he started jumping up and down while shrieking at me through the door's plate glass to leave him alone, to get out of there, and to do. *"Do, Jay!"* he kept screaming, again and again. *"Do! Do! Don't you understand me? Just do! Do! Do! Do! Do! Do! Do . . . !"*

In September, before I reached California, Robert was hospitalized at Creedmoor again—his fourth breakdown, and fourth hospitalization in less than five years.

Six months later (and five years after his first breakdown), he telephoned me in Palo Alto to give me his good news—he had just been discharged from Creedmoor, and was moving back to his apartment at 152 West 76th Street, where his roommate Charles was still living. That week, Robert sent a new poem:

> out of one night into another
> Hello father, goodbye mother
> time flows through me and I
> through time
> a mime actor, I watch from dead lands.

When, in September 1967, after a year at Stanford, I returned to New York and then left, by ship, for Europe, Robert was at the dock to see me off.

I would stay in Europe for the next eighteen months, living mostly in Spéracèdes, a small village in the south of France. During these eighteen months I worked on several books, including a volume of memoirs *(Parentheses,* mostly about my activities in the civil rights and antiwar movements, and my coming of age as a writer), which I wrote (or so I told myself) in order, by exorcising things personal and political directly, and not through the indirection of fiction, to return, more freely, to the writing of novels and stories without being infected by the madness—in me, in the world around me—I feared could destroy both me and my writing.

For a chapter ("Pictures from an Institution") in which I wrote briefly of Robert's hospitalizations, and in which I lied, stating that "largely through his own courage, his own humor," Robert had "emerged whole, himself . . . back again for better or worse in the 'real' world"—I chose an epigraph from one of Vincent van Gogh's letters to his brother Theo:

For cooping up all these lunatics in this old cloister becomes, I think, a dangerous thing, in which you risk losing the little good sense that you may still have kept. Not that I am set on this or that by preference. I am used to the life here, but one must not forget to make a little trial of the opposite.

9

" 'THROW AWAY your Sigmund Freud, Mrs. Neugeboren!'
the doctor told me," my mother said, " 'because I am going
to cure your son!' "

It was a gorgeous afternoon in late May 1968, and my
mother was sitting on the balcony of my house in southern
France, going on, at length, about what Robert's new doctor
had been promising her. Although I had sent several telegrams
telling her not to visit me (as I suspected, she was once again
considering divorcing my father, and wanted my "opinion" as
to whether she should or not; she had made a similar visit to
Palo Alto the previous year), she had managed to get a seat on
the last plane to land at Nice Airport before the national strike

and uprisings then taking place throughout France had shut all airports down.

And while she was on a balcony in Spéracèdes, telling me about Dr. Cott, a man who, she claimed—like Dr. Laqueur before him—was working "miracle cures" with schizophrenics like Robert, Robert and my father were living together in the Queens apartment. ("Robert will be with me while mother is away," my father wrote, "so do not worry about me.")

Shortly after my mother left France and flew back to Queens, she wrote to tell me that Robert's progress was, according to Dr. Cott, "splendid, splendid," and to explain why his cure was going to be "permanent":

> . . . from the looks of things this treatment of vitamins is spreading & hopefully down will go very much of past psychiatric-therapeutic treatments—all now geared to "change of metabolism" and biochemistry as the cause & so the cure is in sight. "My cup runneth over" that we lived long enuf to reach this goal. Of course, Robt has a way to go, but its all uphill [sic]— no more therapy sessions, no more doctors—he only goes to pick up "RX" if necessary—no more bills except for the inexpensive drugs. Unbelievable! But a fact! And spreading rapidly thru all mental hospitals!

In addition to taking the megavitamins, Robert was once again "under strict orders," she wrote, "*not* to see or communicate with any former patients—& he has followed these orders and I assure you it has been difficult for him to cut so many ties but I'm happy to say he *is* doing it." Even when the mother of one of Robert's friends urged my mother to let Robert visit with her child, my mother reported that Robert obeyed the doctor's orders ("Robert said to me, 'she finds it difficult to understand that I cannot see anyone who has been a former patient' ").

Dr. Cott believed that the secret to curing schizophrenia lay in giving patients massive doses, not of drugs (or insulin comas), or of psychotherapy ("Useless! Useless!"), but of vitamins. Robert had begun his "megavitamin treatment" (also called orthomolecular therapy, or, more accurately, megadose-vitamin therapy) with Dr. Cott a month before, in April 1968.

The rationale for megadose-vitamin therapy put forth by doctors like Cott derived from their belief that there was *a* chemical that produced schizophrenia and that this chemical could be absorbed by the introduction of large doses of vitamins, especially niacin. The theory, pretty much disproved by the late sixties, was given new life in 1968 (and again in 1972) by the endorsement of Nobel Prize winner Linus Pauling. It was Pauling's belief that "mental disease is for the most part caused by abnormal reaction rates, is determined by genetic constitution and diet and by abnormal molecular concentration of essential substances." Megadoses of vitamins, especially niacin and vitamins B-6, B-12, and C, could counteract these abnormal conditions by causing "a rearrangement of abnormal molecules."

By the late sixties, however, even those researchers and psychiatrists most disposed to favor a biochemical basis for schizophrenia did not take megavitamin therapy, or doctors like Cott, seriously. In fact, all controlled double-blind studies not only produced negative results, but demonstrated that the vitamins were inferior to placebos. In addition, studies showed that megavitamins had markedly harmful effects on those receiving them. Still, despite the universally demonstrated lack of therapeutic effects, the therapy, even in 1975, was, according to the *Contemporary Textbook of Psychiatry,* nonetheless being "widely touted by self-styled 'orthomolecular' psychiatrists with a proselytizing fervor not entirely devoid of pecuniary considerations."

But how discourage any parent from believing in miracles, especially when they were being proffered by doctors who produced scientific rationales, and (alleged) scientifically based and proven cures, and who, by claiming that the cause of the child's illness was chemical, absolved parents of a portion of the guilt and stigma that seemed, inevitably, to pervade the lives of most families in which mental illness occurred?

The problem with doctors like Laqueur and Cott was not merely that what they prescribed didn't work (lots of things, in medicine and elsewhere, don't work—and we can't know this until we try them; and lots of things work—e.g., drugs that successfully treat epilepsy, colitis, migraines, and some forms of arthritis—without our understanding why), but that they believed, and in ways that encouraged large and false hopes, that they had definitive, and simple, answers to problems which, then as now, simply do not allow for definitive and simple answers.

Had they been less arrogant, and merely said what some other doctors were saying—that we know very little about how the human mind works, and very little about the cause, course, and cure of what we call mental illness, but we think this drug (or this combination of drugs, or this combination of drugs and psychotherapy) *might* be helpful to your child—how much less painful life would have been for Robert, and for our family, and for all those families like ours that, despairing, had had their despair intensified by the sudden introduction (and failure) of some new cure-all.

But by this time Robert had been in and out of hospitals for a half-dozen years, and the most dreadful and salient fact of his condition, a condition that was proving both unpredictable *and* chronic in its course, was that there seemed nothing anyone could do about it. Certainly, by this time, we knew what *didn't* work.

But what did work, or *might* work? Robert had been hospitalized in both private and state institutions, had been given old and new forms of treatment, while being condemned by some doctors to a lifetime of institutionalization and promised complete recoveries by others. Given an illness which seemed to vanish for months at a time, and for whose reappearances no timetable or determining cause or causes had been found—

an illness that showed itself forth not in lesions or physiological symptoms, but in erratic, often dangerous forms of human behavior—how not hope for some theory, drug, or program that would make a difference?

In recent years I've talked with a childhood friend, Jerry Friedland, about Robert. Jerry has been, since 1991, medical director for AIDS treatment and research programs at Yale Medical School, and I recall my surprise when he said to me some years back that there would never be a cure for AIDS. "Never?" I said. "The virus is too smart," Jerry said. "We'll be able to manage the disease better, and make genuine gains, but, as virtually all doctors and researchers in the field know, it is unlikely there will ever be a cure."

Still, Jerry pointed out the first rule known to fund-raisers in America: "People want to give to Winning Causes, not to Needy Institutions." Americans tend to give more readily, that is, if they believe their donations will help bring about a cure, rather than if they are asked to give money (merely) in order to care for those who are ill. Thus, when scientists and fund-raisers talk about AIDS to the public, they frequently find themselves talking about a cure, since if they don't, they find that interest wanes, and they often come away empty-handed.

Why, then, in their hopes and dreams, should the family of a mentally ill person be different from other American families? Why shouldn't any mother and father, then as now, have wanted and hoped for what didn't exist, and what may never exist? Why weren't they, too, entitled to Winning Answers, especially when the attempts to deal with, and live with, disease were forever being put forth in warlike rhetoric—we seem, always, to be either "winning" or "losing" *battles* against cancer, muscular dystrophy, or heart disease. How ever convince any parent, spouse, child, or sibling that this strange, bewildering condition we used to call madness and lunacy, and now call by various medical-sounding names (schizophrenia, bipolar disorder, atypical depression), is a condition that has no cure (as such), and may never have a cure (may never be "conquered" or "overcome" or "defeated"), and will—like diabetes, or multiple sclerosis, say, though with nothing remotely like their somewhat predictable courses—simply (*simply?!*) have to be managed, and endured—by the person afflicted, and by all those who love and care for this person—over the course of a lifetime? And why be surprised that the longer the condition persists, and the more chronic it becomes, as with Robert—the more its sad, wild, and daily ups and downs terrify, terrorize, and dishearten—the more desperate will the desire be for something—for *anything*—that might magically arrest and reverse its course?

When I read books by people such as Kay Jamison and William Styron, in which they talk about their experience of manic depression, and how they have found partial cures in drugs, therapy, and friends, and when I read of others who have responded well to medication, I wonder: Why not Robert? *Is* compliance the central issue? Would Robert have a larger, happier, fuller life today had lithium been available in 1962? Have I done him a disservice, through the years, by not encouraging a more purely medical approach to his condition? If I had had the means to get him into good private facilities, would that have made a difference? And would people like Kay Jamison and William Styron (and Patty Duke and Josh Logan, and others) have recovered to the extent they did had they not had access, because of their talents and their accomplishments (and the will that enabled them to cultivate their talents), to doctors, friends, funds, hospitals, researchers, and private clinics that most of us lack?

For the next two years, during which Robert was hospitalized at a private Manhattan hospital (Gracie Square) by Dr. Cott at least three times, and at enormous expense to our parents, Dr. Cott continued to be optimistic about Robert's potential for becoming "completely normal," and my mother continued to be hopeful. "More & more is coming to light re: the change in chromosomes, metabolism," she wrote. "Dr. Cott is pleased—& all of Robts testing (which was Positively Abnormal when treatment was started—is now recording as NORMAL. I am most grateful & hope, hope."

Although Robert dropped all his courses at CCNY early in 1968 (at the time he started treatment with Dr. Cott), he was able to hold down part-time jobs, and early in 1969, a year after he began megavitamin therapy and a month before I returned to New York from France (to teach at the The State University of New York's new campus at Old Westbury, a few miles east of Creedmoor), he enrolled once again for courses at CCNY.

Two weeks before my return, my mother wrote that he had begun a job at the post office, working six to ten in the evenings, Monday to Friday. "He really is moving towards good mental health, slowly, surely—& it is becoming so 'secure'—I could weep for seeing my hopeless hopes becoming a hopeful reality," she wrote. "Again, word from Dr. C—positively, absolutely—he will be 100% OK—Don't we have much to celebrate?"

Robert's views were more measured. "I saw my doctor yesterday," he wrote, "and he thinks that I am doing so well that I'll only have to see him once every two months, which is somewhat of a relief. I mean after all these years of talking to doctors and pretending doctors I have run out of problems. My biggest problem now that I have almost reached a state of satori is digesting all the pills he has prescribed for me three times a day. I have to swallow these enormous dosages of vitamins."

"Hey did you ever think of becoming a writer?" he added, at the end of this letter. "Jay, reading over your last two letters and they are quite well written—if you're not doing anything why don't you try writing?" (My own letters from these years seem, in fact, insufferably coy and self-conscious—filled with effusions, evasions, and exclamation points. I was, as Robert frequently noted, ever "the good son," and cloyingly so—e.g., "My wifikin's painting course is marvelous—wait until you see her productions!! . . . stay well, send us all the news that's fit to send—")

"It seems that Dr. Cott is going to be on [David Susskind's television show] and he wanted me as an example of the fine work he is doing with schizophrenics and their cure," Robert wrote in February 1969. "I half toyed with the idea and then thought better of it, not wanting to make a public spectacle of my delusions and not wanting to be deluded into thinking that the publicity surrounding the show would be about anything but my previous sickness(es).

> I did ask him if he thought therefore that I was cured. He said not exactly cured but at least the illness was arrested, and that if after five years i stayed about the same on the vitamins with a reduction in them over that time and then afterwards he saw no reason why that term could not be applied. The pills are working fine and much more fun than making up stories for doctors and pseudodoctors. I am repulsed by all the talking that I once did and really don't know what I talked about and how those "professionals" could sit there and listen. But then i guess when you're getting paid at the rates that they [are] you can sit. I only have to see the good doctor once every two months and then only for a half hour and then I just about have enough to say to him. But he does have nice pictures in his office (among them original Klees, Picassos and Braques).

In the same letter, he wrote about his new job ("I took the job with the Post Office because of the money and also returning to school—I'll be able to go full time finally, in the fall, and just work summers"), his hopes ("Perhaps someday I'll be in the position you're in and be free of bosses and busy work"), and with the news that his roommate Charles was getting married ("Of course I wished him the best, but god only knows what I'm going to do with all the junk left in the apartment").

The warmth, sensibleness, and good humor of his letters

seemed to return to his life as well during this period, and while I was living and teaching at Old Westbury in 1969 and 1970, Robert was completing thirty credits at CCNY, with an above-B average (getting grades of A in Drawing I and in Writing of Poetry), while working twenty hours a week at the post office. He often stayed overnight and for weekends with me in Old Westbury, and he seemed, if sometimes shakily (but how not, given the previous half-dozen years of his life?), to have returned not only to himself, but to a self that could survive and thrive in the world outside hospitals. I remained skeptical about Cott and his Cure, but was delighted Robert was doing well (whether he did or did not take his pills). Who knew *what* worked, and why, and when?

In the summer of 1970, six months after my first child, Miriam, was born, I quit my job at Old Westbury and returned to Spéracèdes, where I would spend a year before taking a position as writer-in-residence at the University of Massachusetts in Amherst. By this time I had published three more books—another novel (*Listen Ruben Fontanez*), a collection of stories (*Corky's Brother*), and *Parentheses*—and though I entertained fantasies of never having to teach again (and of remaining forever in France, living on the income from my writing), I knew this possibility, especially with a growing family, was unlikely.

At the same time that I was returning to France, and planning a move to Massachusetts (I bought a house there before the move to France), our parents announced that they were making definitive plans to leave New York and retire to Florida.

Robert's reaction to my leaving, and to this news, was swift. A few days after my departure for France, he declared that he was no longer mentally ill, discharged himself from Dr. Cott, and flew to the island of Bermuda. My mother wrote, in detail, about how Robert got into four motorcycle accidents on the island, how these accidents "threw his psyche off," and how

Dr. Cott kept assuring her that if only Robert continued to take his vitamins, he would be all right.

Robert wrote me from Bermuda, telling me about his accidents, about how the police showed up at his door to tell him to telephone home, and about his long-distance conversations with Dr. Cott. "He suggested I be a plutocrat and take taxis," Robert wrote. "I muttered back, very easy for you to say. Doctors always seem to think that if you can afford them, you can afford life."

Several months after his return from Bermuda, I received an aerogram from him, his handwriting shaky and oversize— "Shitting in Bach class next is Poetry with sum Greek pantheist Konstantinos Lardos—Look up Schmerner (?) Gesellshift #122 Bach—Das Neugebor' ne Kindelein"—and shortly after this, my mother wrote to tell me he had been hospitalized at Gracie Square again. She also wrote at length of the arguments she and my father were having about leaving New York (our father, she said, "would not go and leave Robt, so I did what I wanted and told Dad this time I will further resent Robt coming between us").

Robert recovered quickly this time—"so fast," my mother wrote, "it seems miraculous! Is it the vitamins? I don't know! but he was really what is normal for Robt. . . . Need I tell you Robt is so well liked in the hospital—it makes me feel hysterical when they say to me—'it's a pleasure to have him here'—funny, eh?"

In late January 1971, Robert left Gracie Square and once again began making plans to return to work and to school. A week after he moved back into the Queens apartment, however, our father was hospitalized at Booth Memorial Hospital, this time for emphysema—and when our father came home, Robert moved out, to an apartment on East 99th Street. (One Sunday afternoon a year or so before, my mother had called and asked if she and my father could come out to Old Westbury for a visit. I said we had plans, but my mother insisted. "It will do your father good if he can see Miriam," she said. Miriam was then two or three months old. Do him good? "Well, he's not breathing," she went on, "but I know that whenever he's with her, he breathes well." I instructed my mother to get my father to the hospital, and to call me after a doctor had seen him.)

Six months later, in June of 1971 our parents made a down-payment on a garden apartment in West Palm Beach's Century Village, and Robert wrote me about their plans to journey to "shangra-la," about school (he had completed the semester successfully but had made a decision not to return in the fall), and about his new job as an assistant substitute teacher ("all we really do is tie shoe laces, watch sesame street, break up fights and watch 25 3, 4, 5, 6, 7 and 8 year olds urinate and defecate about twenty times a day. I figure if i start with nursery and kinderhopsgardten I should graduate about the same time as if I just stayed at CCNY").

At the end of the summer—shortly after my return from France and my move into my new home in Massachusetts—Robert was hospitalized at Gracie Square again, and at the end of October, when he visited me, he was in dreadful shape. He screamed a lot (mostly about all the things I'd done to hurt him and exploit him), scurried from room to room, and kept making threats—demanding, among other things, that I pay him large sums of money for what I had written about him and the family. For the first time in my life I became frightened he might harm me, my wife, or Miriam, who was then twenty months old.

When he talked about visiting a friend in Stockbridge, an hour west, I didn't hesitate—I got him in the car, drove him to Amherst, and put him on a bus. (If it was terrifying for me to be in his presence at times like these—should I shout back? leave him be? get my wife and daughter out of the house?—how much more terrifying for him, especially when feeling disoriented and out-of-control, to feel possessed of the *power* to terrorize, even if he was only dimly aware of this power.)

A few days later, I received a letter from him, barely legible and written partly in Hebrew, partly in pen, partly in pencil, on stationery from the Red Lion Inn in Stockbridge, and addressed to Jacob Mordecai Neugeboren:

> i accept all rights
> to my character as-
> ass-ass noted or in bound
> -mimeoded or otherwise reproduced
> "FICTIONS"
>
> if you continue to have such poor (as in poverty)
> tastes and misuse of your better judgements as to *use* not friends
> unfathom seulemente but living persons in your "WORKS";
> then please at least offer them (the living or surviving that is)
> some sort of token. . . .
>
> Frère Jacques—
> u know that the autumn
> winds Blow
> Many leaves
> How about $um of
> those green leaves
> my way?

It was a month or so after this, when Dr. Cott discharged Robert as a patient, declaring he could not treat him successfully if Robert would not take his pills, that my father asked him where the pill was to make Robert want to take the pills Dr. Cott said he should be taking.

And a few months after this, Robert was arrested in New York City and taken to a hospital for the criminally insane, the Mid-Hudson Psychiatric Center, in Beacon, New York.

"At Gracie Square," Robert says, "they gave me gas treatments—they were called Endeclen, or something like that. They put you up on carbon dioxide and let you down on oxygen. It was crazy. Dr. Cott ordered the treatments. He said that before he let me go, he wanted me to have something under my belt."

(The gas treatments—also called "inhalation treatments"—were made up of 30 percent carbon dioxide and 70 percent oxygen, and, like insulin-shock treatments, were intended to produce unconsciousness. Some doctors gave patients up to 150 treatments. The rationale for the treatment remains obscure, and the results were not only negligible, at best, but often fatal. By the early seventies, the treatments had been discontinued throughout the United States.)

"One time I went with Dr. Cott to this house, so he could show me off as a cure," Robert says. "It was Teddy Roosevelt's house once. He thought I was so successful—but he spoke loud and I spoke softly."

Robert remembers lugging around large batches of vitamins. "They were bulky, and I hated carrying so many pills with me everywhere I went. It was embarrassing," he says. "The vitamin C's were supposed to digest the vitamin B's, I remember, but the amino acids depressed me, so I went to his office and he gave me shots, I don't know what." He pauses, glances at his lap. "I'll tell you something, though—I could shoot further when I was taking it."

Robert also says he was on pills which, because they were not yet approved by the FDA, our parents had friends smuggle in from Canada.

"It was called Linodel," Robert says. "Or something like that. They had to sneak it in as vitamins. Dr. Cott prescribed it, I think. I'm not sure. I didn't know what it was and I took a *lot* of it."

Robert says that whenever he had a session with Dr. Cott, Dr. Cott would spend the time opening his mail. "It was also his telephone hour," Robert adds. "The phone kept ringing all the time and he would talk with patients. The parents gave him a *lot* of money."

Did he and our father talk much during the time he was living at home?

"Oh yes," Robert says. "He'd wake up when I got in at two A.M. from my job at the post office, and he'd make dinner for me—hamburgers, steaks, lamb chops. I'd call at eleven to tell him when I was coming home, and we'd talk while I ate.

"I'd go to Dr. Cott early in the morning with Dad sometimes, and Dr. Cott would say, 'I'm glad somebody canceled an appointment!' That meant me. Dad took me there. Mrs. Cott was a bitch. She ran the office for him. Remember how Dad said he would never work for somebody whose wife ran the cash register?

"And I remember this one time Mother visited me at Gracie Square when I was pretty out of it, and she met this other woman and was going on and on to her about her son Jay and all your accomplishments, and then I walked in and the woman asked who I was and mother said, 'Oh, him—he's my other son.'"

"I bet you're bragging to all the other kids on that block of yours about your big time criminal of an uncle," Robert wrote Miriam (then two and a half years old) in June 1972, from the Mid-Hudson Psychiatric Center. "Well, I regret and I now declare that I shall never again (if there was a first) assault and battery (what a charge—I made a pun! I made a pun!) even a police officer."

A week or so later, he wrote to Miriam again: "Well believe it or not 'Oncle' Robert has a new number. Every time you write to him you must include it. Also I am on Ward #1. There R only two wards and wouldn't you know it, I made #1."

All mail to and from Mid-Hudson was subject to inspection (patients "may receive any communication sent to them which in the judgment of the Director would not be injurious to their welfare"), and Robert's letters to me were all initialed by hospital staff. I was given a long list of what could not be brought or sent (gum, salad dressing, cheeses, spices, nuts with shells, etc.). "In order to protect [their] legal rights while undergoing treatment," patients were forbidden to sign checks or documents, or to enter into any business transactions. They were not allowed to receive phone calls. They were, however, permitted to "call collect to a member of the immediate family up to four times a month, between the hours of 6 P.M. and 8 P.M., if written approval has been given in advance by the family member, and approval by the Director." Calls were limited to five minutes, though exceptions, if approved by the director, could be made for emergencies.

Although the effectiveness of lithium in the long-term maintenance therapy of bipolar mood disorders (manic depression) was established, most notably in Denmark and Australia, by the early fifties, the U.S. Food and Drug Administration (in part because of lithium's diastrous misuse as a salt substitute for cardiac patients) did not approve the labeling of lithium for the treatment of mania (and bipolar disorder) until 1970, and for "maintenance therapy" in patients with a history of mania until 1974.

Robert, however, was receiving lithium regularly during his stay at Mid-Hudson, at least as early as 1972, and, since it seemed to be effective in calming him—and with fewer side effects than antipsychotic drugs such as Thorazine and Stelazine—he began at this time being diagnosed as manic-depressive, and not as schizophrenic. (He also thinks Dr. Cott may have been giving him lithium—was this the illegal Linodel?—in the late sixties, but, given lithium's toxicity, and the consequent need for regular blood-monitoring, which Robert did not receive, this seems unlikely.)

"No news here," Robert wrote me during his first month at Mid-Hudson. "I either sleep or read, also eat and take my Lithium like a good boy. I'm told I look good so there must be a Bar Mitzvah soon. The folks came by Shabbos with the chicken and all the news about who's dying and who isn't."

He said he had put himself in charge of a newspaper, but couldn't get anyone to write for it. "Please write," his letter ended, "type and send pictures as every day I wait for mail like some P.O.W."

His letters to me during his first months at Mid-Hudson were warm, witty, and lengthy, and seemed, especially given their place of origin, remarkably clear and coherent:

> There is some hope that I can get a pass and Burt Brody will probably take me somewheres in the neighborhood. . . . Listen, one favor—I would like to correspond again with Ben Saltman, my old friend and teacher at Emerson. In the edition of "Works" that your short story was in (Elijah?) there was an ad from some out of the way publisher for a small book of poetry of his. Maybe they would forward a letter from me. Thanks. Keep well, don't work too hard and forget about the publishers—let 'em publish crap. . . . your languishing frère.

"If you show your face [at a family wedding]," he wrote, "and they ask after me (you know, Jay, didn't you once have a brother and there was something wrong with him, there was even a book about his painting his pictures out of an institution) tell them I smoke cigars and really do love them and that with my next face lift I'll look better than ever."

He looked forward to getting out and moving back home to Queens ("I know i shall have to stay as a skeleton hangs in a crowded closet"), and when I received a less than positive review in *The New York Times Book Review*, he had a suggestion: "Why don't you just tell these guys that you're R. Gary Neugeboren's Big Brother and you used to answer his questions about Albert Camus. Get the Pictures?"

I visited Robert at Mid-Hudson several times, and was surprised to find that the hospital did not seem anywhere near as dreadful and frightening as Creedmoor had. His fellow inmates seemed less mad and confused, their behavior less bizarre, and though Robert's rights were severely restricted, and his medical treatment minimal, he himself seemed rational and calm (he was dressed neatly, our conversations were easy and natural), the hospital less oppressive than Creedmoor: less wildness, menace, and clutter, and—the impression that stays with me mostly—everywhere more bright light coming in through larger, cleaner windows.

In early August, my mother wrote to tell me she had asked the staff at Mid-Hudson to inform Robert that he definitely "will *not* be coming home to Union Tpke," which meant, she said, that he would have to be transferred back to Creedmoor.

"Know any good foster parents?" Robert wrote me a week after the hospital conference at which our parents confirmed their decision. In the briefest of all the notes I received from him that year, he could barely hide his disappointment and rage: "Listen I love you, you love me, so *write*!!!! send things anything except of course hack saws and TOBACCO. Tell Miriam whatever you damn please. But this ain't no home or house it's a fortress."

After a silence of more than two months, he wrote to tell me my attitude toward the American Book Business seemed healthy. "It is good to be healthy, mon frère," he commented. "Take it from one of the favorite subsidy patients of all forms of insurance in New York State (I am applying for Social Security and bet I retire before the folks!)."

By December 1972, a month before my son Aaron was born, Robert's letters were filled, mostly, with expressions of his loneliness: "Just a short note to say I still love you and miss you and would like to get the hell out of here. I'm writing on one of those innumerable Mondays which I think was inserted into the calendar on the account of Blueness. I'm not Blue just depressed which of course everyone enjoys except me. I really could go for a good manic state. . . . please send books as I am finally through most of what wasn't stolen.

"I wonder," he added, "how many more years I shall have to spend in these Young Age Homes."

In March 1973, charges against Robert were dropped (in my memory the charges were for assaulting a policeman; Robert says he was arrested in a restaurant for throwing ashtrays at everyone), and in April he asked for a pass so he could visit me in Massachusetts, for Passover: "Please send to Dr. Tebken a permission slip so that I can come visit you for the Pesach holydays—it would do so much for me and I guess the whole family for us to once again be together and on my birthday yet."

He was allowed out, and the visit went well. "You have no idea how great I felt at your place," Robert wrote me afterward. A few sentences later he added, "Please tell me what to do with my feet. They are still bothering me like crazy. I am writing this letter with my left leg pinned underneath my seat—it seems to calm me, that position."

Whenever I was with our parents in the months preceding their move to Florida, they fought about the move. My mother kept insisting she had done enough for others, and that staying in New York would not help or cure Robert. She was entitled, after a life of hard work and suffering, she said, to some peace.

My father did not disagree, but he pleaded with her that they not leave Robert, especially when he was so sick. I had seen my father cry only twice before in my life—when his brother Hymie died, and when his nephew Joey died—but one Sunday afternoon before a trip to Mid-Hudson, when I walked into my parents' living room, I found him on his knees in front of my mother, weeping away. "I'm begging you, Annie," he kept saying through his tears. "I'm begging you, I'm begging you—one doesn't abandon a son! One doesn't abandon a son . . . !"

My mother remained firm. My father was entitled to live in a climate that wouldn't kill him, she said, and she was entitled to live in a place where she was not forever taking care of *two* sick men. From now on, the state could take over, and I could be in charge of Robert. But with or without my father, she was going to Florida. He could choose.

In the years since, when I recall my father weeping and pleading, and when I conjure up all the other arguments and sufferings my parents endured and inflicted upon one another,

I have sometimes found myself wondering about other families who have been torn apart by the illness of their child. How, not living with chronic mental illness, day by day and year by year, can anyone know what it is like to have a child one wants, at one and the same time, both to cure and comfort . . . and to run from and never see again? How know the infinite ways the presence of a child with such a condition exhausts, strains, and informs *all* the moments and relations of a family's life? How, in such a life, find time and space for the ordinary, natural expression of affection, gentleness, playfulness, and lovingkindness? And how, ever again, think of one's own needs in an easy, uncomplicated way?

Robert was transferred from Mid-Hudson to Creedmoor that summer, put on a waiting list for Boerum Hill, a halfway house in Brooklyn, and, after a while, given passes on a regular basis to leave Creedmoor for visits to Boerum Hill, as well as for classes at a drafting school.

In late August, about six weeks before our parents moved out of New York, Robert met us for lunch at Junior's, a restaurant in downtown Brooklyn. We were all tense, weary, angry— we argued and accused in old, familiar ways—and Robert finally walked out, saying he couldn't take any more, and that he was going to go to Boerum Hill to pick up his prescription. My mother ran out after him. My father paid the bill, and then he and I left.

It was a broiling summer day in New York, and at one point my father stopped, said that he couldn't go on. He stood in the doorway of an office building, dripping sweat and trying to catch his breath while yelling at me to go on ahead without him. When I told him to calm down and take his time, that I would wait, he began stamping his feet like a frustrated child. *"What do you want from me?"* he kept repeating. *"What do you want from me? What do you want from me? He's my son, he's my son, he's my son . . . !"*

When, in mid-October 1973, at the time of their thirty-seventh wedding anniversary, our parents left for Florida, Robert was still at Creedmoor.

"Thanks for a copy of your new book [*Sam's Legacy*]," he wrote, several months later. His letter was six pages long, and at the top of the first page he drew a heart around the date ("Feb 14, 1974/ St. Valentine's Day"), and a Cupid (the Cupid, like Robert, curly-haired and in eyeglasses) next to the heart. "Have been waiting for mail for so long from either you or the folks and now this Big Black book arrives. It looks terrific and you should feel proud. I shall try and start reading it tonight. I hope the folks are alright. I haven't gotten any mail from them in over a month, then I haven't written to them either, but they do usually write. I was *very worried* but I guess all is well with them."

He ended his letter with disappointing news: "It seems," he wrote, "I shall be here for an awfully long time as there has been a holdup and delay in Welfare on account of the transfer from NY City to Federal funding, with me caught in the middle. I don't think Boerum Hill would be that much better but I would like to get out of here and away from these sick people."

(Before our parents left New York, my mother had had Robert "grandfathered" into the new Social Security law. Since Robert was permanently disabled before the age of twenty-one, he would, under the new law, be supported by Social Security for the rest of his life. My mother had also asked our Aunt Mary to take care of any bureaucratic problems, in New York City, that might arise concerning Robert, in part, Mary told me recently, because, she quoted my mother as saying, "I know that Jay doesn't really care about Robert.")

Robert stayed in Creedmoor for over a year this time. In late September 1974, he left Creedmoor for Boerum Hill (again), and on September 24, two days after my son Eli was born, he typed a long, congratulatory letter on the stationery of the Amchute Manufacturing Corporation, where he was working part-time, doing clerical work ("I *do* hope everything is going well and as expected. I bet Miriam is anxious though to see her new sybling. Me, I already bought a box of cigars . . .").

Less than a month later, however—on October 16, 1974, during the week of our parents' thirty-eighth wedding anniversary, and exactly a year after their move to Florida—Robert was hospitalized at South Beach Psychiatric Center on Staten Island, which was now the state's "catchment area" for Brooklyn's mentally ill. A "Notice of Status and Rights—Involuntary Admission" was sent to me, "Jacob Neugeboren—brother (Nearest Relative)," as was a "Notice of Hearing," from the New York State Supreme Court ("Demand having been made for a hearing in the matter of an application for the involuntary retention of the above named patient . . .").

A dozen years had now passed since Robert's first hospitalization—he was thirty-one years old—and the first or second time I spoke with him after he was admitted to South Beach, instead of asking him if he was feeling better or worse, or about his doctors and medications, or if things were improving or not, or what had happened that had led to his hospitalization, or if he thought he might be getting out soon, I found myself asking, simply, how his day on the ward had been: What had he eaten? What was his room like? Did he have a roommate, and what was his roommate like? Did he have a social worker assigned to him yet, or a therapist? What had he watched on TV . . . ?

"One time at Mid-Hudson," Robert says, after telling me of the time he tried to set himself and his straitjacket on fire, "they doped me up with so much Thorazine—and sometimes it has an opposite reaction, you know, so I kept jumping up and down and up and down so much that they gave me Prolixin by injection, but then there was all this water pouring out of me—floods of it—so they had to hook me up to an IV of water. I really thought my life was going to end.

"Creedmoor was a waste of time, but Mid-Hudson was

worse. At this conference we had, with Nurse Gallagher and Dr. Tebken, Dr. Tebken said they'd let me out if Mother would let me come home, but Mother said, 'Well, I have my husband, and he's a problem to me already, and I just can't put up with *both* of them anymore.' So they sent me to Creedmoor, and I stayed there for another year and a half."

Robert remembers Mrs. Gallagher warmly. "When I was in seclusion, she came to me once and brought me a whole green pepper. Just to eat. Whenever I eat a green pepper, I think of her."

He says that Shirley and Jules Brody came to his rescue. The Brodys had lived in the apartment house two buildings away from ours on Martense Street, and their sons, Gary and Burton, had been our best friends. In the early fifties, when I was in my first year of high school, the Brodys bought their own home in the Bellerose section of Queens, thus becoming our first friends to leave Brooklyn for the suburbs.

"At Creedmoor, when I was on line in the cafeteria one time, this woman who was dishing out the food—it may have been a holiday, or some kind of collation for the rabbi—she looked at me and I looked at her—she was a volunteer—and I realized it was Shirley Brody. She couldn't believe it was me."

The Brodys invited Robert to their home when he had passes, and when Robert was at Mid-Hudson and Burton (who had graduated from Columbia while Robert was at Hillside) was teaching nearby at Bard College, Burton spent time with him.

"On their last day in Queens," Robert says, "Mother gave me all her change. I was supposed to be on my way out of Creedmoor at the time. Mother didn't really want to go to Florida, you know. She went there for Dad, because of his health." He looks away. "And then she bumped him off."

Bumped him off?

"He was very sick, very sick." Robert shakes his head, then suddenly shouts, "*He was sick and tired of living with his first wife, Annie!*"

Did Robert know about the times our father wept because he didn't want to leave New York for Florida—because he didn't want to leave Robert behind?

"Aw," Robert says. "I'll have to speak with him. But listen, Jay, I have a question. Do you think there's a heaven?"

I say that I don't.

"Me neither. When we die we disintegrate, right?" he says. "But listen—what happens if you're cremated?"

You turn to ashes, I say.

"Is that all?"

I say it is, as far as I know.

"I'm glad Dad was buried," Robert says. "I mean, in case there is a heaven, I wouldn't want him wandering around forever as ashes."

I laugh, tell him he's very funny.

"You think so?"

Yes.

He nods. "Don't tell anybody," he says. Then: "Only tell me this: What's the moral of this book you're writing?"

I begin to say something about there not being a moral, that I just want to tell the story of his life so that . . .

"And *you?*" he exclaims, cutting me off. "Why just look at you—and at your age too!"

He stands, starts to leave the room (we are in my living room, in Northampton), turns back. "The moral is—" he declares, *"Take Your Medicine!"*

He is wearing a lime-green T-shirt, baggy shorts, argyle socks, and black loafers, and he holds a juice glass in one hand. He does a graceful soft-shoe across the living room, and at the doorway he twirls, turns toward me, waves. "And—*Face the Music!*"

He dances out of the room.

10

FROM THE TIME I left New York in 1966 until the fall of 1974, when our parents celebrated the first anniversary of their move to Florida—years during which Robert traveled from Creedmoor to Gracie Square to Mid-Hudson to Creedmoor (again) to South Beach—I published five books (and wrote one other, never published). I sold stories, essays, reviews, screenplays. In the eyes of others (and sometimes in my own), I was a writer. I seemed, that is, to have been doing just what Dr. Laqueur had urged me to do a decade before: getting on with my life without being so concerned about my brother.

As writer-in-residence at the University of Massachusetts, I earned a salary sufficient to support me, my writing, my family.

I was the father of three healthy children. I had a handsome home in a peaceful, rural setting. I had, it seemed, a life very different from the life I had known as a child, and very different from any I had ever believed might one day be mine. To my (constant) amazement, I had not, it seemed, failed at the things I cared most about, I had not killed anyone, and I had not gone mad.

These were also years during which, when people asked about Robert—about how I dealt with him, about how I dealt with my feelings about him, and with my fears for him and for myself—I would sometimes say that though I still broke down after visits occasionally, or second-guessed myself (what I'd said, what I hadn't said, what I'd brought, what I hadn't brought), I found myself getting through these visits by acting as if there were two Roberts: the brother I grew up with, and the brother who was now hospitalized. It was as if, I would say, the brother I grew up with had died. Was this too cruel? Perhaps. But it was what I often felt: the brother I grew up with had died, and now another brother had taken his place— a brother who looked very much like my first brother, and who shared many things with him—a history, a wonderfully idiosyncratic sense of humor, a love of books, movies, and art, a sweet generosity of spirit, memories, feelings, desires . . . but who seemed, sadly, a very different person, with a much grimmer, narrower life.

(In the fall of 1990, after being found wandering around a Staten Island cemetery with a bunch of flowers in his hand, Robert tells his social workers and doctors that I am not his "real" brother. We had two different mothers, he insists, and she has been keeping this secret from us her whole life long.)

To imagine that there were two Roberts, I would explain, enabled me to be with Robert and to care for him without, while I was with him, feeling undue (*undue?!*) sadness, or hope. But by imagining Robert this way I seemed, often, able to make things easier for both of us: I could spend time with him in the here and now, accepting him as he was without grieving over what had been, or what might have been, or what might never be—without, that is, having any expectations other than that we be together.

By imagining there were two Roberts (as it were), and by having no hopes or expectations for the one who was alive now other than that, if possible, he have a bit more comfort and pleasure—and much less misery and pain—I found I could spend time with him, most of the time, without making things harder for him *or* for me (though often my patience ran thin, and all I could do during a visit was to think about how and when I could get away). I could spend time with Robert without making him feel that he (or I!) was somehow *to blame* for his fate. I could spend time with him without making him feel that he had, by becoming a mental patient, somehow failed me, or himself, or life.

(What did it mean, I would say to friends, when Robert said about his life and his actions, "I wasn't myself," or "I was far gone," or "I was out of my mind"? If he was out of his mind, whose mind was he in, or who was in his mind? And if he was far gone, who was close and here? He might not *seem* to be himself, but since he was always Robert, if he wasn't being himself, who, then, *was* he?)

Imagining that there were two Roberts, as it were—one who had died, and one who was (still) living—helped for a while. But it wasn't so. Robert had never died, nor had I ever, in my imagination or my feelings, killed him.

During the first three years after our parents moved to Florida, I saw Robert several times a year (sometimes at South Beach, sometimes in New York City), and we spoke by phone—sometimes two or three times a week, but sometimes only two or three times a month. Far from the home Robert and I had grown up in, I was, during these years, in my new home and new life, devoting most of my energies to raising my children, teaching my students, becoming active and involved in my community, and writing my books and stories.

Our parents saw Robert not at all, and in long letters my mother often made no mention of him, or referred to him in only a single sentence. There was either no news ("Haven't heard from Robt," she wrote shortly after she moved to Florida, and added a sentence she would repeat in letter after letter, "so believe no news is good news")—or good news ("Robert called—sounds good as new again")—or bad news ("Guess you know Robt is back in hospital—Staten Island").

The bad news, however—the chronic nature of Robert's life—gradually drove out the good news, and encouraged my mother to hold more and more to a belief she had been nurturing for years: that Robert be kept "permanently" in a mental hospital, and be given work there ("Robert called . . . and he is back in Staten Island—sick, sick, sick. It seems to me he should be given a job in the frame-work of a hospital and kept there—I said this so long ago, and now repeat my thoughts. So what's new?").

In the spring of 1975, on the day I sent off the manuscript of a new novel (*An Orphan's Tale*), I felt suddenly, to my surprise, as if I could not go on with my life. I was on my way home from the University of Massachusetts and had just deposited the manuscript in a mailbox when I found myself having an enormous and uncontrollable urge to step out in front of an approaching bus.

I felt exhausted in a way that puzzled at least as much as it frightened. Since my life was truly over, I reasoned, why go on? I was, I knew with certainty, going to destroy either myself or others, and I was going to do so soon. I stood at a street corner, near the mailbox and bus stop, trembling slightly, feeling distinctly lifeless, and wondering what was going to happen next.

If nothing moved me, I did not know how or when I would move. If somebody pushed me into the oncoming traffic, why resist? If nobody pushed me, I might stand where I was forever. If I drove home and one of my children (then ages five, two, and one) resisted me and said no to something—*anything*—I asked one of them to do, I saw myself turning maniacal—saw myself picking up that child by the ankles and smashing the child against a wall, or hurling the child through a window.

Realizing that this was so—that not only could I imagine myself hurting (or killing) one of my children and/or myself, but that my imagination could, the way I was feeling, swiftly *become* reality—that the boundary between imagination and reality seemed to be swiftly dissolving—stirred me momentarily.

Still, I felt dizzy, limp, tired, and, as I recall, unbearably sad and life-weary, as if all the disappointments, betrayals, and burdens of my life—with family, publishers, friends—were there with me, paralyzing me. But why was I feeling this way *now,* I wondered, when I should, if anything, have been celebrating the completion of a new novel—when I should have been taking pleasure from the good life I seemed to be living? Didn't I have everything I thought I wanted in life—a marriage, a home, a family, children, friends, a good job, published books . . . ? And if I had these things, and they were good, and I had worked hard for them, why were the awful and terrifying feelings that had been with me, intermittently, my whole life long, especially those of shame, guilt, and rage, still with me, and—with this sudden, frightening rush—more *powerfully* than ever?

Traffic stopped, the bus moved away. I stepped from the curb, and walked across the street with others, and it was then—back in the literal flow of life—that I realized I was feeling very much the way I had felt on the night, thirteen years earlier, almost to the day, when I had received the call from my parents telling me Robert had had a psychotic breakdown and had been hospitalized.

My greatest fear was about to come true, I sensed, and it might not be so different from my greatest wish: that I would soon be where Robert was, physically *and* emotionally, and that once there, surely—given my lack of goodness and character, my inability to love, my unworthiness to be loved, my cowardice, my selfishness, and my transparent fraudulence—I would not deserve, as he did, to be helped by anyone, or cared for, or loved. Since, like others, I had abandoned him, why would everyone *not* abandon me? My good life had, clearly, been bought at the expense of others, and now it was time to pay up. The only solution—the price—was obvious: for me to disappear from the face of the earth.

For years, when I felt feelings, and intimations of feelings, like these, I had resisted the idea that I was, in fact, more like Robert than I sometimes feared I was—and I surely resisted the idea that I needed psychological or psychiatric help in any way, or that I could not work any and all problems through on my own. (For most of my life, too, until this point, it had never occurred to me that I possessed anything resembling an imagination, or a gift for storytelling. Robert had been the imaginative and creative child, I believed, and despite the evidence of the books and stories I had conjured up and written, I also believed—in what was doubtless a way of keeping what imaginative gifts I had separate from my fear that *any* imaginative gift was inevitably and fatally informed by madness—that I had written them, and come to publish them, only because I worked hard and persisted—because I was, in the prose narratives I invented, being solely and essentially *prosaic*.)

Until this point in my life I had believed that I could, by sheer force of will, win at and accomplish most things I set my mind to (thus, my books, my family, my political activities, my job). Then, too, I had, for thirteen years, known and witnessed the worst of American psychiatry, psychotherapy, and psychopharmacology, the worst mental hospitals, the worst and most inept therapists. What, in any sustained way, in this world, had *ever* helped Robert?

When I arrived home, I quickly closed myself in my office, telephoned my family doctor, and, getting through to him, told him about what had happened, and made an immediate appointment. In his office, my hands trembling, my heart pounding away in my ears, my teeth actually clicking, I told him I felt spent and suicidal—that all my resiliency seemed gone, that I felt I could not go on alone, and that I feared I would never write again.

Had I had feelings like this before? he asked.

Only twice, I said. The first time, in 1962, when Robert had been hospitalized; and the second time, in 1963, a half year later, when, a few weeks after Betsey and I had become engaged to be married, she called from Indiana (where she was finishing her last year of college while I was in New York, teaching at Columbia) to tell me she had, several nights, gone back to her old boyfriend.

When the doctor asked what I thought had precipitated the feelings that brought me to his office, I said that it was the completing of the novel (a novel that told the story of a thirteen-year-old boy who runs away from an orphanage that is closing—because of the new abortion laws, there are not enough orphans to keep it going—in order to enlist the aid of the orphanage's alumni in *saving* the orphanage). I had, I said, reviewing my literary history for him, been devastated two years before when an earlier novel, *Sam's Legacy,* on which I'd worked for six years, and for which I'd had enormous hopes, had pretty much died, as if stillborn, in the marketplace. I had lifted myself up from the floor of my feelings, plunged ahead, and written yet another novel—this new novel, which I loved as if it were one of my own children—but the instant I put the manuscript of the novel in the mailbox, all my strength seemed to slip from me, and fears—especially of failure, madness, and humiliation—had come roaring up from within.

My family doctor referred me to Jean Franklin, a psychiatrist who had recently begun to practice in Amherst (and who had, I later learned, been a concert pianist as well as the first woman appointed chief psychiatric resident at Harvard Medical School), and, a few days later, I went for my first therapy session.

I had through the years, I thought, come back again and again from failure and rejection. (Although I was getting my books and stories published, in the decade between the publication of my first novel and the time I sent off the manuscript of *An Orphan's Tale,* in addition to the more than two thousand rejections I received before *Big Man* was published, I accumulated over a thousand additional rejections.) Despite the vagaries of the literary life (who had asked me to write? Who had promised that if I wrote, I would be published? Who had promised that if I were published, my work would be read or treated fairly?), I had continued to do the work I loved. I had not gone mad like my brother, or failed like my father, or put on what I had come to see as the often sadistically narcissistic personality of my mother. Why, then, I asked Dr. Franklin, did I suddenly feel so fearful, murderous, ashamed, and—most of all—*depleted?* Why so forlorn, and so terribly sick at heart? Why this constant, bone-deep, nauseating feeling that no matter how much I did, for myself and others, I, somehow, had no existence, no *right* to exist?

I could *understand* my fears and my history well enough, I thought: I had, clearly, invested an enormous amount of actual and psychic energy in my writing, and in my identity as writer—if, then, my writing failed (in the marketplace), what, of me—of who I was—would be left? If I wasn't a writer, who and what was I? If I wasn't, in the eyes of others (as I perceived them looking at me), a worldly success, was I nothing at all (the nothing our father had been)?

And if I had written the books I wanted to write, and made them as good as I was able—and if I had become a parent who had *not* visited upon my children the confusion and misery that had often been visited upon me and Robert—and if I knew such things to be so, why oh why did this knowledge suddenly seem worthless?

When, at the end of the first session, I got up to leave, Dr. Franklin smiled, and urged me to return. "I think you'll see," she suggested, "that it will be worth your while."

A few sessions later, I recall saying that I often felt as if there were a curse in our (Jewish) family that was not unlike the curses in Greek tragedies, and that this curse had been passed down from generation to generation, strewing casualties along the way: from my mother's parents and grandparents to my mother (and her sisters and brother) to Robert (and our cousins). What I wanted, I screamed through my tears, my stomach grinding against itself, was for the curse to stop with me. *I want it to stop!* I cried. *I just want it to stop! I want it to stop with me. . . .*

The immediate feelings that overwhelmed me on the day I sent off the new novel faded after a few months, but I stayed in therapy for the duration—three times a week for six years (and, later on, two times a week for an additional eight years), accomplishing work there that, I believed, not only saved my life, but made small, slight changes in me, and in the way I understood my life, and in the way I lived it. (My wife, Betsey, though grateful for the changes, saw my sessions with Dr. Franklin as a betrayal of our marriage and declared early on, and throughout my years in therapy, that she would never rest until I was out.)

How I made these changes—the process that brought them about through well over a thousand hours in Dr. Franklin's office, and in the life beyond her office, where our work made itself felt slowly and surely, if with enormous fluctuations, and with what often seemed only a mild lessening, in my daily life, of struggle, doubt, tantrums, and intermittent depression—is another story, about which, while getting on with the story of Robert's life, and of how it affected my life and was in turn affected by it, I will, here, note this: that, along with my parenting and my writing, the work I did with Dr. Franklin was the hardest and most rewarding of my life.

In the summer of 1976, shortly after *An Orphan's Tale* was published, I arranged for a conference with Dr. Bilby, Robert's therapist at South Beach. Dr. Bilby, like Dr. Franklin, was a bright, attractive woman in her thirties. We talked about Robert's most recent breakdown and what might have precipitated it. We agreed that in his wanderings during the previous fourteen years—from hospital to hospital, ward to ward, therapist to therapist—one of the cruelest facts of his life was the very itinerant nature of that life.

Given Robert's life and history—its ravages and its fragility—how much harder when there was no professional person— no doctor or social worker—whom Robert could depend upon in good times and in bad, on ordinary occasions and during crises. How much more unsettling for him, we agreed, was the absence in his life of constancy and continuity.

With great feeling, Dr. Bilby told me how much she *liked* Robert, how determined she was to stick by him. No matter what happened, she said, or where her duties took her, or where Robert was—*now and forever*—she was going to be Robert's doctor, she promised, a constant presence in his life from this time forth. And this very fact—of knowing, day after day and year after year, that he would have a doctor who would always care about him and be available to him—might itself make all the difference in the years, and the life, to come.

Then she asked me about my own life—my children, my teaching, my therapy, and, especially, my writing—telling me not only how much Robert talked about me and my books, but how fascinated she was by novelists and by "the creative process." She asked where she could obtain copies of my books.

When I rose to go, she smiled warmly, shook my hand, and then, as I was about to leave her office, she called to me.

"Mr. Neugeboren?"

"Yes?"

"You're really quite different from your brother, aren't you," she said.

"I guess," I said, and though in part flattered—pleased to have my difference and achievements appreciated, especially by a bright, attractive woman—I remember, at once, feeling strangely helpless. I said nothing, but shrugged, as if to say: What do you mean—*different*? I have my life and he has his.

"It's really remarkable," she said.

•   •   •

"Well here I am again," Robert wrote from Mid-Hudson, in late September 1976, "and it's not a short story. The truth is 'the' parents reneged on my visit [to Florida] and now Aunt Mary . . . [is] listed in the N.Y. Supreme Court as not only my codefendant but also: as 'my mother;' meanwhile I always thought I favored Uncle Arnold but I at least I made it thru bailhood."

"Jacob I miss you very much," he wrote a few weeks later, at the close of what turned out to be the last letter he would write me for a dozen years, "please write or type a response." He signed the letter "Robert Schleeta, your kid brother, frère Robt Gary." He drew a self-portrait, and added a PS: "I forgot to add that I loved your new book [*An Orphan's Tale*] and so did Dr. Bilby—could you please phone her—I also could receive calls."

On the morning of December 23, 1976, our father, who had not seen Robert since the day in October 1973 when he and my mother left New York, died. He was seventy-two years old, and he passed away in his sleep, in a hospital in Florida where he was resting—his emphysema acting up—after having had his lungs pumped out.

A year before, in December 1975, when I was visiting my parents in Florida, I had found that my father and I were able to talk with each other in a way that was wonderfully new—easily, frankly, naturally. During a walk together one afternoon in Century Village, we stopped and sat by one of its canals and he told me that he hoped I wouldn't take what he was going to say the wrong way, but he wanted me to know that he was really quite happy in his new life here. His one regret was not being near Robert, he said, and his one wish, he confided, was that he be able to die without seeing his wife put away in a mental hospital like Robert.

For most of his life, he had believed he was the major cause of my mother's unhappiness. But now, he said, gesturing to the palm trees and the sunshine, she had everything she wished for, and she was no different. "You don't know what she's like, Jay," he said then. "How she'll be fine one minute, and then the next, it's like a wind blows through her, and she's a different person. She wakes up some days and just starts walking from room to room, all day long, going on and on about how this one hates her, and that one is against her, and how everyone's ganging up on her, and then she starts phoning every person she knows. She opens her address book and starts from the letter A, and goes through it from beginning to end, and if I try to get her to calm down, it only makes things worse and the next thing I know she's banging her head against a wall, or sitting down on the living-room carpet and tearing at her hair, or telling me I'm as bad as the rest—that all I really do is wait for the chance to criticize her and tear her apart. . . ."

Now, a year later, the news of my father's death tearing me up, I called and asked for Dr. Bilby, but was told to speak, instead, with a social worker newly assigned to Robert's case. I did, after which I spoke with Robert and gave him the news. Robert said he wanted to come to the funeral.

When I told my mother that Robert would be coming, she screamed that she didn't want Robert to come—it would only make things harder for everybody! What, seeing him, would people *think*? There was enough suffering in the world—why should Robert come and have to suffer more? I said that my father was Robert's father too, and that if Robert wanted to be there and could be there, I would help him to get there.

I spoke with Robert and his social worker, and made arrangements: while I would be flying to Florida with my wife and children, Mary and Arnold would see that Robert was taken to their house in Brooklyn. Together, the three of them would take an airplane to Florida.

When I met Mary and Arnold at the West Palm Beach airport the next day, however, Robert was not with them. Dressed in jacket and tie, he had walked from the hospital, suitcase in hand, opened the door of the car Mary and Arnold sent for him (the driver was a social worker Robert knew), then shook his head, closed the door, turned, and walked back into the hospital.

My father was buried the next morning, and my mother spent the hours before the funeral wandering around her apartment, talking to the walls as if she were talking to Robert, and then, in Robert's voice, answering herself.

"Robert, my love-child, where are you, darling? Why weren't you here today? Where are you? Where are you, sweetheart? . . . Here I am, Momma . . . here I am! . . . Can I bring you a wash cloth for your headache, Momma? . . . Can I get you a pillow? What can I do for you, Momma? . . . Tell me . . . tell me, my beautiful Momma. . . ."

When we returned from the cemetery, my mother's first act was to unkosher her kitchen—to mix the meat dishes and silverware with the dairy dishes and silverware. I suggested she not do something she might, in a few days, regret, but she shot back that she'd kept her kitchen kosher for *him* for forty years, that she was sick and tired of doing things she didn't believe in. Now, at last, she was going to live her life the way *she* wanted!

Later that day she invited me into her bedroom, apologized, said she would try not to act so impetuously again. She asked me to go through my father's belongings, to take what I wanted. (I went through his possessions and discovered that, after seventy-two years of living, the only things in the world he had that were his own—the only things in their apartment that bore the least impress of his personality—were a few drawers of cheap, stained clothing, and two narrow shelves of books: prayer books, and books I had given him as gifts.)

I called Robert that evening. He was flying—no two sentences connected, a dozen subjects crashing against each other in any one sentence: had I seen the new Orson Welles movie, and did I want a mink coat, and I should be careful about letting my arm get cold if I was trying out for the baseball team, and were my children still alive, and Mayor Lindsay was the best mayor but the Kennedys were all cousins like the Ruben-sohns—but when I told him that at the graveside while I recited the Kaddish I had imagined him beside me and had said Kaddish for the two of us; when I said something about being proud of him, and about how hard it must have been for him—when I said, simply, that our father was gone, that we had loved him and he had loved us, and when I added, "And I love you, Robert," his manic stream of words stopped abruptly, his voice dropped into one that was completely natu-ral—"I know, Jay. I know. Thanks. . . ." Then he was off on his flight of words again: about King Kong and pogroms and stamp collections and Ali Hakim and lithium levels and bank accounts and life insurance and baseball gloves . . .

"Oh, Robert darling," my mother said, first thing, when she got on the phone, "I'm so *disappointed.* We were all expecting you!"

A week later, when the *shiva* period was over and I drove my mother around West Palm Beach to take care of financial matters, she talked with me about how hard on my father she had been, about how terrible their marriage was. Driving around in an air-conditioned, locked car, from bank to bank, along vulgarly built-up commercial strips, she seemed calm and focused in a way I had rarely seen her.

"I know he loved me," she said. "I never doubted that. Maybe he loved me too much. Can you love somebody too much?" She laughed. "I never should have married him, but he just wouldn't take no for an answer, and he kept pursuing me and pestering me so much—and I liked it. Let's face it, Jay—I needed to be worshiped and told I was loved a thousand times a day. But it was no good between us and I used to worry about how it affected you and Robert, that we stayed together through all he years and all the battles. Maybe it would have been better if we hadn't, but times weren't so modern then, and—you know what?—I'm not sure I ever really knew what I wanted. I'm not sure if *anything* would have satisfied me. It's the way I'm built, I guess. I like to think I've done pretty well in life, given my childhood and what I was up against afterwards, only"—she looked away—"only sometimes, I guess, I'm not so proud of myself."

Three weeks after this, Dr. Bilby telephoned to tell me she had been given an opportunity she felt she couldn't refuse—a promotion to an administrative position elsewhere at South Beach, and that she would not be able to see Robert any longer. I said something hard and direct, about broken promises and broken lives. She assured me that Robert's new therapist would be excellent, and our conversation ended.

A few months after this, in a long letter about her life in Florida, my mother wrote to tell me of how she had solved the problem of dealing with Robert and his history: "Have not heard from Robt—so have to assume no news, is okay too. That last phone call made me sick—when he told me how he was beaten up because they caught him 'peeping' into a doctor's window and thought he was Sam." (Sam—"Son of Sam"— whose real name was David Berkowitz, the same name as one of Robert's psychologists [for a while, when "Son of Sam" was his psychologist, Robert also had a psychiatrist whose name was Dr. Pavlov], terrorized New York from July 1976 to August 1977, killing six and wounding seven.) "I do get Robt nitemares," my mother went on, "and they don't help my feelings. However, the last job application I finally was able to say '1 child' to the question 'how many children' 'any mental illness, etc.'—answer to latter 'no.' Dad would be proud of me finally being able to tell the 'white lie.' "

In the year following our father's death, Robert was let out of hospitals six times, and readmitted seven times.

"I remember being awakened one night by the police," our Aunt Mary writes. " 'Do I know a Robert Nugent? He has gotten into a street brawl.' I went out to see him. He was well bruised—all he wanted from me was cigarette money. When I spoke to the doctors at Bellevue they said he was badly overdosed and they would dry him out. Another time I got a call from Kings County. When I saw him it was the same picture—he had broken a window with some books, got into another fist fight. He was very glad to see me—and asked me to bring him some cheese blintzes and cookies—I came the next day with his requests. Guess what he did? Handed every one in his ward most of what I brought."

The conditions on the wards Mary visited were "not to be believed," she says—patients living in their own excretions, rats and mice crawling over people. "But no matter how confused and banged up he was," she writes, "Robert was always very glad to see me."

From the time our parents left New York in 1973 until the mid-eighties, when, in his forties, Robert began to spend longer periods of time outside hospitals and to be able, increasingly, to care for himself, the elements that had made up his life and the story of his life during the dozen years that followed his first breakdown became the constants of his life: hospitalization and discharge and readmission, a college course or two, a vocational rehabilitation program, a part-time job, a welfare hotel, a halfway house, a run-down apartment, a violent episode, a court hearing, a journey through the madness of New York City emergency psychiatric wards (Kings County, Bellevue) before being returned to his designated "catchment area" (South Beach), where he would be treated by (yet another) new doctor, new therapist, new social worker, new drugs . . . in and out, out and in, breakdown and recovery, recovery and breakdown, breakdown and recovery . . .

By 1978, when deinstitutionalization reigned and Robert was being treated now with one drug and now with another (and with enormous variations in dosage), was now in one hospital and now in another, now out and now in and now out again, the three places that had previously promised the greatest hope for cure were gone: Dr. Laqueur's unit at Creedmoor had been abolished; Dr. Cott and his megavitamin therapy had been discredited; Hillside Hospital had locked wards, and most patients were permitted to stay there for no more than ninety days (or until their insurance ran out).

And by this time, too, my parents and I were gone from New York, and, for the most part, from Robert's life.

When I began to write about these years—the years when I was not a daily, or even weekly or monthly, presence in Robert's life—I found that though the elements of his life seemed apparent enough, repeating, as they did, their sad themes and variations, I could not, on my own, or with Robert's help, make much sense of this period other than to note what I have already noted: that his life was rich in confusion and unhappiness, and that, if with a more complex accrual of memories and experiences, it kept returning, again and again, to a sad and familiar series of disasters.

Whenever I have asked Robert about these years, his answers have been, at best, curt and cryptic, and when I asked him about the possibility of going through his medical records— to corroborate dates, medications, doctors, et al.—he rejected the idea at once. "No!" he said, and he turned away from me. "What for? I mean, what for, Jay? What would you see in them except that I went to sleep and ate and got up and took drugs? No and no, so don't ask me again."

Though I persevered with work on the book (and though Robert continued to ask how the book was coming along, and if I needed to know more; he often telephoned, collect, saying to the operator, when asked to identify himself, "This is Imagining Robert, and I'm calling for William Morrow"), I continued to have doubts about the enterprise. I thought, too— especially when I would ask Robert about his life and times in mental hospitals—of a review I had read years back by Paul Goodman of Robert Coles's book about the survivors of Hiroshima, in which review Goodman said, simply, what has always made enormous sense to me: that it *was* a bit much, after all, to drop a bomb on people and then to ask them how they felt about it.

• • •

"When I was on Stelazine, all I talked about was bowel movements," Robert says. "Then I was at Beth Israel—I'm not sure how I got there, but I was only there for a few weeks. And there were the SROs—no, not Standing Room Only, but Single Room Occupancy. There was a shelter on the Lower East Side I stayed at, and one night I rode the subways all night, and then I went from hotel to hotel. The Granada, and the Nevins, and to some YMCAs."

Robert mentions other places he stayed at: the Brooklyn House of Detention, the Rikers Island prison, Mrs. Binum's apartment (a foster home), an apartment on Pierrepont Street, a cooperative on the Lower East Side, an apartment on East 25th Street.

"The worst place was where I put down my pants to take a shower, and when I got out, my pants were gone. The rooms were terrible—small and seedy, and they smelled.

"Then I got my Social Security money and I bought a motorbike! I didn't like it, so I gave it to a boys' club. The brake and the starter were on the same handle and I couldn't figure out how I would know the difference, so I gave it away.

"I was living on Staten Island then. I went to DVR [Department of Vocational Rehabilitation] and drafting school, and they put me in a place called the Institute for the Crippled and Disabled, so I said to them: 'That's an awful name, don't you think?' So they changed the name to ICD—that was because of me. I did piecemeal work for them.

"I also worked at Altro—I learned some printing, and got twenty-two or thirty-two cents an hour." He raises his eyebrows. "And they took out for Social Security too."

How did he get to Rikers Island?

"Ah," he says. "That was the famous Norman Morrison affair! I was preparing to set Pierrepont Street on fire. In those days I was ringing a lot of alarms. I had a little room, and he claimed I wasn't supposed to be living there, so I started a fire and they arrested me for arson. They took me to Rikers Island, to await trial, and I was there for three months." He sighs. "I thought it was the end of my life. Really. It was awful, Jay. It was very rough there. You don't want to know."

Buggering?

"At least," Robert says. "I was in a cell by myself. I thought it was a luxury, but it wasn't. Me and a potty and a window. I looked out at the play yard and thought it would be fun to go there, but it wasn't. . . .

"They had a library and I filled my cell with books: Joyce and *Remembrance of Things Past* and Dostoevsky. Then they took me to trial, I think for being put into South Beach. I was also in the House of Detention then . . . I don't remember it very clearly. I started hoarding books again, and when I was discharged to the streets I was given a subway token. That was all. I went to my friends Grover and May."

Robert is still friends with May (they met when they were both patients at South Beach), who is disabled by multiple sclerosis and lives in a nursing home in Queens, where Robert continues to visit her about once a week (the round trip, by bus and subway, takes him four to five hours) whenever he is living outside hospitals.

"I remember this one time, walking through Manhattan with my shoes off, having fantasies, and just walking and walking, early in the morning. I just kept walking—up to Columbia. I had shorts on—they were beige—and my fly was open. And then I stopped and took my pants off, and I laid out all my cards—library cards and credit cards and the rest—and they arrested me and took me to Gracie Square."

And the long scar, on his cheek?

"Oh, that! One morning I made a joke with some prostitutes and they didn't get the joke, I guess, because one of them broke a Coke bottle and cut me with it."

He asks if I'm going to put everything he says in the book, and I say no—that I won't put anything in the book he doesn't want in it.

He rubs his chin. "Even though I hate you, you're still good to me," he says. "You always took care of me, but you know I hate you, don't you?"

I laugh, say yes—that we're brothers: think about all the brothers in the Bible, I say: Cain and Abel, Jacob and Esau, Isaac and Ishmael. We're carrying on a tradition.

"Well, I love you too," he says, and then his voice shifts and he begins asking me a series of questions—how big will the book will be, and what are we going to call it (he has two new suggestions for titles: *A Stigma on my Back,* and *The Romances of Robert Gary Neugeboren*), and how much money will we get for it, and will it have pictures.

"I think there should be pictures," he says. "But of places, not people, or maybe some line drawings, like the ones I used to do."

I say that I like the idea of pictures, and that in the hundreds of letters I've been going through I've found some marvelous drawings and self-portraits he made.

"Isn't it wonderful to have been sick," he says. Then: "Well, at least I'm getting something out of it." He is quiet for a while before he speaks again. "The only trouble, though, Jay," he says, "is that my world only goes so far."

"I weep when I think of such suffering for Robt and man's inhumanity to man to allow him to go to the outside world and cope," my mother wrote early in 1978, and she went on to say what she had said before about Robert's being kept in a mental hospital permanently ("Call from Robert—revolving door once again to put a sick mind out of secure surroundings once again—such a grief. Why do I meet people who have the same situation—and their child is permanently in Creedmoor . . .").

During these years, however, under the new deinstitutionalization policies governing state hospitals, what my mother wished for was no longer possible for Robert, or for most people with his history and condition.

In 1961, a year before Robert's first breakdown, the Joint Commission on Mental Health had published a report recommending that the care of the mentally ill be shifted from large state hospitals to community mental health clinics. In February 1963, President Kennedy sent a special message to Congress on mental illness and mental retardation, one in which he blasted the "cold custodialism" of mental hospitals and called for a "bold new" program of comprehensive community care.

In October of that year, a month before he was assassinated, he signed the Community Mental Health Center Act, under which community clinics received federal funds if they provided essential inpatient, outpatient, and emergency services to the mentally ill. Large state and county hospitals began discharging their patients, and so between 1964 and 1973 the population of all state and county mental hospitals in the United States decreased from 452,000 to 252,000, while in New York State, between 1968 and 1974, the number decreased from 84,000 to 38,000. (In December 1995, it was below 10,000.) What generally happened, as with Robert, was that as soon as a patient was "stabilized chemically," he or she was released to places—the streets, hotels, rooming houses—at least as terrifying as the hospitals they had been in, and without any viable plan for their care. Community mental health clinics were either underfunded, understaffed, overworked, poorly run, or— most often—nonexistent.

In New York State, this policy was given greatest impetus by a June 19, 1968, Department of Mental Hygiene directive. The directive called on mental hospitals to send patients like Robert out into the streets with all due speed. ("We therefore request the directors of state hospitals and their medical representatives to scrutinize more closely the condition of persons who are candidates for admission to their hospitals and to determine prior to their admission whether or not such persons are suitable for care and treatment. . . .")

The vast majority of those called "candidates for admission" were, of course, those who, like Robert, already had histories of previous (and multiple) admissions. (In 1978, for example, of 2,759 people admitted to Creedmoor under the new guidelines, 1,853 of them had previously been at Creedmoor. And in the summer of 1992, three decades after the policy of de-institutionalization was initiated, when my state, Massachusetts, was sued for discharging mental patients and sending them into the community without *any* plan, medical or otherwise, for their care, the Department of Mental Health, and the state attorney general's office, in defending the DMH, claimed it had "no continuing responsibility" for patients released to the streets, and no obligation to protect them, or others from them.)

Under New York State laws, patients could be held for only fifteen days if they were involuntary, and except in very unusual cases for no more than ninety days if they were voluntary. Bellevue, for example, where Robert was hospitalized several times, was, in the early seventies, receiving from 250 to 350 patients a day on its psychiatric ward. The policy that sent most of these patients careening from city wards to state wards to sleazy hotels to the streets and back to city wards was, according to Dr. Alexander Thomas, psychiatric director of Bellevue's ward at the time, "straight out of Kafka."

My own life during these years—my family life especially—was not without its changes and difficulties. In the summer of 1981, shortly after my eighth book, *The Stolen Jew,* was published, and shortly before our third child, Eli, began school full-time, my wife asked for a divorce. In the fall of 1982, she moved out of our home, and not long after that, in the early spring of 1983, I filed for divorce, and agreed to a joint custody arrangement that was, by any measure, insane, unworkable, and especially gruesome for the children. The divorce became final in the spring of 1984.

The following year we went through reviews, investigations, and hearings concerning custody, and a few months after these were over, at the start of 1986, the children's mother decided to move about forty miles north, to a small town near the Vermont border, and the children chose to live with me full-time. In 1989, while the children were teenagers, their mother moved away again, this time to North Carolina.

During the years I was going through divorce and court battles, Robert did not visit me in Massachusetts, and there were times when neither I, my mother, my Aunt Mary, nor South Beach knew where he was. ("Made a few calls," my mother writes on a postcard in May 1983. "Robt is in S.B. Psychiatric Inst. and I spoke with him—he is getting better. So I hasten to let you know since Mary said you have been trying to locate him.")

In late March 1984, shortly after my divorce became final, I visited Robert at South Beach. I had visited him there a month earlier, and when I entered his ward, one of the aides recognized me and called out, "Robert Neugeboren—visitor!" I turned away for a second, dealt with the swarm of patients who crowded me, turned back, stared at a small, hunched-over, toothless man who had wandered into the hallway and who stood, stiffly, about twenty feet away. He looked like one of the many little old men—lost, deteriorated, shapeless—I had often seen at Creedmoor. When the man turned my way, and tried to smile, I realized he was Robert. I spoke his name, and moved toward him. He shuffled toward me, we embraced, and, his mouth against my neck, he began sobbing.

After I returned to Massachusetts, I wrote my mother about this visit, trying, with words, to reassure and comfort her no less than I was trying to reassure and comfort myself. I wrote that Robert was "subdued but coherent," that he "joked and laughed and was able to sustain reasonably normal conversations. We went for a walk down to the beach, got a snack, sat around for a few hours—which tells you something. He is, of course, very heavily sedated, and has deteriorated physically. He has only one tooth left in the top of his mouth, is overweight, etc. But [sic] he has not been out of the hospital for over a year and seems to be getting good supervision. He asked about you and I told him your divorce was finished. . . ." (Our mother had remarried a year after our father's death; she divorced her second husband in 1984.)

Once my children began living with me full-time, I found myself seeing Robert more frequently, and, as before, talking with him by phone most days. In October 1985, when I married again (this marriage lasted only until the fall of 1987), Robert came to Chevy Chase, Maryland, for the wedding. He looked better than he had in two decades. The in-out shuttle from hospital to the streets (and to hotels and emergency wards) had stopped, and he was preparing to move out of South Beach, into an apartment program.

And once my second divorce was final, I found myself making a greater effort not merely to take more active responsibility for Robert (calling his therapists and doctors, finding out about medications, halfway houses, etc.), but, simply, to be with him more often—something I did not out of needs alone (his and/ or mine), but out of desire: because I missed being with him, because I missed having him in *my* life in a sustained and constant way.

Robert began visiting more frequently again—for birthdays, holidays, special occasions (Passover, Chanukah, the Jewish High Holy Days, Aaron's and Eli's Bar Mitzvahs), and for no reason other than that I invited him, or he invited himself ("Listen, Jay," he would say when we spoke on the phone, "Greyhound is having this special round-trip fare this month, so I was wondering . . .").

As my children moved from their early to their late teens, I was able to leave them by themselves more frequently, and Robert and I spent more time together in New York, often meeting on West 76th Street and hanging out together in the neighborhood where we had lived next door to each other a quarter of a century before. During these years—from the time I saw him at South Beach in March 1984 until the night of Eli's graduation in June 1993—he seemed, if with some faltering, to have reversed the course his life was set upon, and to be making steady gains for himself in all ways. I began to believe—to hope—that perhaps his illness had, in his middle years, somehow, happily, burned itself out. Robert lived outside hospitals in halfway houses and supervised residences most of the time, his hospital stays were of shorter duration (usually for three or four months), and there were some years during which he was not hospitalized at all.

Thus, for example, in June 1987 he was able to travel, by himself, on trains and buses for over a dozen hours, from Staten Island, to Ithaca, New York, in order to attend the Bar Mitzvahs of our cousin Madeline's two sons. At the time he was working across the street from South Beach, at Staten Island Hospital, doing clerical work in the accounting department, and living on the grounds at South Beach, in Beacon's halfway house.

Most of our family—cousins, aunts, uncles—had gathered in a restaurant, a converted railroad terminal called the Station, on the Friday night before the Bar Mitzvahs. My mother had last seen Robert, me, and my children at my second wedding two years before. We embraced, she made a fuss over her three grandchildren, hugged and kissed her sisters, her nieces and her nephews, and then she looked around the restaurant, smiled, reached across the table, extended her hand.

"Well, hello," she said to the well-dressed man sitting across from her. "I'm Anne Neugeboren. Who are you?"

"I'm Robert Gary," the man said. "Your son."

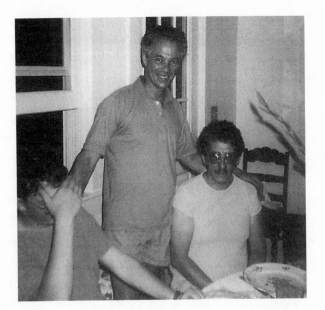

II

ON THE LAST SUNDAY in March 1991, twenty-nine years
after Robert's first hospitalization, I travel to New York City
to visit with Robert and to tell him that I've decided to write
a book about his life. I drive down to Springfield from my
home in Northampton, leave my car parked across the street
from the Amtrak station, and take the train to New York
City.

All the way down, and the next morning, when I take the
subway and ferry, to get from Manhattan to Staten Island,
I think of how I'll give Robert the news, and, to my surprise,
I find that I'm not rehearsing my words the way I often do,
or worrying about his reaction—about whether or not what

I say and don't say will help or harm. I find instead that I'm feeling that when we're together the words will, simply, be there.

If I fear anything, it's not Robert's reaction, but my own inadequacy: I'm frightened I won't be able to write the book because I don't *know* enough to write it—that I don't know enough about writing, or mental illness, or about Robert; that I don't know enough about *anything*, and that I've forgotten and won't ever be capable of summoning up all the crucial matter—all those small incidents and details that were the essence of and made the difference in our lives.

Then, too, I wonder: how make a story out of five decades of someone's *life*? Where and how, since stories end but ongoing lives do not, will I find a beginning, middle, and end—a narrative thread I can pull through? How ever imagine, with any accuracy—with any truth—what any single moment or hour or day of his life has been like for him?

Mostly, too, I find myself wanting to reassure Robert in the way I want to reassure myself: I find myself hoping he will understand that I'm not interested in writing about his life in order to exploit him or embarrass him, to find villains or to designate blame, to come up with answers to how and why he's led the life he's led, or to what mental illness is or is not and what we can or can't do about it, but in order—simply, and most of all—to tell his story as best I can, and thereby be a witness to his life, in all its complexity, uniqueness, hope, and despair—in all, that is, that makes it fully human.

Tell the story, Jay, I keep saying to myself. Always, always. Just tell the story. For in the making and telling of stories there lies, I believe, not anything as grand (or illusory?) as salvation (who is saved, after all, and for what?), but something more fundamental and human: the pleasures that come from knowing, feeling, and remembering. As painful and grim as any experience, or any life, may be, to be able to transform it into story, like the act of remembering (which creates life even as it retrieves it), can often offer us a kind of consolation—and, sometimes, of joy—unlike any other.

I stay overnight at 150 West 76th Street with Harvey Rosen, a friend who lives in the same two-room apartment he lived in twenty-five years ago when he was a law student at Columbia and I was newly married and working, in the apartment adjacent to his, on *Big Man,* and when Robert was living in the building next to ours.

I wake suddenly on Monday morning—it's seven-fifteen, and I realize I've forgotten to set the alarm clock Harvey put out for me. I shave, dress, gather my stuff, phone Robert to tell him I'm on my way—we've arranged to meet for breakfast on Staten Island, at the Country Club Diner—and I'm out of the house, walking to the 72nd Street subway, by seven-thirty.

It's a gorgeous early-spring morning—the sky a pale, cloudless blue—and I take the IRT down to South Ferry, stay in the first car, stand at the front end so I can watch the train rocket through the tunnel. I love the subways as much as I did when I was a boy, still marvel at the worlds that exist below ground, and below rivers, in layers and caves, and in the flickering half-light of enormous curving tubes.

On the ferry I sit outside, and I find that it feels wonderful, simply, to be between here and there, where nobody knows me and nobody can reach me, and to know that I'm on my way to see my brother. My brother Robert has a life of his own, I think, and I smile, hearing the words. *My brother Robert has a life of his own:* a simple sentence that belies the wonder of his life, and fixes itself in my mind. Surely there is an immense and pervasive sadness at the core of his life; it is so much less than he and those who knew him hoped it might be. Still, it is infinitely larger than most of us feared it would be. And in this, as in so many other things, I think, how different from each other are we really?

I picture Robert in his present home, a single-story dwelling supervised by Beacon of Hope, and I imagine him waking and washing, dressing, walking down his front steps and along his street, boarding a bus and showing the bus driver his disability card, paying his reduced fare, and journeying across his island, from an opposite direction, to meet me.

I gaze out at foaming whitecaps, at patterns that appear and disappear on the steel-green, oil-slick water, and I think of marbleized swirls on endpapers of leather-bound books. I remember being told—but by whom?—that in ancient times the Greeks would cure those who were mentally ill by sending them to live on peaceful islands, far from all that was noisy, troubling, and familiar. My feelings float from me, hover in the air above the water: How different are we really?

I live in a hundred-year-old three-story Victorian house paid for mostly by a bank.

Robert lives in a somewhat newer one-story ranch-style house paid for by a Catholic charity.

I live with two teenage sons, Aaron and Eli, whom I love and like, though we drive one another crazy at times.

Robert lives with two housemates, whom he likes, but who drive him crazy at times.

I earn a living teaching students at a state university; Robert earns an income working in the gift shop of a city hospital.

Robert and I are about the same height, we both have curly hair, we both wear glasses, our physical gestures are similar, and our sensibilities—our likes and dislikes in music, art, books, movies, politics, people—are close. When we tease and joke, we delight in similar kinds of nonsense and wordplay. . . .

From a distance, to some creature to whom our civilization is alien, would Robert and I seem less different than two ants working on a trail look to us—than two cows grazing in a meadow?

A cool wind seems to pass through my mind, clearing it of its usual clutter and rush, and I find that I am seeing Robert very clearly, and that he is smiling at me because he sees that I can't stop smiling, and I hear myself saying to him that at the risk of being sentimental about us, I'm wondering about this too: What is love, Robert? Beyond family and memory—beyond affection and attraction and tenderness and passion, beyond sympathy and shared moments and all we've known of each other and experienced together and wondered about when we've been apart: what *is* this impossible, mysterious feeling that seems to pass beyond blood, beyond explanation, beyond memory, beyond imagining, and beyond history?

Then, suddenly, I am seeing a square, illustrated frame, and another, and another, and I recognize the pictures that move across my mind as if on a scroll, and I make a connection so obvious I can't believe it's never occurred to me before. No wonder *The Corsican Brothers* was my favorite Classic Comic when I was a boy. No wonder it stayed with me, made its way into so many of my stories. If one of the Corsican Brothers was hurt or in danger, no matter how many miles apart he was from the other, he would feel the pain. I continue to see the separate frames, in motion on the screen inside my mind in the way they were in motion on the page nearly fifty years ago: I watch one brother leap onto a horse and ride furiously—through forests, across rivers—in order to come to the other brother's rescue. . . .

The ferry docks. I move quickly through the crowd so I can be first off. I follow Robert's directions, take the Number 79 bus, and it caroms through the streets of Staten Island, through Italian, Spanish, and Irish neighborhoods. As we veer around one corner, barely missing parked cars, I see a Salvation Army Dumpster, recall the time I loaded my car with boxes and bags of clothing, rags, and junk Robert had pressed on me. On my way home, I pulled in next to this Dumpster, stuffed into its mouth all that he had given me.

When I arrive at the Country Club Diner, it's nine o'clock—the time we said we'd meet—but Robert isn't there. I sit in a booth, read a Stephen Jay Gould essay in *Natural History* magazine in which Gould reflects on his childhood in New

York, and on how deceptive and inaccurate, when he has gone back to check, his own memory of things has sometimes proved.

The restaurant is as Robert described it—bright, airy, pleasant, busy. I drink my coffee, wonder if I've arrived too early, or if Robert is lost, but then—nine-twenty—I look up and he's coming quickly toward me, loping down the aisle, smiling, talking even before he sits. He looks wonderful.

He is dressed, as ever, with flair—but somewhat more coherent flair than at other times: he wears a rust-colored double-breasted suit, a purple red-and-white-flocked silk hand-tied bow tie, a black beret, an ivory-white silk scarf. The mustache he has had for about a decade is full and neatly trimmed. His hair—wild, close, thick brownish and gray curls—glistens as if threaded with silver, and his skin, despite the scars and the years, seems amazingly soft, like that of a young man just beginning to shave.

His brow furrowed, he leans across the table—he wears thick-lensed eyeglasses like our father's—and tells me he's very nervous about coming to the screening that evening, in Manhattan, to see an *American Playhouse* film, *The Hollow Boy,* for which I've written the script ("Should I wear a *tallis?*" he asks. "Is it like a Bar Mitzvah? Will I have to get up and say something?"), and before I can reply, he is off on a nonstop monologue: about what he did in his home that morning, which buses he caught, how much money he has—to the penny—and expects to have, what he wants to eat and which number breakfasts are the bargains, how much different cigarettes cost, how much he won and lost on scratch lottery tickets the day before, which buses and/or trains he should take when he comes to visit me in Massachusetts the next week for Passover, and what gifts to buy for the children—he doesn't know what to get them, or, for that matter, who they are ("I can never tell them apart, your sons")—and how he *knows* they don't like him even though he's their only uncle, and about how his cholesterol is down to 217 and about his diet ("I *cheat,*

I *cheat,*" he whispers), and about his job at the hospital and how he doesn't want to work there forever, but maybe he could get a gardening job, or a job in food or hotel management, or go back to college, and about how he's smoking a lot and about how much he sells cigarettes for to other patients and what his profit is, and how he doesn't like the ferry but he likes his roommate Dan but can't stand his roommate John, who turns on the TV and starts laughing no matter what's on, but that John claims he's begun looking for another apartment and has finished auto school and is looking for a job in a body repair garage . . . and I sit there silently, amazed at his energy, happy simply to be with him.

"Listen—about my legacy from my *dear* Aunt Pearl . . ." he says, and starts in once more about money, asking if I know how much our mother's sister Pearl, who died a year before, has left him. I say I don't, though I know that other than what she left to her two children, Carolyn and Ronnie, Robert is the only person to whom she left anything. Robert asks why, and I say Carolyn assumes it's because Pearl too had been hospitalized for mental illness.

I start to tell Robert about my memories of visiting Pearl at Hillside when I was six or seven years old, but he interrupts and presses me for details about his legacy (he will, we learn a few weeks later, get twenty-five dollars on the first day of each month for the next fifteen or so years), and then is off doing figures again, about exactly how much he gets from the state and from Social Security and for clothing allowance and from his jobs at the hospital and from finding deposit cans and bottles and from getting cigarettes for Dan, and about how much his coupons and rebates and special deals amount to if he goes back to Atlantic City before the end of the month. . . .

We order breakfast. As soon as the waitress leaves, I take a deep breath. "I have some news—" I begin.

"Oh—am I getting another legacy?" he asks.

"Not quite," I say, "but you will be getting some more money. I'm going to write a book about us."

He smiles broadly. "Am I going to be rich and famous?" he asks.

I laugh, feel some nervousness slip away, though I notice that my hand, holding a fork, trembles. "I don't know about fame," I say, "but I'll be getting an advance and I'm going to give you part of it, of whatever the book earns—"

"I think we should speak with Rudy about this," he says.

Rudy is Robert's social worker, and I've made an appointment for the two of us to see him later that morning. Robert and I talk some more about the book, and what might be in it—Robert is adamant about its *not* becoming a movie ("Everyone will be looking at me and knowing me—I'd have to hide"), but when I say I was frightened he would not want to talk with me about it, he is surprised.

"Why would you think I wouldn't want to talk with you?" he says, and then he changes the subject and for the next twenty minutes or so, while we eat, it is as if I'd never mentioned the book. Robert talks about the people he wants me to meet in the gift shop, and at the day center, where he spends most of his days. He talks about the coffeemaker Rudy gave him, about his VCR (which needs fixing), about what he does when he goes to Atlantic City, about how he doesn't like how gray his hair is getting and how he's started tinting it with hydrogen peroxide, about how much he hates his medications, and about how scared he gets at night if his roommates are gone and he's left all alone in his house.

When he pauses, I find myself talking—trying to explain to him *why* I want to write the book. Given how quickly he changed the subject, I'm afraid I have hurt him with my news; to my surprise, however, the more I talk, the more he smiles. And the more he smiles, the easier it is to say things—directly, feelingly—I didn't know I was going to say: that I love him very much, and that I also admire him enormously. Getting through life on any given day is hard enough for most of us, but to have had your life and history—to have been through all the shit you've been through for thirty years and still to have your energy, your humor, and your desire to get on with things—this takes real courage, I say, and if I can tell your story—if I can get it right—I think it can be a help to many people, and to many families who've been through and are going through what we've been through. Your story is the most important story of my life, I add, and before I leave this planet, I'd like to be able to set it down.

I pause, expecting Robert to object to something I've said, or to make a joke. Instead, he keeps smiling at me. I say a few more things about the book—that I'm not *only* being altruistic, that I'm writing the book for me too, that few things in life give me as much pleasure as writing, as the making of stories—but now Robert interrupts and says we should leave so we can tell Rudy about the book. First, though, he has to go to the men's room.

When he comes back, I go to the men's room, but when I return to our table, Robert is not there. I look around, see that he's at the cashier's booth, and that our check is gone.

"You paid?" I ask.

"Listen, Jay," he says, "you're on *my* island now."

Rudy is about our height, has a scruffy salt-and-pepper beard, a diamond in the lobe of one ear. He wears a striped-blue short-sleeved shirt, and is very energetic and direct. He talks about himself (he loves tennis, loves living in the sun, is going on a vacation to Mexico soon), about South Beach's history (originally its swimming pool was to be open to the general public), about his favorite books (Joanne Greenberg's *I Never Promised You a Rose Garden*, Rabbi Kushner's *When Bad Things Happen to Good People*), and about how he intends to write novels someday. He gives me several bookmarks. Across the top of each, in five horizontal lines, and in various fonts, are a series of names: Abraham Lincoln, Virginia Woolf, Beethoven, Leo Tolstoy, Vincent van Gogh, Isaac Newton, Michelangelo, Winston Churchill, Patty Duke, Michael Farraday, and others; below the names, in bold red letters, there is a message: **PEOPLE**

WITH MENTAL ILLNESS ENRICH OUR LIVES; and below that, an explanation: "These people have experienced one of the major mental illnesses of Schizophrenia and/or Manic-Depressive Disorders."

Robert is mildly restless—standing and sitting a lot—and after a while he tells Rudy that he has good news. When he says I am going to write a book about him, he turns away, but once he has given Rudy the news, he faces him again, and seems to relax. Rudy asks him how he feels about it.

Robert shrugs, looks down. "I don't see what's interesting about me," he says.

Rudy says he finds Robert *very* interesting—and that he thinks my writing the book is a wonderful idea. Why? Because it will reduce the stigma attached to mental illness—because the more people can see that those called mental patients are fully human, the better. He says that the most courageous people he has ever known are the mentally ill people he's worked with—inner struggles are always the hardest and most important ones, aren't they?—and that he wishes people *out there* could understand this.

Rudy asks if I have a title for the book yet, and I say the working title is *His Heart, My Sleeve.* Rudy says he likes it.

What do you think of it? he asks Robert.

"I don't like it," Robert answers.

What would you call it? Rudy asks.

"I'd call it *My-Brother-the-Ex-Mental-Patient,*" Robert says.

Less than three months later, Rudy is transferred to another part of South Beach. Robert and I schedule a farewell conference with him for June 10 (the same day, it turns out, that New York City has scheduled a parade to welcome home American troops from Operation Desert Storm), and before the conference, Robert and I meet at the Country Club Diner again for breakfast.

Robert talks about how his back still hurts from a fall he took on a staircase in my house a few weeks before, and how he went to an emergency ward on Staten Island and waited eight hours for blood tests and X-rays (all negative). He asks if I brought him a check, says he is going to sue me for falling down my stairs, goes over the menu nervously, looking for the best deal, talks about how much he lost on lottery tickets, and about how he wants to buy a condo with the money he gets from the book. When our food comes, he reaches across and grabs food from my plate. "It's just like eating with Mother, right?" he says.

He jumps from subject to subject, is at me constantly for a response (yet never gives me time to answer his questions), and he rarely finishes sentences of his own: about how he is scared about the two Germanies becoming one, about the war in Iraq, about his new "chopped" haircut, about his medications and their awful side effects, about sleeping and not sleeping, about old girlfriends—his and mine—about lottery tickets and subway tokens and the cost of cigarettes and special deals on trips to Atlantic City. . . . Within five minutes of being with him, I feel exhausted: as if I've been immobilized in front of a jet engine that keeps blasting away at me full force.

But Robert is no jet engine, and what fires his stream of worries seems real enough. When I ask about our conference with Rudy, he slows down, becomes thoughtful. "Rudy is the best therapist I ever had," he says. "He's of the caliber of Abe Schwartz." Robert says he liked Abe a lot, but that Abe once confided in him that he thought black people smelled different from us. "I told him it was none of my business how they smelled," Robert says. Then he says that he didn't sleep at all on Saturday night—two nights before—and that he is *not* going to tell Rudy this, and he gives me an elaborately detailed description of how he spent his sleepless night: listening to cars and trucks going by, moving his air conditioner around, rearranging his room.

The day is intensely hot and humid—the temperature and humidity in the nineties—and we walk a mile or so, from the diner to the hospital. Robert stops at every newspaper kiosk, soda machine, candy machine, and telephone booth, to see if there is change in the coin returns. We walk across parking lots and fields of weeds, and Robert keeps looking for money—picking up pieces of paper, going through garbage, showing me the spot where he says he once found a hundred-dollar bill.

On the bulletin board in the day center there is a hand-lettered sign in red, blue, and green about my *American Playhouse* movie, with the time and channel listed, and a notation: "Screenplay by Jay Neugeboren, brother of Robert Gary." When I say that I'm going to meet with some people the next day to talk about the possibility of writing a script for another movie, Robert asks if it's going to be about him.

No, I say.

"Then I'm not interested," he says.

He introduces me to everybody we meet and everybody who passes by—aides, patients, his new therapist, Ellen ("She looks just like Ethel Merman, doesn't she?" Robert whispers), and his new psychiatrist, Dr. Chandra (Robert asks her several questions, none of which she answers).

Robert has brought a farewell gift for Rudy—a wallet and key ring he bought at a yard sale—and he has wrapped it in paper on which he has written "rapping paper." Rudy thanks Robert for the gift, says he will miss him, that one of the downsides of working for the state—for any large institution—is that transfers and changes in personnel occur frequently, and that you have no control over your assignments. He maps out, on paper, an explanation of how South Beach works—how clients are referred from one division to another. He says that there's really not much chance for any therapy on the inpatient wards like Baltic, and if patients don't get out of them quickly, sometimes they "get stuck."

The staff is overworked and outnumbered, he explains. If you have fifteen patients one day and forty the next, and if one is a ninety-three-year-old woman depressed because her husband died, and another is a nineteen-year-old boy acting like a maniac, how can you do anything much except to try to contain the situation? Containment, he says, is all that's possible until a patient gets to the day hospital or becomes an outpatient. And, as all social workers know, anytime you have more than twenty patients on a ward, you're really dealing with crowd control, not treatment. Once a client gets out of the ward, however, he notes, South Beach is probably better equipped than most hospitals to provide support and resources.

Robert has little patience with Rudy's explanations, and he begins complaining loudly that one of his roommates didn't write down a telephone message for him the week before. He tells Rudy he hasn't been sleeping, and Rudy says, "Good—! We want to know your symptoms as soon as possible, so we can help." If Robert doesn't tell them what's going on, Rudy says, it would be like a man with chest pains going to a doctor, not telling him about the pains, and then going home and having a heart attack.

Robert talks on and on about money—how he doesn't want *any* restrictions on how he spends the money he gets—and when Rudy says that he used to go to the supermarket with one of his clients, who was a drug addict, to make sure his client had food, Robert becomes angry, screams that he is *not an addict,* then turns to me and accuses me of "dangling" money in front of him.

I say that I'm not dangling it—I just want us to agree on the best way of giving it to him so his benefits from Social Security are not jeopardized, and so he actually *gets* the money and can use it. Rudy says something to Robert about my also wanting to be sure he is cared for should something happen to me, after which he changes the subject and asks Robert how he feels about this being their last session together.

Robert never answers the question. Instead, he talks at length about being angry with Sally, the social worker in charge of his apartment program. Rudy says he hopes he'll get Robert as a client in the outpatient department someday, when Robert has a job. He also asks Robert how the sessions with me are coming along, for the book.

When Rudy asks this, Robert calms down for the first time. He says that the sessions are okay, that he doesn't always like talking about the past and remembering things, but that he supposes it's good for him, and that it's good—he can't find the word at first—to *exorcise* things. No, he says, correcting himself: to have some *catharsis*.

He turns to me, touches my hand. "Do you know why I cry so much, Jay?" he asks.

I say I don't.

He presses his fingertips to the sides of his eyes. "To relieve the pressure inside my head," he says. And then: "I'm not afraid of dying anymore, though. I used to go to sleep at night and be afraid I'd never wake up. . . ."

Rudy has brought a book for me, Milton Mayeroff's *On Caring,* and he gives it to me now, and inscribes it: "To Jay— This is the most important book I've read in my life and I'd like to share it with you. Sincerely, Rudy Kvenvik."

He says he looks forward to reading our book one day, and that in his opinion the best thing about the two of us working on the book together will be the ways in which, by coming to know each other better, it will bring Robert and me closer.

"You know," Robert says, and he speaks very deliberately, "that what I decided is that I won't finish college. And I'm too old to be a messenger. This is my life—I work at the hospital, and I'm a volunteer, and I'm an uncle, and I go to Atlantic City sometimes."

The ferry is filled with sailors, soldiers, and families on their way to celebrate the victory over Iraq. There are battleships and aircraft carriers in the harbor, blimps overhead advertising insurance companies and doughnuts. I listen to a man ordering his wife around, telling her she never does anything right, while she deals with their small children, shows them how to wave their flags. I hear another woman—a career officer in the Navy, in dress whites—complaining to a fellow officer about the limited selection of cable channels they get on her base, about how "disgusting" it is they can't get Cinemax, how the Defense Department only cares about low bids, not about people.

Robert is mildly antic, threatens to make caustic remarks to some sailors about earning a living by destroying cities and murdering women and children, but he never does. He says that maybe he'll use his money for driving lessons, or for buying a car and car insurance, or for buying a condominium, or for his education—to take more college courses. If he goes back to college, he wants to know, do I think he can still get money from the state scholarship he won thirty years ago?

We talk about Rudy, and Robert shrugs—his eyes are moist, I notice—and tells me that one time at South Beach he had eight different social workers in six months. When we get off the ferry—we see ticker tape falling in the distance, hear bands playing for a parade which, the papers will later report, nearly five million people attend—Robert kisses me, says he has things he wants to do, and runs off through the crowd.

A week later I come to the city again, to meet with Robert and his new social worker, Ellen. I have received the first payment for the book, and have brought a check with me, made out to Robert. I meet him at the day center, and though he, Ellen, and I have our conference in a small lounge, Robert starts the conference by talking in an incredibly loud voice, as if addressing a large and distant audience. Whenever Ellen and I try to talk, he interrupts. There is a scale in the room, and he keeps getting on and off, weighing himself, says his lithium is acting up, making him pee all the time. Then why don't you just go to the bathroom? Ellen suggests. Robert laughs and leaves the lounge, and when he returns he is calmer.

He talks about the things he wants to do with his money: first of all, he wants to pay off a debt he has at the bank; then he wants to buy a hair dryer and a blender, to sign up for cable TV, to join a health club, and—maybe—to take driving lessons.

When Ellen asks him about the book and what parts of his

life it will cover, Robert grins. "Well," he says—a line he uses at the start of almost all our sessions—"I was separated from my mother at a very early age—" He stands. *"It was all mother's fault, you know!"* he shouts.

If only it were that simple, I say.

"Yeah," Robert says, and he sits. "You're right."

Robert, Ellen, and I go over a letter I have written to Robert, stating the terms of our agreement, and the three of us sign it.

"Now can I get the money?" Robert asks.

We talk about Rudy, about what I might and might not include in the book, about Robert's activities at the day center, and about how much they bore him. Ellen says she has read through Robert's case history, and she ends our conference by stating that she thinks Robert is doing exceptionally well in all areas: in his apartment, at his jobs, at the day center, at getting around the city on his own.

After our conference, we visit Rudy in his new office. He is between clients, and we talk for a few minutes—Robert's left hand keeps flapping uncontrollably—and then walk to a bus stop on Seaview Avenue, in front of the hospital, where we wait with about a dozen others who have just come from the day center. Robert introduces me to them. They range in age from their late teens to their fifties, and they are all dressed neatly. Were they going around New York City separately, they might not seem at all noticeable. In a group, however, their differences seem more apparent: they have minor facial and gestural tics, talk either very loudly or very softly, and have somewhat drugged (stiff, sluggish) bodily movements, and there is, in the halting, eager, shuffling way they move—in the timidity, the slight fear, the endless questions they ask and that their eyes ask—something strangely, unnaturally childlike about them.

They seem to be asking of each thing they do—whether getting on the bus, or lighting a cigarette, or going to a meeting, or brushing their hair—*Can I manage this? Will I be all right? If I can't manage it, will somebody help me?*—*or will somebody*

punish me? If I think I can't manage what I am about to try to do,
will you help me? Will you take my hand? Will you lead me
through? Will you stay with me no matter what?—or will you soon
be leaving me too . . . ?

They seem very happy to be together, and they also seem—
in their teasing and their jokes, in their endless bartering of
tokens and cigarettes and transfers—to have a sure sense and
appreciation of one another's qualities and of one another as
distinct and separate individuals.

Robert sells his token to a friend, then uses his Disabled
Citizen card to get a reduced fare (fifty-five cents instead of
$1.15) for the bus. Somebody asks Robert for a loan, and he
says no, but he whispers to me that he has loaned Dan thirty
dollars and that Dan *always* pays him back. When Robert and
I get off the bus to go to the bank, everybody says good-bye
to me, some telling me they have seen my television show,
that Robert advertised it well.

During lunch at a Chinese restaurant, Robert offers me ten
dollars, in case, he says, I can't find a cash machine that will
take my Massachusetts bank card, and I accept the money. We
talk about the book, and Robert begins telling me things he
remembers—about our grandfather, our parents, our cousins,
Martense Street, Camp Winsoki. He asks me, again, about my
cancer, and when I say that after thirty-four years I don't think
I'm in any danger—that the cancer is gone—he asks what
happened to it.

They took the cells out when they operated, I say, and sent
them to a pathologist.

"That's sickening," he says, and then he laughs, and we talk
more, about his jobs, his home, his friends, and it occurs to
me that just as he keeps trying to set himself free from the
prison that has been his life, so I too—by setting down his
story—keep trying to set myself free from the fears and inhibitions that have been with me for most of my life. It seems
lovely to me—a wonder—that we can sit in a restaurant together and talk freely about things we had thought we were

forbidden to talk about, or write about, once upon a time. Robert is as relaxed and happy as I have seen him in a long time, and while we eat and talk and reminisce, it is as if the years have disappeared—as if we are living again on some ordinary day in the time before Robert ever saw the inside of a mental hospital.

When we leave the restaurant, the heat—it is 101 degrees outside—is brutal. Robert walks me across the street, to my bus stop. I will head south, for the ferry, and Robert will take a bus in the opposite direction, to return to his home on Hylan Boulevard. A few minutes after we cross the street, however, he sees his bus coming. He kisses me good-bye, and heads back across the boulevard—across six lanes of traffic—his satchel swinging at his side. The satchel is loaded with cigarettes, with shirts he bought at the thrift shop, with empty soda cans he will redeem, and as he hurries across the street, he seems, despite the heat and despite his age and despite the years—despite his life!—as light and graceful as he has ever been. He runs quickly between cars, dancing across a road that shimmers from the intense summer heat, racing to catch his bus before it leaves, and while he runs—he stops at the island in the middle of the street, turns, and waves to me—I see the graceful boy he once was, alive still within the body of this forty-eight-year-old man who is my brother.

POSTSCRIPT

IN EARLY DECEMBER 1994, when staff members tell
me, several days in a row, that Robert is on isolation and is
not permitted to receive any telephone calls, I call Dan Farrell
at the state's regional office and ask if the hospital is allowed
to take away Robert's right to receive calls.

Two days later Henry calls me. "Well," he says, "you certainly know how to get our attention!" He tells me the hospital
has received calls from the regional office, and that he is upset
because whenever the state gets involved they "kick up a lot
of dust and there's a lot of fallout." After he assures me that
he really *likes* Robert, as the entire staff does, and describes for
me, yet again, what Robert can be like when he uses the pay

phone, I express my concern about the length of Robert's stay on Baltic this time (a reversal of his pattern of the last decade), and wonder, as I have before, about trying some of the newer drugs, clozapine and risperidone in particular, that have proved helpful for patients with Robert's history. Henry says he will look into this, and promises to call me once every two weeks to keep me informed.

Two weeks after our talk, while Henry is on vacation, Robert is four-pointed (for attacking an aide), and, for the first time in the twenty years since he was first hospitalized at South Beach, he is transferred to its maximum security unit.

I write a letter to the director of South Beach, requesting a thoroughgoing medication review, and Dan Farrell speaks to various people at South Beach, endorsing my request, and telling them, among other things, that I am "an investigative reporter with good access." He tells me that he does this not in order to scare them or make them defensive, but to "keep them awake."

Robert is kept on the security unit for ten days. While there, he receives a full medication review, the result of which is that the doctors decide to (gradually) take him off lithium and Klonopin and to put him on risperidone.

His improvement is swift. When Henry next calls me, four weeks after returning from his vacation, he says that Robert is in excellent shape—"the best in years"—and he asks if I have had a reply to my letters from anyone at South Beach. When I say I have not, he tells me he will take care of this.

For about two months, Robert makes steady gains. He is lucid, warm, funny, energetic. He talks about how much less heavy his head feels, how he can taste foods again, how he is sleeping through the night, and—mostly—how *clear* everything is. He gets all his privileges back, sends me and my children notes (and wonderfully engaging self-portraits), consults with me about birthday gifts for Miriam and Aaron, and begins talking about what he hopes to do when he gets out of the hospital.

In the year before Eli's graduation, Robert and I had gone

to Atlantic City together twice, and he reminds me of the time he hit the jackpot there and won over four hundred dollars. "I become electric, Jay!" he says. "I just become electric when I'm playing the slot machines. Can you tell? Can you tell?" Given his breakdown the weekend of Eli's graduation, he is wary of coming to Northampton again soon ("Henry suggested I never visit you again," Robert tells me), but we talk about going back to Atlantic City, and about making a trip together to upstate New York, to visit Camp Winsoki, and to go to the horse races at Saratoga Springs the way we did four decades ago.

He also tells me he's begun reading again. "I can actually read *books*, Jay," he says, "and I'm reading this wonderful book by Robert Somebody about what we learned in kindergarten, and I'll save it for you, and it's the funniest book I've ever read, and can't you see how my concentration is much better?"

Yes, I say. I can.

"What'd you say?" he asks immediately, and then laughs.

He asks often about our mother, who has been transferred to the Morse Geriatric Center. (There, the first thing the staff does is to take her off tranquillizers. Within a few weeks she becomes fully ambulatory again, and begins participating in activities. "Your mother is back to her old self," one of her nurses tells me. "She spends most of her time walking around the home telling everybody what to do." I hear from the staff at Morse regularly, and receive a telephone call each time my mother has any kind of problem—when she bruises her knee, when she falls, when she strikes or is struck by another patient, when she scratches herself in her sleep. In a few months, how- ever, she will no longer recognize either me or her sister Evelyn, and will spend her days, for the most part, wandering aimlessly, and folding and unfolding clothing.)

When I tell Robert about our mother, he asks if he can write to her, and I say I will send him her address, but that she doesn't seem to know who anyone is anymore, and that she forgets everything.

"What does she forget?" Robert asks.

Robert's recovery, alas, is short-lived, and when I visit him in March, he is back on isolation and tranquillizers ("It's the Doctor-of-the-Month Club, and the Pill-of-the-Day," he says), and he has, again, begun peopling his ward with friends and relatives from our childhood. (Henry's agreement with me, to call every two weeks, is short-lived, too; in the four months following our talk in December, he calls only once to report on Robert, and after that, he rarely calls unless I call him first; nor do I ever hear back, by phone or letter, from anyone else at South Beach. Henry also tells me—this happens later—that if and when Robert is ready for discharge, he will go to a residence in Brooklyn, because, he says, "between you and I, Beacon is pretty shitty." It is "not working" for Robert, or for their other patients, and they are trying to find "other places.")

"Why did God create sick people?" Robert asks several times during our visit. "Tell me, Jay. Tell me." And later: "Why did God create mental illness and cripples?"

He asks if I am his doctor, and if I still have cancer. Was mother a prostitute, and have I buried her yet? Was Mrs. Klein our mother? Was our grandfather really W. C. Fields? Is Joey Leifer going to stay on his ward? Can we say Kaddish together for him?

"I hate you, Jay," he says to me frequently, between hugs and kisses (while kissing me, he licks me, tries to suck on my neck). "I hate you even though you're good to me and love me. You know that, don't you?"

I laugh, put my arm around him, tell him he's told me this before—hey, we're brothers, I say, we're family just the way other people are—and when I say this he tells me again that he hates me, but adds that he loves me too (I also tell him never to try to bite me, and he shrugs, says he likes to bite people, he doesn't know why), after which he begins crying, and rests his head against my shoulder.

"Oh please, please, Jay, please get me out of here," he says.

"Please, please . . . it's so awful, Jay. You don't know. You don't know. It's so awful."

When I leave the hospital and walk to the bus stop, for the first time in memory there are no tears in my eyes. Nor do I find myself cursing the hospital, or Robert's therapists, or life, or the universe. I feel, simply, very sad, and enormously tired. On the ferry, I begin making notes, but when I imagine transcribing the notes, I stop writing because it occurs to me that any narrative about our visit—any *list*—by the mere fact of being set down on paper will make our time together seem more coherent than it actually was.

How, on the page, record the various pauses, stutterings, hesitations, repetitions, whisperings, droolings, and touchings—the infinite variety of expressions on Robert's face, the thousands of thoughts, half-thoughts, doubts, imaginings, and memories that pass through either of us—without being false to what seems, even a few minutes after our visit, a time marked mostly by randomness, and an utter lack of ordinary continuity?

During this visit, as during all visits since Eli's graduation, Robert talks openly about his homosexuality. He tells me he thinks his operation, at thirteen, didn't result from our fight, but from the fact that he had heard about something called a blow job, but he didn't know what it was and was afraid to ask, so he put a straw into his penis, and kept blowing into it.

He asks me if I have ever had a man fuck me up the ass, and when I say no, he describes what it feels like ("It's like you have to take a bad shit, but you can't"), and then describes his present lover's penis: "It's like this beautiful Tootsie Roll that peels back, only it has a pink tip." (A few weeks later, he tells me that he has lost most of his privileges, and is on isolation again because they caught him "doing it." I ask if he had a good time, and he says yes, but that Henry got very angry with him. I ask if *Henry* lost his privileges. Robert laughs, and when he talks about getting out, I say what I've often said: that he knows what he has to do to get the staff to let him out—that as arbitrary or infuriating as their rules may be, if he wants to get out, he's going to have to obey them—to obey their fucking rules. "But that's what I was doing, Jay," Robert says. "I was obeying their *fucking* rules.")

When I get back to Harvey's apartment, and Harvey asks why I think the new medication stopped working, I shrug. I gesture to West 76th Street and say the first thing that comes to mind: that there are hundreds of thousands of people out there on Prozac and lithium and antipsychotics like risperidone, and that most of them are getting on with their lives because these drugs really do help them to get through. But that's because most of them *have* ongoing lives they come from and go back to, while with Robert, I suggest, given his history, it's as if he is suddenly all dressed up, but with no place to go.

It's possible that in a week, or a month, Robert will start to feel better again, and will get out of his locked ward again, and—who knows?—maybe he'll stay out for a long time this time. But when he begins to feel better, he's not out here with us—he's locked up with thirty psychotics, and if, after a day, or an hour, or a week, he becomes restless, or bored, or if somebody gets in his face, or if he gets in somebody's face, the staff reacts by punishing him—taking away his privileges, sedating him, isolating him.

And then too, I add, there are all those years, all those wards, and all those medications.

What would make a difference, even now? Harvey asks. I have thought about this, since the time, a month or so before, a psychologist friend of mine asked the same question, and I give Harvey the answer I gave to her. Three things, I suggest: competent professionals who would be a constant in his life, and who would have the skills to work with him—steadily and steadfastly, through all his ups and downs; a pleasant place to live, like the supervised Beacon apartment he lived in on Hylan Boulevard; and some regular work that drew upon his mind and capabilities.

Did providing for such basics seem an impossible task? Wasn't it, for example, worth a try, solely on economic grounds, to give him individual psychotherapy once or twice a week? At even a hundred dollars an hour, for, say, two or three years—let's say a cost of twenty to thirty thousand dollars—wouldn't that still be a bargain if it would help him to lead even a minimally productive life outside an institution (where the costs, estimated by New York State, are approximately $125,000 a year per patient)? We don't think twice about paying for medical equipment and surgical procedures that cost staggering sums (and often have only marginal chances of prolonging life), yet we deny people like Robert the (labor-intensive) care that might make a difference across their entire lifetimes—care that, if it accomplishes nothing else, might alleviate, through the years, a measure of their anguish and misery.

A day after my visit with Robert, I take the train down to Philadelphia, to meet my daughter, Miriam, who takes the train up from D.C., so the two of us can go to UMass's post-season basketball tournament (my children and I have been season-ticket holders to UMass basketball games for more than a dozen years), and spend a few days together. Between New York and Philadelphia, and after I meet Miriam at the train station, and during our time together, I continue to reflect on my time with Robert, and to recover from the fatigue that invariably sets in after hospital visits.

I've never been one to believe in quick fixes, and though I remain skeptical about the claims being made for breakthrough medications—the miracle drugs and magic bullets others maintain will soon be curing mental illness—I am also aware that I feel so tired and sad, in part, because I'd been hoping the risperidone *would* work some kind of magical transformation in Robert's life.

For more than thirty years now, I've been resistant to much in the medical model of mental illness (a model that diagnoses

Robert as being *"medication*-resistant"), and to all those forms of diagnosis and treatment that see a person as somehow having a disease (instead of the disease having the person)—and to seeing the disease as something that is *wrong* with the person: a problem, or an error of a genetic or physiological nature that can somehow be eliminated, exorcised, or *fixed*.

When it comes to our feelings and identities, and to those conditions that, as for Robert, bring lifelong grief and suffering, not only are there no quick fixes or easy answers, but, it seems to me, there may *never* be answers. What we know about conditions such as Robert's is mostly, as ever, that we don't know very much—except that these conditions bring great sadness and misery, and that they do not allow Robert, and those like him, to live with the rest of us in *our* world.

But why should it follow from this that there is something innately *defective* about Robert, or that his behavior (whose causes remain unknown) is proof that he has somehow been contaminated? And why do so many people continue to believe that being near people like Robert may contaminate *them*? Why oh why do people still remain so fearful of what is unfamiliar, strange, or, merely, different?

Although I find the rhetoric and research that seek mechanical and chemical answers to what are and probably always will be human problems—that dead-end scientific materialism that would reduce Robert to a flawed, heretical biological inheritance that somehow determines his behavior *and* his fate—I realize that I, too, like my mother and father, and like the families of millions of those afflicted with what we call chronic mental illness, am enormously *disappointed* when the risperidone stops being effective.

Although the notion of "no-fault brain diseases" seems absurd to me, I find myself less inclined, now, to argue with or refute those who believe in it. Surely, blaming parents, siblings, or childhood for causing mental illness rarely helps anyone. Though surely, too, the complex of love, hate, envy, dependency, rage, memory, resentment, shame, bitterness, joy, and confusion that are the matter of all families and communities, of all long-term relationships that possess any substance, cannot be eliminated by catchphrases, or by a deterministic materialism as reductive as it is unimaginative.

For if and when Robert's medical condition is stabilized chemically, as it is, briefly, in the spring of 1995, and is again in the winter of 1996, what then does Robert do with his life on the morning *after* he is stabilized? What does he do with his history? What does he do with his memories, doubts, habits, and fears? The sad truth is that who he is—his identity as Robert Neugeboren and nobody else, a human being forever in process, forever growing, changing, and evolving—is made up, to this point in time, largely of what most of us have come to call his illness. And if he gives that up, as it were—if he denies that this so-called illness is central to his life and being (and if he merely *fixes* its symptoms instead of also understanding their causes), and does not hold on to his illness and its history as a legitimate, real, and unique part of his ongoing self—what of him, at fifty-two years old, will be left?

Which is only another way of saying that just as we cannot separate the mysterious ways in which mind and body interact—the ways in which history, memory, and behavior influence the chemistry of the brain, and the ways in which the chemistry of the brain influences behavior—so we can never separate who Robert is, and how he came to have the life he had, from the life he has, in fact, had, and may yet have.

When, in the late winter of 1995, his medical exam shows no significant kidney, liver, bladder, or gastrointestinal problems, and when, on risperidone, he begins recovering, I find that I am still hoping against hope, and fantasizing a future for Robert in which he will have a life at least somewhat better, day to day, than the life he's had. I don't *expect* my dreams to come true, but I do imagine the following: that Robert will continue to make gains, will leave the hospital in a few months, will live in a halfway house, will get an apartment and a parttime job, and will, within, say, a half-dozen years—when he is about the age I am now—begin to live the way many people his age live: in retirement, spending his next twenty or thirty years, into his seventies and eighties, the way any other person his age might. Who knows what life may yet bring, for him, or for me?

When I walk around Philadelphia with Miriam, and we talk—grown-up to grown-up, father to daughter and daughter to father—in a frank, easy way I never imagined was possible for the two of us a few years back, and when she asks about her Uncle Robert, and I tell her that he's not doing well, I add that it seems to me that what is important about the medical exam, the medication review, and the slight leverage I now have via the state's regional office is not the medications, the brief recovery, or the intervention of the state office, but, more simply, that because of these things Robert sees that we have not given up on him. His life may be sadder and narrower than ours, I say, but neither he nor his life is *less* than ours.

I say this after a conversation in which Miriam has been telling me about her work in the Big Sisters program in D.C. (when Miriam visits her Little Sister Lisa in the projects, Miriam is always the only white person on the bus), and asking my opinion about how to handle a sensitive situation with Lisa. While we talk, it occurs to me, too, that to give up hope for Robert—or for Lisa—would be to do the same thing for *us;* and it also occurs to me that maybe Rudy knew what he was talking about when he said that the most important thing about writing this book would be the ways in which—simply by working together, and coming to know each other better—it would bring Robert and me closer.

The more I know about Robert—and the same, surely, is true about Miriam—the more I keep wanting to know. I think of what a miracle it is that this young woman—my daughter—has a life, mind, and history all her own (one not, at twenty-six, without its own dangerous moments, its unexpected terrors), and a most fascinating and radiant one. I think of how, like her brothers, she keeps surprising me by the ways her actions, choices, and opinions continue to prove thoughtful, responsible, generous, delightful, and—best of all—unpredictable.

So that, as we make our way around Philadelphia together, I sense once again, with my daughter Miriam, as with my brother Robert, that I may just be beginning to understand—beginning, only beginning—the mysterious and unnamable ways in which, no matter the joy or sadness of our lives, knowledge and love often prove to be one.

AFTERWORD

On September 1, 1999, after six consecutive years of living in state mental hospitals, Robert moves into the Clinton Residence, a supervised residence run by Project Renewal on West 48th Street in the Hell's Kitchen section of New York City. The following day, I drive down from my home in Northampton, Massachusetts, and move into a one-bedroom apartment (a sabbatical sublet) six blocks north on West 54th Street. It is the first time in more than thirty years that the two of us are living in New York City at the same time.

Three years later, on September 1, 2002—and forty years after Robert's first hospitalization—we go to dinner at a local restaurant to celebrate the third anniversary of his freedom. This is the longest stretch in his adult life that Robert has lived outside a mental hospital or psychiatric ward. Jim Mutton, the director of the residence, is with us, as he has been for the past two anniversary dinners. After we raise our glasses and toast Robert, Robert thanks us, then announces in his best theatrical manner, "Well, what I want to say is that I'm very happy to be here—," he pauses, then talks more softly, "and I hope I never have to go back to a hospital again."

Robert now spends most days at Fountain House, a community center for people in recovery from mental illness, around the corner from his residence on 47th Street. He has friends, he goes to museums, he shops in the neighborhood, he makes trips out of the city—excursions with groups from his residence and Fountain House—and gets around the city on his own by subway, bus, and taxi. He takes classes—horticulture, poetry, photography—and he also works for pay, as a receptionist and in the training unit at Fountain House, one day a week.

When people ask about his life now he often says that he is "semi-retired." "But how do you spend most of your days?" a cousin asks at a Passover Seder. "How do I spend my days?" Robert replies. He shrugs and gives what seems to him an obvious answer: "I smoke and I drink coffee." Then, seeing the surprise on our cousin's face, he laughs.

Early on in our time back in the city together, when we go to a Chinese restaurant for dinner one night, I tell Robert that the daughter of one of our cousins is going to be married and that there's going to be a family function. "But Jay," Robert says, "our family *doesn't* function."

When I make dinner for us in my apartment one evening, Robert goes on at great length about his friend Bella Shapiro (they were neighbors when Robert lived in the Beacon of Hope home on Staten Island) and how they are getting engaged and are going to be married soon. "But Robert," I interject, "what's with all this talk about you and Bella? I mean—you like *guys*!"

"That's just for practice," he says without missing a beat.

Two years before, shortly after Robert arrived at Bronx Psychiatric Center from South Beach, Dr. Alvin Pam, the director of psychology, telephoned me. Everybody, he said, was laughing about what Robert had done earlier in the day. Asked to provide a urine sample, Robert had gone into the bathroom, filled the flask, brought it to the nurse's station, started to hand it to the nurse, then took it back. "I'd like a receipt," he said.

The fact that Dr. Pam and the staff at Bronx State appreciated Robert's humor and that Dr. Pam called to tell me about what had happened, augured well, I knew. And the fact that Robert could still find ways to laugh about those very things that have been at the heart of so many of his hard times—with regard to his status as a patient on a locked ward, with regard to our family, or to his homosexuality—spoke eloquently of his extraordinary powers of resiliency.

Robert had come to Bronx State because of *Imagining Robert.* After the book appeared we received hundreds of letters and calls, including some from people like Dr. Pam, who offered to help. "No promises," Dr. Pam said, "but if Robert is willing to give us a chance here at Bronx State, we'd like to work with him. We think we can do better."

Robert and I visited Bronx State several times. In appearance it was not nearly as pleasant as South Beach; it was a warehouse-style state hospital, one with large, gated windows and old surgical units for lobotomies. Nevertheless, Robert enthusiastically agreed to a transfer. Dr. Pam later told me, though, that when Robert first arrived at Bronx State it was the general consensus of the staff that Robert would *never* be able to live outside the locked ward of a state hospital.

Dr. Pam disagreed. There was always hope, he believed—he never gave up on what might be possible for any individual—and he and his staff worked with Robert patiently, firmly, and with kindness.

Two years later, in the summer of 1999, when Robert was ready to be discharged from Bronx State, our book again proved a tangible force for good. Arnold Unterbach, Vice President of Mental Health Services at the Odyssey Behavioral Health Care

Residence in Harlem (a halfway house for individuals with dual diagnoses: mental illness and substance abuse problems), had called after he read *Imagining Robert* and, like Dr. Pam, had offered to help. He said he felt a particularly strong connection to us since he too had a brother who had suffered from mental illness, though his brother, Kenneth, had, at the age of forty-nine, killed himself. When I asked Arnold about places in the city he thought might provide good homes for Robert, he said he knew just the right place—the Clinton Residence, home for fifty to sixty men and women, all of whom, like Robert, had experienced long-term serious and persistent mental illnesses—and he offered to call the home's director, Vicky Miller.

The Clinton Residence was a handsomely furnished, seven-story red brick building built in 1990, adjacent to one of the city's more beautiful neighborhood-run gardens. A month or two after Robert's arrival, I met Vicky Miller on 48th Street while on my way to meet Robert for lunch. We talked for a few minutes about our children and the fact that Vicky was in her last months of pregnancy with her second child, and would, alas, be leaving Project Renewal soon, after which she told me that the staff had been discussing Robert that morning. "People kept talking about his symptomatology," Vicky told me, "and finally I said, 'You know what? If you ask me, he's just a pain in the ass.'" Vicky assured me that her opinion would in no way compromise the care Robert was getting—*everybody* at Project Renewal got the best care the staff could offer, but, as in the rest of life, you liked some people more than you liked others. There was illness—sure—but there was also personality. "I mean, this is no secret to you, Jay, but sometimes he's rude, and he's nasty," she said, "and if he's this way with us, how is he ever going to get along with people out here in the world?"

I touched my fingertips to my lips and blew a kiss to the skies. At last, I thought. They are dealing with my brother as a real, vibrant, troubled and often troubling human being, and not as a set of symptoms. They are responding to *him*, glory be, and not merely to his "diagnosis" or "condition."

A month or so later, Jim Mutton called to tell me that Robert had struck a female staff member when she refused to give him a cigarette. Could I come to a meeting the staff was going to have concerning the incident?

I came and sat in with Robert, Jim, Ralph Aquila (Robert's psychiatrist), Rhonda Kudel (Robert's case manager), and Marianne Emmanuel (the staff nurse). Rhonda told me that earlier that day, Dr. Aquila—a dedicated, no-nonsense guy from New Jersey—had called Robert into his office and told him he'd heard about what he'd done. "I'm the head man here," Ralph said to Robert, "so if you're angry, you come and be angry with me. Because I *will not let you abuse my staff*. Do you understand?"

In the two and a half years since, Robert has never again struck anyone at the residence. What impressed me at the time was not Robert's rage and lack of control—I had seen these before—but the staff's reaction. In most other institutions, I knew, had Robert done what he'd done, he would have been sent to an emergency ward or a mental hospital, had his medications increased (sedatives especially), had "privileges" taken away, been four-pointed, put on isolation, or punished in a combination of familiar ways. But the staff here, while letting Robert know that his behavior would not be tolerated, also let him know that they were not going to deport him, punish him, or abuse him—that they were committed to working with him, with all his ups and downs, for the duration. And knowing that he would not be abandoned when his behavior became difficult—being treated honestly, fairly, and humanely—seemed, with time, to enable Robert to act more humanely.

In 1997, during the last few weeks of Robert's stay at South Beach, Larry Hott and Diane Garey had begun making a film based on *Imagining Robert*. For four and a half years they filmed me and Robert in various places, including Project Renewal, Fountain House, South Beach, other hospitals where Robert had been confined (Creedmoor, Hillside), and our old Brooklyn neighborhood.

On April 28, 2002, a week after Robert's fifty-ninth birthday, he drove up to Northampton with Kathleen Rhoads, Director of Training at Fountain House, for the premiere of the film at Smith College. (I had arrived a day earlier.) The last time Robert had been in Northampton was on the weekend of Eli's high school graduation.

Several hundred people attended a reception before the film's screening, and Robert, in a handsome new blue pin striped three-piece suit, greeted one and all with charm and with flair. He made jokes, he talked about our book, he surprised old friends and family members by remembering things about them they had forgotten, he told women how gorgeous they were and what lovely names they had, and, in his most chivalrous manner, he kissed the backs of their hands.

The film, shown to a standing-room-only audience of more than five hundred, was a triumph: not only because it was an accurate, moving, and visually compelling portrayal of us and of our lives, but because Robert and I were able to watch it together outside a hospital, while surrounded by friends and family. When the film ended, Robert reached over and took my hand in his. The lights went on, the applause grew, and then Robert stood, turned to face the audience, and suddenly lifted both arms high in the air, the first two fingers on each hand extended in *V*s, for victory.

The applause grew louder and louder. (At a screening six weeks later at Mount Sinai Hospital in New York, Jim Mutton would present Robert with a gift from his friends at the Clinton Residence: an Oscar. To the crowd's cheers, Robert would hold the Oscar aloft in both hands, then lower it, close his eyes, lean forward, and kiss the Oscar on its forehead.)

A week or two after the Northampton premiere, Robert and I were having dinner in our favorite Japanese restaurant when I said something I would soon hear Robert say to others—about how I thought the film was going to do a lot of good, for it would show people that no matter how far down you've been, there is always hope. Robert nodded, after which he said something he had never said before in such a simple and direct way.

"Well, none of it would have happened if not for you."

I tried to deflect his gratitude, but he persisted, "Let's face it, Jay, if not for you, I wouldn't even be here. I'd be dead."

For a few moments, I could not speak. I was deeply touched to hear Robert say this—how could I not?—not least of all because the fact that he could express his feelings to me so openly, unequivocally, and warmly was a sure sign of the distance he had, in recent times, traveled.

When through the years, people would ask what my hopes for Robert were, I would usually say, "I just hope he has more good days than bad." These days, this hope has been realized. Still, the gains Robert has made hardly wash away the pervasive sadness and loss that have marked his life.

After the premiere in Northampton when the two of us were standing outside the auditorium and most people had gone home, a friend of mine approached and told Robert that ever since she read *Imagining Robert* she had been remembering him in her daily prayers. She was honored to meet him, she said, and pleased he was doing so well. She spoke about her love of God, and of God's love for us—of how the Lord was a loving, merciful, and compassionate God.

Robert nodded. "He's also a God of wrath," he said.

New York City
September, 2002